W. C. Bruson

Fresh eggs and yellow butter

W. C. Bruson

Fresh eggs and yellow butter

ISBN/EAN: 9783743377165

Manufactured in Europe, USA, Canada, Australia, Japa

Cover: Foto ©Andreas Hilbeck / pixelio.de

Manufactured and distributed by brebook publishing software (www.brebook.com)

W. C. Bruson

Fresh eggs and yellow butter

FRESH EGGS AND YELLOW BUTTER.

A TREATISE

ON EGGS AND BUTTER, SHOWING METHODS OF PRESERVING

EGGS, BUTTER, MEATS, ETC.

WITH THE PROCESS OF

DEOXYGENATING AND INSULATING EGGS.

AND OTHER NEW AND

VALUABLE INFORMATION

USEFUL TO THE PRODUCE DEALER, GROCER, DAIRYMAN, CHEESE-MAKER, FARMER, DRUGGIST, MANUFACTURER, Etc.

BY

W. C. BRUSON,

PRACTICAL CHEMIST.

Consequitur quodcunque petit.

CHICAGO, ILL.:
WESTERN NEWS COMPANY, 121 AND 123 STATE STREET.

Entered according to Act of Congress, in the year 1870, by W. C. BRUSON, in the Clerk's Office of the District Court of the United States, for the Northern District of Illinois.

Evening Journal Print, 46 Dearborn Street.

TO THE

FARMERS' DAUGHTERS OF AMERICA,

Who take pride in gathering fresh eggs, and are accomplished in the
art of making sweet yellow butter, and by their energy and
enterprise stimulate the hardy sons of the soil to
cultivate the fields, that they may teem with
golden heads of wheat and waving corn,

THIS VOLUME IS RESPECTFULLY DEDICATED,

With the compliments of

THE AUTHOR.

Fresh Eggs and Yellow Butter.

EGGS,

DEOXYGENATED AND INSULATED, REMAIN IN A FRESH STATE.

BUTTER.

PRESERVED AND COLORED. RANCID BUTTER RESTORED.

EXPLANATION OF TERMS.

Compound.—A mass or body formed by the union or mixture of two or more substances. *A chemical compound* is composed of two or more bodies united in certain invariable proportions. Thus 49 parts of sulphuric acid, and 28 parts of quick lime form *sulphate of lime or plaster of paris.*

Deodorizing—Depriving of odor.

Deozygenating—Depriving of oxygen.

Digest—In chemistry, to soften and prepare or dissolve by heat.

Diluted—Made thin or weak by adding fluids.

Endosmosis—Passage *inward* of liquids, vapors, or gases through membranes or porous substances

Exosmosis—Passage *outward* of liquids, vapors, or gases through membranes or porous substances.

Insulation.—Non-communication with other substances. Insulated eggs are not liable to endosmosis or exosmosis.

Maceration—Softening in water, or soaking in a fluid.

Mixture—Ingredients blended without an alteration of their substances. A mere mechanical union of bodies. For instance, corn and oats may be mixed, but not combined.

Solution—Dissolving a solid in a fluid. Thus, salt disappears in water, its solution takes place. The liquid is called a *Solution of Salt in Water.* Solution is a true chemical union.

Saturated Solution.—Solution is the result of attraction or affinity between the fluid and the solid. This affinity continues to operate to a certain point where the fluid no longer possesses any solvent properties; it is then saturated and the fluid is called a *saturated solution.* Thus, one gallon of water will only dissolve three pounds of common salt. It is then saturated. Any additional salt will remain undissolved.

Saponified.—Converted into soap.

Specific Gravity.—Density of bodies as compared with an equal bulk of water. Water is the standard for solids and liquids, common air for gases.

Water-bath.—A kettle or vessel of water, over a fire, in which is placed another vessel containing fluid that requires only a heat below the boiling point of water. Water boils at 212° F. Water in *the vessel* in a water-bath can only be heated to 207° F.

PREFACE.

The subjects which this volume is designed to elucidate have, in their consideration and investigation, engaged my attention for the past fifteen years. Their importance, and that of the improvements and discoveries made, have constrained me to undertake the task of placing them before the public in the form of a book.

While I have aimed to secure enough accuracy in the details of these processes and directions to insure their successful application, it has also been my endeavor to render the language and style as free from technicalities as possible.

In order to subserve the interests of not only Produce Dealers, Dairymen and Farmers, but also of several other classes of industry, a large amount of information not suggested by the title has been introduced.

In every department and subject discussed, not only have my own discoveries and processes been faithfully stated, but the cream of all that is known thereon has been transcribed for the benefit of the reader.

The processes of DEOXYGENATING AND INSULATING EGGS, preparing kerosene oil and other barrels and vats by insulation, the insulation of egg-preserving solutions and mixtures, the restoration of rancid butter, and the preservation and coloring of white and streaked butter, as well as many others, are wholly new and original, and are herein, for the first time, given to the public. It is believed that these discoveries will inaugurate a complete revolution in the art of preserving eggs and butter.

The information regarding the preservation of wood, metal, stone and meat, tanning, soaps, inks, sirups, vinegar, wines, cider, aniline dyes, etc., etc., is reliable, and considered the best for practical purposes.

Indeed, it has been the object of the author to make the work worth many times its price to those engaged or interested in any department of industry of which it treats.

With the confident hope that my efforts to diffuse reliable information on the topics which most intimately concern our happiness and prosperity will be appreciated and appropriately rewarded, this work is respectfully submitted to the judgment of an intelligent public.

THE AUTHOR.

FRESH EGGS AND YELLOW BUTTER.

In the multiplicity of methods to preserve eggs in a state of freshness, and to restore rancid butter, it is well known that, heretofore, there have been no successful and practical processes which meet with general approval.

To keep eggs in a fresh and healthy condition from spring to winter, at a reasonable expense, is a great *desideratum* to the public.

Nor is it of less importance to know how to preserve good butter, and how to redeem sour and rancid butter by a process of purification which is effectual, cheap and expeditious, answering the needs of the Grocer and the Produce Dealer in every particular, so that they may be able to supply the public with fresh eggs and sweet, yellow butter.

Almost every Produce Dealer, Grocer and Farmer has tried one or more processes for preserving eggs, but to all these there are more or less objections.

It is claimed by some that the edible substance of the egg known as the yelk (*vitellus ovi*), and the white (*albumen ovi*), should be preserved by chemical agents that will penetrate the porous substance of the egg-shell, and thus cure the egg, without imparting to it any unpleasant flavor; but various obstacles have arisen which renders this method very objectionable; as, for instance, the conversion of the albumen of the egg into a watery substance, and the hardening and drying of the yelk. Others claim that hermetically sealing or covering the egg-shell with varnish, liquid glue, gum, etc., which renders it impervious to air, is sufficient to keep the egg long enough for all practical purposes.

Before setting forth the processes which may be relied upon, we propose to show the chemical effects on the egg of the principal agents now in use.

First—The common quicklime, (*Oxyd of Calcium*), has been the chief agent used in almost every quarter of the globe. It has been tried in its pure state and with various compounds, and the question now arises; how does lime act upon the egg?

It is believed by some that when lime-water is too strong, it "cooks" the egg, and "eats" the shell, as commonly expressed. Others contend that when the lime-water is too weak, the eggs are spoiled, and indeed there seems to be no settled rule for using lime in the preservation of eggs. Lime-water never dissolves any portion of the shell, which, being composed of carbonate of lime, is not soluble in alkalies, but, on the contrary, when exposed to the action of lime-water for several months, is increased in thickness, caused by a deposit of carbonate of lime on its surface; for example, the interior surfaces of tea-kettles and boilers are incrusted by the carbonate of lime from hard water in a similar manner.

Acids and not alkalies dissolve the shell of the egg.

Some prefer to use the fresh lime (*Oxyd of Calcium*),

slaked in an excess of water; others take the freshly slaked lime, (*Hydrate of Lime*), slaked with about half its weight of water, and to which, when used for eggs, more or less water is added.

We will now treat of the properties of Lime. It is well known that its solution possesses caustic properties, but of the weakest class. For instance, one pint of either slaked or unslaked lime, stirred into a barrel of water, renders it just so strongly impregnated as if a half-bushel, or any greater quantity of lime, was added. This statement may appear incredulous, but it is a well-known fact to chemists.

Water dissolves but a minute fraction of lime, and, contrary to the general law, less is dissolved in hot than in cold water.

A gallon of water at boiling point (212° Fahr.) dissolves 45 grs. of Lime.
" " .... (60° ") " 74 "
" " at 1 deg. above ⎫ (33° ") " 90 "
" " freez'g point or ⎭

A barrel of 32 gallons of water, at 60° Fahr., the average temperature of water in the summer months, requires only 5 oz. of pure lime to make a saturated solution, which renders it just as strong as if a bushel of lime had been used; but the lime water, by exposure, attracts carbonic acid from the atmosphere, and becomes covered with a thin pellicle, or coating, of insoluble carbonate of lime, which, subsiding after a time, is replaced by another, and so on, successively, until the whole of the lime has become insoluble. Hence, in order to keep lime-water of a uniform strength, *i. e.* a saturated solution, it must be kept in closely corked bottles, or the vessels must contain an excess of lime. To illustrate:

in order to keep a barrel of saturated lime-water for six or eight months, when it is exposed to the air, it will be necessary to add a few ounces of lime every few days, or else put into the barrel a peck of lime at the beginning, which will require stirring every few weeks, as some lime contains more or less clay and magnesia, which cause the lime that has settled at the bottom to become more or less hard. In such cases, the water does not dissolve any more lime, unless frequently stirred. This accounts for lime-water losing its strength, even when there is an excess of lime present. When a cold, saturated solution of lime-water is heated, a deposition of lime takes place, but upon cooling it is re-dissolved. Lime-water is colorless, inodorous, and of a slightly disagreeable alkaline taste. It changes reddened litmus test paper and vegetable reds to blue, and forms an insoluble soap with oils. Carbonate of lime, as above mentioned, is lime which has lost its strength or caustic properties by exposure to the air, and it is of no utility for making lime-water. Hence, air-slaked lime should never be used for this purpose. By the absorption of carbonic acid from the atmosphere, the lime is gradually converted into a carbonate, and is thus rendered insoluble in water. Marble, chalk, etc., are among the carbonates of lime. In regard to the effect of lime upon the egg substance, if an egg be broken into lime-water and allowed to remain in it at any temperature from 55° to 100° Fahr. for three weeks, the result will be a completely spoiled egg.

The best method heretofore used for preserving eggs with lime has been to mix a sufficient quantity of lime with water, to the consistency of cream, and immerse the eggs therein.

It is a well-known fact that eggs, after remaining for some length of time in lime and water, undergo a chemical change. Decomposition of the white of the egg, or albumen, takes place, and it becomes watery.

The chemical composition of the white of eggs is about 85 parts water, 2 parts gluten, and 13 parts pure albumen, or animal mucilage.

The egg-shell being porous, after remaining in a lime mixture sufficient length of time, the lime-water percolates or soaks through the shell, and dissolves more or less of the white of the egg, rendering it watery.

Some eggs, having a close, compact shell, are not soon affected by the alkali, but the majority of limed eggs are affected in about forty or fifty days, but may remain even longer with but slight change, according to the freshness of the eggs and the temperature at which the mixture is kept.

Eggs, having been kept on hand two or three weeks, in warm weather, and then put into the lime-mixture at a temperature above 70°, will usually spoil in a few weeks. If strictly fresh eggs are put into the lime mixture, and it be kept at a temperature below 50°, they may be preserved for about eighty or ninety days without very material change, and may keep from spring to winter with but a partial loss or decomposition of the albumen. After the decomposition of the white of the egg, the yelk necessarily becomes involved; it is the last portion of the egg that spoils. When the white becomes watery, its specific gravity is lessened, and, being less buoyant the yelk settles till it rests on the shell, where not being protected by the albumen, endosmosis of atmospheric oxygen, and other substances abnormal to the egg, soon hastens decomposition and putrefaction.

A few weeks after eggs are put into lime-water, the pores of the shells become partially closed by a deposit of the carbonate of lime on the surface of the shells, rendering absorption of the lime-water slow; and though decomposition may have commenced, as is explained before in reference to stale eggs, the supply of atmospheric oxygen is lessened, it being only partially excluded by the lime. Lime-water will not prevent decomposition of the substance of the egg when it has commenced.

This fact is known by the experienced buyers when such eggs are offered for sale, upon examination they are found to be watery, and many of them spoiled.

They are called "*limed eggs*," and have a slow sale; their market price is from ten to thirty per cent. less than for fresh eggs.

Various substances have been used in combination with lime, with a view of rendering it more efficient as an egg preservative, but without the least success, if we may except common salt.

An *excess* of salt with lime, however, causes a more rapid dissolution of the albumen, and at the same time hardens the yelk. Such eggs are generally, though erroneously, said to be "cooked" by the action of the lime, when it is mainly due to the effect of the salt.

For a proof of this statement, place eggs in a saturated solution of salt in water. After remaining in it forty or fifty days, at a temperature above 60°, the whites of the eggs will be discovered to be very watery, and the yelks preternaturally hard and tough. The solvent properties of the lime, as before stated, dissolve or disintegrate the albumen and yelk, and a small proportion of salt may be properly used, to partially correct this effect.

The presence of salt may readily be detected by the taste in both the white and yelk of the egg, as soon as its absorption takes place.

It is an established fact that either a lime or a salt solution, or both combined, will dissolve the white of the egg, in a time proportioned to the firmness of the egg-shell and the freshness of the eggs, and the temperature at which they are kept, which, if below 40° Fahr., wholly retards decomposition, while at 50° Fahr. decomposition is slow. At from 60° to 70° decay is more rapid, and so increasing with a higher temperature at from 80° to 100° Fahr. *but a few weeks are required to spoil eggs by the best "lime process"* known.

A series of experiments have determined the quantity of salt required to prevent the yelk from being dissolved by the lime-water.

The following is considered the best formula for the "lime process," which is not generally known:

> Take of fresh unslaked lime, 40 lbs.
> Common barrel salt, 2 lbs.
> Cold or hot water, 20 galls.

After the lime slakes or dissolves in the water (which will require from twenty to thirty minutes), stir it occasionally for about an hour; and then for one or two days stir, from time to time, in order that the solution may cool down to the temperature of the surrounding atmosphere. The above quantity of solution (which may be called the "Cream of Lime Compound") is then ready, and is sufficient to cover about 150 dozen of eggs, the usual number required to fill a 42 to 45 gallon barrel. As the specific gravity of this mixture is considerably greater than water, eggs will not readily sink in it; hence it will be best to put the eggs into a clean empty barrel, of the capacity of 45 gallons, placing them in carefully, so that they may not be broken. The last layer of eggs should be about three inches below the top of the barrel; then pour on the "Cream of Lime Compound," which has been previously prepared in another barrel. Just before dipping it out, stir it thoroughly, so that it may be evenly mixed. When the eggs are covered with the mixture, spread over them a thin cotton cloth, so that they may be entirely covered; and pour on the top of the cloth the "Cream of Lime Compound," to the depth of at least two inches. Then pour over all one quart of refined paraffin oil (see process for refining the oil), and cover the barrel closely with a couple of thicknesses of paper and a board cover.

The cloth is spread over the eggs to receive whatever sediment of lime may subside from the additional solution poured over them, which sediment will feed the solution from above, and thus tend to keep it of a uniform strength, and by its weight prevent the eggs from rising to the surface.

The oil is added to prevent evaporation, chemical change, and absorption of impurities and gases from the atmosphere. As ordinary barrels are liable to leak, and as it is essential that their contents should not be lessened, for the eggs would then be liable to spoil, they should be examined every week, and more solution added, if necessary.

By all means, prepare the barrels or vats for holding egg-preserving solutions according to the method of preparing kerosene oil and other barrels, as it will save much anxiety about leakage.

Do not use any more salt than is prescribed in the formula, nor any more lime, as it would render the mixture too thick; nor a less quantity, as it would render it too thin, and the lime, settling to the bottom, would produce a chemical change in the solution. The quantity of lime given in the formula will keep the mixture about the consistence of cream, and thus preserve a uniform strength.

Repeated experiments have enabled us to give the following rule:

To each gallon of water add two lbs. of fresh, unslaked lime, and an ounce and a half of common salt.

The water should all be poured on at one time, and we prefer to have it at the boiling point, in order to expel any oxygen it may contain in solution. Be particular to have the "Cream of Lime Compound" *cold* and well stirred just before pouring it upon the eggs as directed. Do not use, on any consideration, preparations of soda, potash, borax, saltpetre, cream of tartar, tartaric acid, or any other acid or alkali, in combination with the "Cream of Lime Compound," as they are not egg preservatives.

Some persons have used these prohibited chemical agents in combination with lime and salt solutions with comparative success, but this was not owing to their employment, for had they been used in excess, the destruction of the eggs would have been greatly accelerated.

The addition of soda, potash, or any other alkali, to the mixture of lime, as before mentioned, only renders it more caustic, and it therefore dissolves the albumen, or white, of the egg in less time than if lime alone were used. When tartaric acid and cream of tartar are used with the lime solution, they are converted into the tartrate of lime, an inert compound. Therefore the addition of these articles are useless.

Before dismissing the subject of lime, we will give the following, which is a decided improvement over the old lime formula, and which we denominate, for convenience, the

IMPROVED LIME PROCESS.

Take fresh, unslaked lime, 40 pounds.
Pure tallow, cut in thin slices 5 "
Paraffin wax, " " 1 "
Boiling water, 29 gallons.

(NOTE.—Cold water should never be used, as the combination will not be perfect.)

Mix these together in a suitable barrel, and, as soon as the lime begins to slake, stir occasionally for an hour, and, afterwards, three or four times a day for two days, by which time the mixture will be cold.

The mixture is now ready, and is sufficient to cover 145 to 150 dozen eggs—the usual number required to fill a 43 to 45 gallon barrel.

As the specific gravity of this mixture is considerably greater than water, eggs will not readily sink in it; hence, it is best to put the eggs into a clean, empty barrel, of the capacity of 45 gallons, placing them in carefully so they may not be broken. The last layer of eggs should be about three inches below the top of the barrel. Then gradually pour on the mixture, previously prepared in another barrel, but just before dipping it out, stir it thoroughly, so that it may be evenly mixed throughout.

When the eggs are entirely covered with this mixture, spread over them a thin cotton cloth within the barrel, and pour on the top of the cloth more of the same mixture, to the depth of two inches, and then pour over all one quart of the refined paraffin oil (see process for refining the oil), and finally cover the barrel closely with a couple of thicknesses of paper and a board cover.

The cloth is spread over the eggs to receive whatever sediment of lime may subside from the additional mixture poured over them, which sediment will feed the solution from above, and thus tend to keep it of uniform strength, and by its weight prevent the eggs from rising to the surface.

The oil is added to prevent evaporation, chemical change, and absorption of impurities and gases from the atmosphere. As ordinary barrels are liable to leak, and as it is essential that their contents should not be lessened, as the eggs would then be liable to spoil, they should be examined every week, and more solution added, if necessary.

By all means, prepare the barrels or vats for holding egg-preserving solutions according to the method of preparing kerosene oil and other barrels, as it will save much anxiety about leakage.

The above is far superior to the ordinary lime process, as by the chemical combination of the ingredients an insoluble soap is formed, which prevents, in a great measure, the lime from settling and adhering to the egg-shell, as is usually the case in the ordinary lime process.

In place of using tallow and paraffin with lime in the improved lime process, we have tried lard, stearin, spermaceti, linseed oil, olive oil, cotton-seed oil, and other oil and fats, but they do not answer so well.

None but the *purest* and *sweetest* beef or mutton tallow should be used.

Paraffin may be substituted for tallow; but six pounds of paraffin, at 40 cents a pound, amounts to $2.40, which, with the expense of 40 lbs. of lime, makes the whole cost for preserving 150 dozen eggs about two cents a dozen, which renders the use of paraffin objectionable to the large dealer. In this case five pounds of pure, sweet tallow may be substituted, as set forth in the formula, and will answer for all ordinary purposes, when eggs are kept at a temperature below 60° Fahr.

When all paraffin is used, the composition will resist a higher temperature, in consequence of the paraffin being a bad conductor of heat.

Hence it is advisable that some paraffin be used, as a better combination is made by its addition.

We will now give the best

DRY PROCESS.

Take coarsely powdered charcoal, 1 bushel, carbolic acid crystals, ½ oz., dissolved in 4 oz. of alcohol, 95 per cent. This solution must be carefully sprinkled over and well stirred into the powdered charcoal. It is now ready for use, and should be kept in covered barrels or boxes, in a dry place, where it will not be liable to attract moisture, till required for use.

Prepare the eggs before packing them in this compound, by the *deoxygenating* and insulating process.

Pack in common flour barrels or boxes firmly, and in the same manner as when packed in oats, and they may be shipped in this dry packing to market.

To prevent the charcoal from sifting out, paste paper, with common flour paste, on the inner surface of the barrel or box, and allow it to dry thoroughly before using.

Head up the barrels securely, and keep them in as cool a place as possible, and every two weeks they should be inverted.

We find that this packing preserves the eggs better than any other dry packing, while the cost of the materials is trifling.

It is well known to chemists that charcoal and carbolic acid are among the best antiseptics and deodorizing agents used. Another advantage which this method possesses is, that, in case of breakage, no injury will accrue to the sound eggs, as all tendency to putrefaction of the substance of the broken eggs is arrested by the use of the carbolic acid and charcoal. The egg-shells being thoroughly coated by the refined materials used in the *deoxygenating* and insulating process, no fears need be entertained that the odor of carbolic acid will be communicated to the egg.

Eggs, if strictly fresh when put up by this process, will remain in a good condition for a long time, in any climate.

THE EFFECTS OF CERTAIN CHEMICAL AGENTS UPON EGGS.

It is proper to state that, in some instances, persons have kept eggs in a passably good condition for several months in certain chemical mixtures; but it is to be borne in mind that the credit belongs to the freshness of the eggs and the lowness of temperature at which they are kept, instead of to the virtues attributed to those compounds.

SALT—ITS EFFECTS UPON EGGS.

Eggs have been kept a long time packed in dry salt, at a low temperature; but this method is unreliable, as many failures are reported. Were the salt deprived of its water by calcination, eggs packed in it, and kept at a temperature below 50° Fahr., in a close vessel, would be preserved a long time.

Salt is a bad conductor of heat, and therefore has a tendency to keep eggs cool, but if once heated it remains so a long time.

DRY ASHES—THEIR EFFECTS UPON EGGS.

Dry ashes have also been used, with the view of preserving eggs, but unless kept at a temperature below 50° Fahr., the process is unreliable.

OATS—THEIR EFFECTS UPON EGGS.

Grains of various kinds have been used. Oats, if old, perfectly dry, and free from must, will preserve eggs, if kept in a cool place. Oats, being an imperfect conductor of heat, are doubtless, of all the cereals, the best for dry packing. But they may be used with much better effect if the eggs are first prepared by the deoxygenating and insulating process, in the manner recommended for charcoal packing.

It is advisable to invert the the barrel or box in which eggs are packed once in two weeks.

The liability of oats to attract moisture, and become heated and musty, renders it necessary to use none but old, dry oats.

KILN-DRIED SAND—ITS EFFECTS UPON EGGS.

Kiln-dried sand may be used with success at a temperature below 50° Fahr.

BRAN, CUT STRAW AND CHAFF—THEIR EFFECTS UPON EGGS.

Bran, cut straw and chaff have also been used to preserve eggs. But as these agents are very uncertain, and often heat, especially if damp, they are decidedly objectionable, unless kept at a low temperature and in a dry place.

SAWDUST AND SHAVINGS—THEIR EFFECTS UPON EGGS.

Eggs should never be packed in sawdust or shavings, under any circumstances, as these substances readily communicate their odors to the eggs, and render them unfit for use.

LIQUID SILICATE OF SODA—AS A DRY COATING FOR EGGS.

We will now treat of silicate of soda as an egg preservative. It has a great affinity for, and readily combines with, various preparations of lime, clay, sand, and other substances of an alkaline or neutral character; but it must never be used with anything of an acid nature, common salt, saltpetre, alum, etc., as it is incompatible with such substances.

We have made many experiments with this preparation for the preservation of eggs. In consequence of its affinity for carbonate of lime, we have applied it as a coating to eggs in a cold, warm and hot state, of various degrees of density, separately and in combination with other agents. When used for coating eggs, enough water must be added to reduce it to about 25° Baume, which is about the consistence or density of thin syrup or varnish. In this form it may be applied to the eggs by a common varnish brush, or they may be dipped into it. It readily unites with the carbonate of lime of the egg-shell, and upon exposure to the air dries in a few minutes, forming an insoluble silicate of lime, a hard, transparent, glass-like coating, unless the egg has been in contact with grease, oil, varnish, acids, or common salt.

Although the silicate of soda renders the shell impervious to water or air, by forming, as it were, an air-tight casing, yet, like all air-proof agents, it can only be used with success when the eggs are strictly fresh, or on the day they are laid; in which case they will keep for a long time.

But as it is impracticable for dealers to get this class of eggs in large quantities, it is not recommended for general use as a dry coating for them.

The question will naturally occur to many of our readers, why the silicate of soda solution, or other air-proof coatings, will not preserve stale eggs as well as *decidedly fresh* or new-laid eggs? Because stale eggs are already in the incipient stage of decomposition, and contain a much larger percentage of atmospheric oxygen, the principal exciting cause of decomposition, which, once commenced, will continue, unless the eggs are deoxygenated, or the temperature at which the eggs are kept be below 50° Fahr; therefore the mere air-proof coating of stale eggs will not long preserve them.

CREAM OF TARTAR (BITARTRATE OF POTASSA)—ITS EFFECTS UPON EGGS.

A solution of cream of tartar in water will spoil eggs in about forty days, causing them to become sour.

Cream of tartar, when combined with lime, is entirely neutralized by the alkaline properties of the lime; hence cream of tartar, an expensive chemical, is useless as an egg preservative, either alone or in combination with other chemicals.

DILUTED SULPHURIC ACID—ITS EFFECTS UPON EGGS.

Diluted sulphuric acid has been recommended as an agent for preserving eggs, by the immersion of the egg for a few moments.

The theory is, that the acid combines with a portion of the calcareous substance of the shell, forming with it sulphate of lime, but this chemical change from the carbonate to the sulphate of lime produces no perceptible effect of closing the pores of the shell.

We have tried this method with various strengths of diluted acid, and different lengths of time for the egg to remain in the solution; but it will not answer practically, as the acid corrodes and weakens the shell, and hastens decomposition.

ALUM—ITS EFFECTS UPON EGGS.

A saturated solution of alum will spoil an egg in about three weeks.

The sulphuric acid contained in the alum, (about 30 per cent.), dissolves the shell, composed principally of carbonate of lime, in a short time.

Alum has been used, in combination with lime and water, as a preservative, but the alum, being acid in character, is neutralized by the lime, and is therefore useless.

BI-SULPHIDE OF CALCIUM, BI-SULPHIDE OF SODIUM, SULPHATE OF LIME, VINEGAR, TARTARIC ACID, MURIATIC ACID, OXALIC ACID, ACETIC ACID, ETC., ETC.

The effects of these substances are similar to that of diluted sulphuric acid, and they should never be used for preserving eggs.

CARBONATE OF POTASSA AND CARBONATE OF SODA (SAL SODA)—THEIR EFFECTS UPON EGGS.

The solutions of these salts possess stronger alkaline properties than lime, but their admixture produces a compound more caustic and destructive, and therefore more powerfully solvent to the white of the egg, which renders the egg unfit for use in fifty or sixty days, at a temperature from 60° to 70° Fahr.

BORAX (BI-BORATE OF SODA)—ITS EFFECTS UPON EGGS.

Solutions of borax in water, of various strengths, have been used. As borax is of a feeble alkaline nature, with a sweetish taste, it was hoped that it would be found superior to lime for keeping eggs, but they will spoil, by the white souring, in about sixty days, at a temperature from 60° to 70°. A pound of borax to a gallon of spring water, at a temperature of 60° Fahr., forms a saturated solution which will keep the eggs a few days longer than a weaker solution.

SALTPETRE (NITRATE OF POTASSA)—ITS EFFECTS UPON EGGS.

The effects of this agent are nearly identical with those

of common salt, causing the white to become red and watery, and rendering the yelk hard in about sixty-five days.

SULPHITE OF LIME, CHLORIDE OF CALCIUM, CHLORIDE OF LIME, BI-CARBONATE OF SODA, SULPHITE OF SODA, SULPHATE OF SODA, HYPO-SULPHITE OF SODA, PHOSPHATE OF SODA, TARTRATE OF POTASSA AND SODA, CHLORATE OF POTASSA, TARTRATE OF POTASSA, CARBONATE OF AMMONIA, BI-CARBONATE OF POTASSA, ETC.

The above chemical substances, being of an alkaline or neutral character, exert no specific effect in preserving eggs.

CARBOLIC ACID AND PYROLIGNEOUS ACID—THEIR EFFECTS UPON EGGS.

By the use of these agents, diluted with water, eggs may be kept a long time, as these materials are highly antiseptic; but the objection to their use is, that they impart a strong, smoky taste to the eggs.

GLYCERINE—ITS EFFECTS UPON EGGS.

Glycerine is a valuable agent for preserving animal substances. It is preferable to alcohol, inasmuch as glycerine does not cause the substances preserved in it to shrink or change color, nor does it lessen its bulk by evaporation. With a knowledge of these properties, and the known antiseptic qualities of glycerine, we have made numerous experiments with it. On account of the expense of this preparation, it is not practicable to employ it in its concentrated form. Diluted with water, in various proportions from 2 oz. to 16 oz. of glycerine to a gallon of water, we find no difficulty in preserving eggs.

But its use is open to serious objections, as it is a most powerful solvent, acting with great force upon the yelk of the egg, dissolving it and rendering it fluid, and combining with the albumen in a most unsatisfactory manner, so that when the egg is broken the yelk does not retain its form, but is spread out and intermixed with the albumen.

SUGAR—ITS EFFECTS UPON EGGS.

A weak solution of sugar in water soon becomes converted into vinegar, and the action of the acid thus obtained destroys the egg in a few weeks' time.

If thick syrup be used, eggs may be kept a long time, but the expense of such a preservative renders it impracticable.

AIR-PROOF AND HOT WATER PROCESSES.

It is alleged by some persons that, by dipping eggs into hot water for a few seconds, the albumen and membrane which line the shell are coagulated—"the pores of the shell closed," and the egg thus canned in its own covering.

We have made numerous experiments by dipping eggs into water of different degrees of heat; but we find it uncertain and difficult to practically render eggs air-proof by this means.

Among other experiments, we have immersed them in hot oil, lard, tallow, beeswax, liquid glue, common furniture varnish, damar, copal, and shellac varnishes, solutions of india rubber, gutta percha and gum arabic.

We have applied these at various temperatures, from cold to boiling heat, at different seasons of the year, to perfectly fresh eggs, and to those one, two, and three weeks old;

but most of these "air-proofing" methods leave an adhesive coating, which sticks fast to all substances with which the eggs come in contact while drying.

In making our experiments, we have placed eggs on points or pegs to dry, so that but a small portion of the coating would be abraded or broken; but we found the varnish, or gum coating, removed wherever they came in contact with the pegs, and these exposed points admitted sufficient air to render the process inoperative.

When eggs which have been coated by many of the above substances are put into alkaline liquids, to preserve the shells in a fresh state, the varnishes, oils, etc., become more or less saponified, and the result is a coating of soap, which is far from being water-proof. Eggs thus treated will not keep in a fresh and marketable condition from spring and summer till winter, unless at a temperature below 50° Fahr.

Again: as the coating of these substances may be readily detected by the purchaser when the eggs are exposed for sale, they are therefore classed with preserved eggs, which renders this method decidedly objectionable, as well as unprofitable.

HATCHING AIR-PROOF EGGS.

From repeated experiments, we find that exclusion of air from the egg does not destroy the embryo or prevent the egg from being hatched, but, on the contrary, preserves the animal life of the egg, provided it be strictly fresh when coated and subsequently kept at a moderately cool temperature; it may be hatched a year afterward by the careful removal of the coating, and subjecting it to the required incubating heat.

WHY CLOUDED EGGS USUALLY APPEAR CLEAR AFTER REMAINING IN LIME-WATER OR OTHER ALKALINE SOLUTIONS.

It is well known that a strictly fresh egg presents a certain *clare-obscure* or semi-opaque appearance, when held before a bright light, and that in a few days longer, according to its state of preservation, the egg, if then "candled," will present a turbid or *clouded* appearance. Such are properly stale eggs, which, although not unfit for cooking purposes, are in the first stages of change, and less liable to keep than strictly fresh eggs.

This fact accounts for the disappointment of egg dealers upon opening a package of preserved eggs, when they find them in every condition, from quite fresh to very bad.

It is also known to dealers in eggs that when clouded or turbid eggs have been kept in lime or other alkaline solutions, they become *clear* and lighter in color in a few weeks' time. We will explain the cause of this, as we are frequently interrogated upon the subject.

This change is due to the solvent effects of the alkaline fluids upon the *semi-opaque membrane* which lines the shell, and upon the albumen, which having become thick and more opaque by age, gives the egg that peculiarly turbid or clouded appearance when examined before a *strong light*. Such a light is necessary to show the "cloud" or "float," unless it is very large and dark.

When eggs do not readily show this "cloud" or "float" and are immersed in lime-water, or other alkalies, for a few weeks, it becomes visible by the action of the alkalies.

WHY EGGS SOMETIMES CRACK WHEN IN EGG-PRESERVING SOLUTIONS, OR AFTER BEING REMOVED FROM THEM.

If eggs are stale, and sour when put into the solution of an alkaline carbonate, it infiltrates through the porous shell, acting chemically upon the acid already generated in the eggs, and causes the evolution of carbonic acid gas, which forcibly bursts the shells, although thick shells will frequently prove strong enough to confine the gas for sometime. Eggs may therefore crack when not in the putrid fermentation, and the apparent fullness, or excess of substance of the egg, is due to the mechanical retention of carbonic acid gas within it.

Eggs in this condition, for the same reason, crack more readily upon being handled, although when strictly fresh or but slightly stale, if placed in an alkaline solution, they are not liable to be thus affected.

HOW TO PREVENT PRESERVED EGGS FROM CRACKING WHEN BOILING.

Prick the egg-shell, just before boiling, with a sharp point, or immerse the egg a short time in vinegar or diluted acetic acid, which will readily dissolve the carbonate of lime that fills the pores, and thus allow the hot air to escape.

This deposit of carbonate of lime is much less firm than the shell itself, and is readily dissolved. However, should the egg be allowed to remain in the vinegar twenty-four hours, the entire shell will dissolve, leaving a tough membrane containing the contents of the egg.

To prevent varnished or gummed eggs from cracking, puncture them with a sharp instrument.

WHY DO THE SHELLS OF PRESERVED EGGS CRACK WHEN BOILING?

This very common inquiry we will answer by an illustration: Put an egg that has not been preserved in hot water, and immediately air bubbles will be discovered rising to the surface of the water from the egg, caused by the action of the heat in expelling the internal air through the pores of the egg.

When a limed or other preserved egg is placed in hot water, it usually cracks before it is cooked, because the pores of the shell are nearly filled with carbonate of lime, which being insoluble in water, partly obstructs the passage of the hot rarified air from escaping through the pores, as in the fresh egg. The confined air finds vent by bursting the shell.

WHY FRESH EGGS SINK AND STALE EGGS FLOAT ON THE SURFACE OF WATER.

The specific gravity of a fresh-laid egg is 1.085; water being 1.000. Hence a fresh egg readily sinks in water. When a stale egg has lost a sufficient portion of its contents by evaporation to swim on the surface of water, it should not be used for preserving, as eggs of this class are on the verge of putrefaction.

STONE JARS FOR KEEPING EGGS.

Eggs have also been kept in stone jars and crocks, in various chemical solutions, as well as in dry packing, and generally with better success than if kept in wood, as barrels, boxes, etc. This arises from the fact that the earthen or stone jars are generally placed on the ground in a cool place, and, the earth being colder, absorbs heat or caloric, and of course eggs will keep much cooler than if placed in wooden vessels, which, if not perfectly seasoned and clean, are liable to give out offensive emanations that are absorbed by the eggs.

THE PHILOSOPHY OF KEEPING EGGS FRESH.

It is proper at this time to communicate to our readers, as the result of our investigations, the interesting fact that neither acids, alkalies, nor any other chemical agents, *by their own specific qualities,* contribute to the preservation of the substance of the egg.

This is the secret of so much disappointment in the use of "egg preservatives" now employed, which, when not positively prejudicial to the egg, have failed to meet the requirements of the egg dealer.

But when such comparatively innocuous preparations are used, and the eggs are found to be preserved, it is simply owing to the result of checking the evaporation of their fluids, by keeping them at a comparatively low temperature, in either dry or liquid preparations that are bad conductors of heat.

The great secret of preserving eggs consists in excluding everything abnormal to their health, and preventing the evaporation of their fluids; or, in other words, protecting them from enemies without and the loss of vitality from within, by which means the eggs will remain in an unchanged condition for an unlimited time.

Most egg dealers have not the conveniences for keeping eggs at a temperature below 50° Fahr., and it is well known that they will spoil more rapidly at the higher, and more slowly at the lower temperatures. At any temperature between 35° and 45° Fahr., they may be kept, unaided by artificial means, a long time without material change, as decomposition rarely takes place at a temperature below 50° Fahr.

Therefore, to preserve eggs effectually for a long time, it is absolutely necessary to prevent either endosmosis of atmospheric oxygen, or of the vapors of substances abnormal to the egg, which would communicate to them flavor or odor; or the exosmosis of any of their normal constituents, whether water, mineral salts, albuminoid, or oleaginous matters.

The large end of an egg, when first laid, contains a cavity within the shell about the size of a small pea, which is filled with nearly pure oxygen. This cavity is increased with the age of the egg, by the evaporation of a portion of the water of the albumen through the porous shell, its place being supplied by atmospheric air. If the egg be kept at a temperature between 50° and 100° Fahr., it possesses all the conditions requisite to induce putrefaction—viz., heat, air and moisture.

If fecundated eggs be kept at a temperature ranging from 100° to 110° Fahr., the conditions are favorable to the germination and production of animal life, and if the heat be continued with but slight intermissions for twenty-one days, a chicken is produced.

During incubation, or the hatching of eggs, they part with about one-sixth of their entire substance. Of this loss only five or six per cent. is water; the balance is the result of chemical decomposition, or probably of combustion, caused by the union of oxygen with carbon, producing carbonic acid, which escapes through the shell.

If eggs, just laid, or within an hour afterward, are deoxygenated by our process, as recommended in the following pages, they will remain in the same fresh condition in the equatorial or any other climate upon the face of the earth, however variable.

At a temperature above 155° Fahr., the heat would coagulate the albumen.

The commercial egg dealer cannot generally obtain eggs of this class, *i. e.*, one hour old, and must necessarily take eggs which are from one day to two weeks old for the preserving process, at which age they have lost by evaporation a portion of their fluids, and have absorbed atmospheric oxygen to such an extent that they may be said to be in the incipient stage of organic dissolution; and in accordance with the established chemical law of nature, that when once the disorganizing process has begun it continues, unless arrested. In a few weeks the eggs are in a condition past recovery.

To help the egg dealer out of this dilemma is one of the main objects of this work; and by adopting our deoxygenating process, which expels the accumulated atmospheric oxygen from the eggs to be preserved, (thus arresting and preventing further decomposition by the most simple and cheap methods, and preserving them in all their original freshness and natural appearance), the dealer will be enabled to realize all the advantages of dealing in sound and fresh eggs at all times.

Both theory and practice confirm us as to the great importance of preventing the evaporation of the egg fluid, and the absorption of gases or substances abnormal to the egg, and at the same time preserving the shell, with all its new and fresh appearance, intact from color or blemish. To accomplish this the eggs must be perfectly excluded from the atmosphere, which subjects them to oxydation and discoloration.

We have already mentioned many of the materials in which eggs may be preserved, if kept at a temperature below 50° Fahr., and which may answer well on a small scale; but we have now to deal with a matter of more importance, and of a much more extensive and practical nature, than the keeping of a few dozens of eggs for family use. We allude to the wants of the grocer and commercial egg-dealer and packer, who are annually collecting many thousand dozens of eggs, and who must keep them, without failure, from spring and summer to winter.

To meet the necessities of the egg dealer, who is required to keep eggs in a fresh condition an unlimited time, has been one great object of our investigations for many years.

We have considered, also, the disadvantages which many egg dealers labor under, in being unable to keep their eggs at even a moderately low temperature during the summer months, when eggs are generally the cheapest, and which is the most convenient season for preserving them.

The atmosphere of their cellars or rooms ranges in temperature, during the summer months, scarcely ever so low as 50°, but more frequently from 60° to 80° Fahr., and often higher, for many days successively.

NO. ONE (or Hot) PROCESS OF DEOXYGENATING AND INSULATING EGGS.

WE WILL NOW GIVE THE BEST PROCESS KNOWN FOR KEEPING EGGS IN A FRESH CONDITION FOR A LONG TIME, AT A REASONABLE EXPENSE:

Place the eggs in a wire basket, or other convenient, perforated vessel, and immerse them in pure Paraffin Wax, heated to about 200° Fahr. by a water-bath.

The water-bath may be simply and easily arranged, by placing a large kettle with some water in it over a fire, and then putting into it a tin pail half-filled with Paraffin Wax. Heat the water in the kettle, which should be almost full, boiling hot, or nearly so; when the wax in the pail is melted, and of the required temperature—about 200° Fahr.—it will be ready for the immersion of the eggs.

The eggs, having been placed in the wire basket or perforated tin vessel, are now to be sunk in the pail of hot wax, so as to entirely cover them, and allowed to remain immersed two minutes. Then raise and lower the basket in the heated wax a few times, occupying a few seconds, so that the entire surface of the eggs may come in contact with and be covered by the wax. Finally, lift out the basket, and allow the eggs to cool.

Instead of using the hot Paraffin Wax, the refined Paraffin Oil (see process of refining) may be heated and used in the same manner as the wax, except that the eggs should not be allowed to remain longer in the hot oil than thirty seconds, which is a sufficient time to complete the process of deoxygenating.

The reason the eggs are permitted to remain so much longer in the hot Paraffin Wax than in the hot oil is, that the eggs being cold when immersed in the hot wax, chill the wax which comes in immediate contact with them. The wax, being a bad conductor of heat, requires about one minute to re-melt it, and another minute is required to deoxygenate the eggs; after which they *must be immediately removed, in order to prevent partial cooking.*

[Copyright secured.]

Either Paraffin Wax or the refined Paraffin Oil may be used, as best suits the convenience of the packer.

After the eggs are removed from the Paraffin Wax, or Oil, and allowed to cool at least half an hour, they may, at any subsequent time within a few days, be put into a barrel about half-filled with the Silicate of Soda Solution, which is prepared as follows, and which we denominate

"THE NEW COLORLESS LIQUID PROCESS."

Liquid Silicate of Soda, 36° Baume............1 gallon.
Cold Water...............................20 gallons.

Stir continually for some time; then allow the mixture to stand two or three hours, giving it only an occasional stirring.

This new colorless solution, which should be prepared in a barrel of the capacity of from forty-two to forty-five gallons, is now ready for use, and is sufficient to cover about one hundred and fifty dozen eggs.

If more convenient, the eggs may be placed carefully in another suitable barrel, of the same dimensions, and the preserving solution gently poured over them until the top-layer of eggs is covered to the depth of two or three inches. Or the eggs may be placed in the solution in the first barrel, in the same manner. A thin cotton cloth is now to be spread on the surface of the solution, and allowed to settle down upon the eggs. Finally, pour over all a quart of refined Paraffin Oil, and cover the barrel tightly with paper and a good board cover.

The object of pouring the refined Paraffin Oil over the solution is, to prevent evaporation and the absorption of impurities by the solution from the atmosphere.

Keep the barrel in a cool place, as in a cool cellar, where the thermometer ranges from 35° to 60° Fahr. The nearer the temperature approaches the first figures, the better; but freezing (which occurs a little below 32°) must be avoided. Although the solution cannot freeze until reduced in temperature to several degrees below the freezing point of water, eggs will freeze at about 32° Fahr.

As has been previously stated, eggs placed in alkaline solutions are more or less affected by the alkali, which dissolves the albumen, thus rendering them "watery."

Of all alkaline solutions employed to preserve eggs, whether they are deoxygenated or not, preference must be given to the Silicate of Soda, which (in the case of eggs not deoxygenated) combines with the carbonate of lime of the egg-shell, rendering it less porous, thus preventing the alkali from permeating it. It does not, however, wholly prevent endosmosis of alkaline fluids, or exosmosis of the substance of the egg, especially when the liquid is kept at a temperature above 50° Fahr.

[Copyright secured.]

In order to make the process perfect for preserving eggs, they should be (as we have before remarked) immersed in the hot Paraffin Wax, or hot Oil, before placing them in the Silicate of Soda Solution.

The egg-shell is permeated by the hot wax, which entirely fills the pores, and thus hermetrically seals them. By this operation the shell is rendered impervious to air, water, or alkaline solutions.

The egg is deoxygenated by immersion for a very short time in the heated wax or oil, which, by rarefaction, (the effect of heat), expels most of the atmospheric oxygen of the egg—an element well known to be the principal cause of decomposition in the egg, under favorable circumstances.

We have now given the best practical processes for preserving eggs. These are the results of many years' experiments, and by carefully following our instructions, clean, fresh and wholesome eggs, at all seasons, may certainly be secured.

WHY IS PARAFFIN WAX THE BEST SUBSTANCE KNOWN IN CHEMISTRY FOR DEOXYGENATING AND INSULATING EGGS?

Because it is tasteless, inodorous, colorless, non-absorbent, and a non-conductor of heat.

It is not in the least affected by air, cold water, alkalies, or acids.

Therefore for insulating eggs it has no equal in the wide range of resins, oil, wax, gums, etc., at present known.

WHY IS THE REFINED PARAFFIN OIL THE BEST SOLUTION KNOWN FOR INSULATING EGGS BY THE COLD PROCESS?

This oil is possessed of properties similar, in many respects, to those of Paraffin Wax. It is the only oil proper to be used for immersing eggs preparatory to preserving them in alkaline solutions.

Paraffin Oil is a vegetable oil mineralized, and is not saponified by weak alkaline solutions, as are the vegetable and animal oils and fats.

When it is not convenient to use the hot deoxygenating and insulating process, the cold refined Paraffin Oil should be used for insulating the eggs. (See the cold insulating process, on page 37.)

A HIGH DEGREE OF HEAT FOR DEOXYGENATING EGGS.

The Paraffin Wax, or refined Paraffin Oil, may be placed in a vessel directly on a stove, or over a fire, and heated to 400° or 500°, at which temperature the eggs may be immersed therein, and they will be deoxygenated in much less time than when subjected to a heat of about 200° in a water-bath, as elsewhere recommended.

But to successfully deoxygenate eggs at high temperatures of 400°

[Copyright secured.]

or 500° requires experience and the use of a thermometer suitable for the purpose, as the whites of eggs will cook in a few seconds at 500°. Further, the process is attended with the danger of igniting the hot oil or wax at these high temperatures, and is consequently objectionable.

We therefore strenuously recommend the use of the water-bath, in which water can only be heated to 212° Fahr. (the boiling point); and liquids set in a water-bath cannot be heated above 207° Fahr. Hence no thermometer is needed for a water-bath when about this temperature is required.

[NOTE.—Only the true, or genuine, silicate of soda should be used for the preservation of eggs. For the process of its manufacture and properties, the reader is referred to page 227, and for its market price, to the last page.]

[Copyright secured.]

PRESERVING EGGS BY THE COLD INSULATING PROCESS.

Place the eggs in a wire basket, or other convenient perforated vessel, and immerse them in refined paraffin oil of a temperature between 70° and 80° Fahr. Let them remain in the oil about five minutes, raising and lowering the basket a few times, that the surface of the eggs may be completely covered with the oil. They should then be removed and put into the New Colorless Solution, within a day or two, or at once, if preferred.

A better plan is to fill a barrel half-full of refined paraffin oil; then fill the barrel with eggs as long as the oil will cover them, and allow the oil to remain at least five minutes; but we prefer to let it remain two or three hours. Then draw it off by means of a faucet at the lower end of the barrel.

Let the eggs remain undisturbed twenty-four hours, so that the oil may become partly dried on the shell. Then fill up the barrel with the *new colorless solution*, so as to cover the eggs to a depth of two inches above the top layer, and whatever oil is left in the barrel will rise to the surface of the solution. There should be, in all, about one quart of oil on the surface, to prevent evaporation, chemical change and the absorption of impurities and gases from the atmosphere.

The barrel should be covered with paper and a board cover.

Keep the barrel in a cellar where the temperature is below 60° Fahr., and in a year after you may expect to find the eggs in as sweet a condition as when put into the barrel.

This process for preserving the ordinary eggs of commerce is probably the best for a cold process that has been discovered.

[NOTE.—One or two hours before putting the eggs in the new colorless solution, add fifteen or twenty pounds of ice, broken up in small pieces, to half a barrel of the solution, and as soon as it is dissolved, and when the temperature is about 40°, pour it on the eggs, and if the barrel is insulated, closely covered as directed, and kept in a cool cellar, the temperature of the solution will remain below 50° Fahr. for weeks, or even months.]

By adding ice to all lime mixtures, or solutions, before putting in the eggs, as above directed, to reduce the temperature to about 40° Fahr., eggs will keep in a fresh condition a much longer time.

Especial attention is called to the fact that eggs will remain fresh in the new colorless solution, even if they are not coated or insulated with oils, etc., provided that the temperature of the solution is kept below 55° Fahr. And it is greatly to be preferred to the lime mixtures as a preservative.

INSULATING EGGS WITH THE REFINED RESINOUS LINSEED OIL FOR DRY PACKING.

Eggs, if designed for dry packing, must be insulated with the refined resinous linseed oil, at a temperature of from 50° to 70°, by immersing them for a few minutes, or they may remain in the oil twenty-four hours without detriment. They must then be taken from the barrel and dried in the open air for two or three days. Or eggs may be *deoxygenated* and *insulated* for dry packing by the use of the refined resinous linseed oil, at the temperature recommended for the deoxygenating process on page 33.

The eggs are then to be packed in the No. 1 dry compound (see pages 16 and 17), or in old, dry oats, and kept in a cool, dry place. Fresh eggs thus prepared will remain in a good condition for a long time.

A COLD PROCESS FOR DEOXYGENATING EGGS BY SUBSTITUTING CARBONIC ACID GAS FOR THE ATMOSPHERIC OXYGEN WHICH IS EXPELLED, EITHER BY RAREFACTION (AS DIRECTED BY THE NUMBER ONE PROCESS), OR EXTRACTED BY MEANS OF AN AIR-PUMP.

Fill a substantial barrel, prepared by the insulating process, with fresh eggs, tightly close it (by fastening the head with screws), and then cover it all over with the insulating composition. Exhaust the air from the barrel by means of an air-pump. As a vacuum is produced, the air in the cavity at the large end of the egg will escape, together with a portion of the air in the substance of the egg. When a moderately good vacuum is secured, carbonic acid gas must be slowly admitted from a suitably charged reservoir, which must have been previously connected with the barrel of eggs. Great care must be exercised to slowly admit the carbonic acid gas, which can be done best by means of a stop-cock, in corresponding quantity with the amount of air extracted, as the egg-shells might otherwise be broken by a too great and sudden pressure of the gas, especially over the cavity at the large end of the egg. By this process, if properly performed, the eggs become filled with an inert gas, which must be retained by a substantial and impervious covering.

Let the eggs remain at least twenty-four hours in this carbonic acid gas. Then inject refined paraffin oil into the barrel until it is full, allowing the gas to escape from the top. Permit the eggs to remain in the oil twenty-four hours, when they may be removed, or the oil may be drawn off by a faucet.

Within one hour after the oil is drawn off, fill up the barrel with the new colorless solution, which should be cooled with ice to 40°, just before pouring it upon the eggs, (as directed in the cold insulating process). When filling up the barrel containing the eggs, carefully pour in the new colorless solution, so that the oil will not be washed from the eggs. After the barrel is full, plug and seal up the apertures made for the faucets, etc. Keep the barrel hermetrically sealed and in a cool place until required for use.

Eggs, after being deoxygenated and charged with carbonic acid gas, if desired for dry packing, must be immediately insulated with the refined resinous linseed oil, (instead of refined paraffin oil,) at a temperature between 50° and 70°. Let the eggs remain in the oil for twenty-four hours; then remove and dry them in the open air for two or three days. They are then to be packed in the No. 1 dry compound, or old, dry oats, and kept in a cool, dry place.

If fresh eggs are used in this process, they will remain in a fresh condition for an unlimited time.

It should be borne in mind that eggs, after being charged with carbonic acid gas, *must not be immersed in hot oils or other hot preparations* to obtain a coating, as the heat will expel a portion, if not all, of the carbonic acid gas, which would vitiate the result.

WHY DEOXYGENATED EGGS SHOULD BE KEPT IN SOLUTIONS.

After being deoxygenated by our process, which hermetrically seals or closes the pores of their shells, the question will doubtless arise: Why is it necessary to put eggs in the cold silicate of soda solution?

Our answer is, first, to prevent an accumulation of dust on the shells, which would give them the appearance of age, and, secondly, to keep the eggs at a more even and lower temperature, as the liquids are not readily affected by slight atmospheric changes. Otherwise, if the eggs are exposed in boxes and barrels, without any other protection, and as some of the eggs may be several days old and contain a large quantity of atmospheric oxygen that has not been wholly expelled, but sufficiently deoxygenated for their preservation if kept at a moderately low and uniform temperature, an immersion in this solution will render them less liable to change.

To illustrate: The cellar where the eggs are kept is 50° Fahr. in the morning; at noon the temperature is increased to 70° or 80°; while at night it is down again to 50°. If the eggs are not protected by some non-conducting substance, many of them not being fresh, they will become affected by these atmospheric changes. If they are in the solution, however, they will be but slightly affected by these changes of temperature. If the solution be kept in the prepared or *insulated barrels* (see method of thus preparing barrels), it will require a long continued summer heat to affect its temperature.

WHY THE SILICATE OF SODA SOLUTION IS PREFERABLE TO LIME-WATER FOR MERCHANTABLE EGGS.

The question may be asked, why lime-water will not answer, in place of the silicate of soda solution, in which to keep eggs after they are deoxygenated.

Answer: Because lime-water is constantly depositing the carbonate of lime, which settles on the eggs and, partially adhering to their surface, gives a roughness to their shells, causing the appearance of limed eggs. Such when offered for sale will not bring so high a price as those having the appearance of fresh eggs. But for family use, the rough appearance of the shell being no objection, the deoxygenated eggs may be preserved quite as well in lime-water or lime mixture as in the silicate of soda solution.

TO RENDER EGGS LESS LIABLE TO BREAK, AND THEREBY INCREASE THEIR DURABILITY AND VALUE.

Additional strength and durability are imparted to the egg-shell by the insulating process, which renders it much less liable to break when handled, or during transportation.

WHY DO LIMED EGGS SOON SPOIL AFTER BEING REMOVED FROM A LIME SOLUTION?

Because they are generally exposed to a higher range of temperature after being removed from the solution, which accelerates decomposition. Eggs with very thick shells are generally the last to spoil. The deposit of carbonate of lime from lime-water upon the shell of the egg does not entirely prevent the endosmosis of atmospheric oxygen affecting the egg substance. Strictly fresh eggs put into lime solutions will keep longer than if they were stale when immersed.

Stale eggs, with thin shells, will keep but a short time after being removed from a lime solution, unless kept at a low temperature, because they are in the incipient stage of decomposition, as all eggs are, unless preserved in their original freshness, or less than one day old.

Therefore, the reason why some limed eggs will keep for weeks, or in some cases months, after being taken out of a lime solution, is the fact of their original freshness when put into the solution, and their possessing thick, compact shells, which receive a deposit of carbonate of lime, rendering them still less porous, and consequently much less liable to suffer from the evaporation of their fluids and the absorption of atmospheric oxygen.

EGGS KEPT FRESH BY COLD.

Decomposition cannot take place in eggs, or other animal substances, when kept at a temperature below 45°; therefore, if eggs be placed in an ice-house, refrigerator, or other cool place, at a temperature of from 35° to 45° Fahr., they will not spoil. Eggs should be packed, for convenience, in barrels containing powdered charcoal or dry oats, or other bad conductors of heat, which will keep them perfectly sweet by guarding them against atmospheric changes and impure or noxious vapors.

The eggs, when packed, should be placed on end, and when the barrel is headed up it should be turned on its opposite head as often as once in every fourteen days, thus changing the position of the eggs, to prevent the yelks from coming in contact with the shells, which is sometimes liable to occur. But this is not a practical method for egg dealers in general, on account of the difficulty in getting so low a temperature.

We have now given our readers the best practical processes, and if they are careful in following our instructions, which are the results of years of research and experiment, they may depend upon having fresh and wholesome eggs throughout all seasons of the year.

ANATOMY OF THE EGG—WHY THE YELK OF A FRESH EGG SETTLES AGAINST THE SHELL, AND THE EGG SOON AFTER SPOILS.

In considering the anatomy of the egg, we will commence with the exterior and proceed inward.

First—We find the egg-shell (*testa ovi*, or *putamen ovi*), and lining its internal surface is found the *chorion* (*membrana putaminis*), a white, semi-opaque membrane consisting of two layers, which, by their separation at the large end of the egg, form a cavity filled with nearly pure oxygen. This vacuity is caused by the condensation of the egg substance and the entrance of air during the process of cooling at the time it is laid. When the egg is fecundated, this bubble of oxygen serves as a respiratory reservoir for the prospective chick.

Immediately within and adjoining the *chorion*, yet detached from that membrane, is found the *allantoid membrane* enveloping the *albumen ovi*. The office of the *allantoid*, which is a very delicate, transparent membrane, is to hold the fluid contents of the white intact, when the egg-shell and *chorion* are removed.

Next in order is found the *albumen ovi*, a colorless, transparent, glutinous liquid, inodorous and tasteless, inclosed in delicate membranous cells.

The partitionary substance that constitutes these cells is the delicate membrane *oonin* (its office is similar to that of the honey-comb), which prevents the albumen from rapidly spreading when the *allantoid* is ruptured. When one or several cells are broken, the *oonin* partition holds the white of the egg in the remaining cells *in statu quo*. The labor required to "beat up" the white of eggs is owing to the toughness of the *allantoid* and *oonin* membranes.

When they are fully disintegrated, either by mechanical force, or by decomposition from the effects of lime-water, or age, the white of the egg flows readily, and is called *"watery."*

Between the white and yelk of the egg is found the *amnion membrane*, which surrounds the yelk (*vitellus ovi*), subserving the same purpose as the *allantoid*, which envelops the albumen.

Attached to opposite points on the circumference of the *amnion membrane* are the *chalazæ*, consisting of two white, spiral, knotty and tenacious membranous bodies, which extend in opposite directions through the albumen, and are attached to the *allantoid membrane* at each end of the egg, for the purpose of supporting the yelk in the central part of the albumen. But when the *allantoid* and *oonin* membranes are destroyed by the causes above stated, or by shaking an egg violently, the connexion of these membranes is broken, and the yelk gravitates to the lowest part of the egg, finally resting upon the shell. As the specific gravity of the yelk is greater than that of the albumen, it settles in accordance with the laws of gravity.

Hence the yelk of a fresh egg does *not* settle (except from agitation sufficient to break the *allantoid, oonin* and *chalaza*); while that of a stale egg does, owing to the decomposition of these membranes.

When the yelk rests on the shell, it no longer has albumen for its protection, and being of a highly susceptible nature, rapidly absorbs oxygen, which soon causes its destruction.

But eggs which have been *deoxygenated* and *insulated* are not liable to spoil, even after violent agitation has ruptured the membranes so that the yelk settles and rests on the shell, as no oxygen can be absorbed by an insulated egg.

The yelk is a thick, opaque, golden-yellow fluid, inodorous, and of a bland, oily taste. On the yelk is a small white spot, known as the *cicatricula*, surrounded by whitish concentric rings. The *cicatricula* is the germinating or embryonic point of the fetal chicken. A duct extends from this germ vesicle to the centre of the yelk, which contains a whitish, granular substance, designed by nature for the support of the chick during its first stages of development.

THE SIZE AND WEIGHT OF EGGS.

Among other facts of interest to the dealer, and especially to the consumer of eggs, are the following, concerning their size and weight: Those laid by the common barn-yard hen have diameters two and a half inches in length, by one and three-quarter inches in width, and an average weight of one and three-fourth ounces. The yelk constitutes about two-fifths of the whole substance, the albumen forming the remainder. Eight of these eggs ordinarily weigh one pound.

SALT WATER A TEST FOR FRESH EGGS.

Dissolve ten ounces of common salt in one gallon of cold water.

Place eggs that candle clear in this solution, and if perfectly fresh, they will gradually sink, but if slightly stale, they will swim.

All eggs that sink in this solution, the specific gravity of which is about 1.065, may be classed as fresh eggs, which have lost but a small portion of their fluids by evaporation and are quite suitable for preserving.

Eggs that will swim in salt water, of the strength of 8 oz. of salt to 1 gallon of water, must never be used for preserving. Eggs which have passed the test of salt water must be rinsed in fresh water and dried before deoxygenating or insulating them.

Twelve ounces of salt, dissolved in one gallon of water form a solution (specific gravity 1.091), sufficiently strong to float a *perfectly fresh egg*. One gallon of cold water dissolves only three pounds of salt, making a saturated solution of the specific gravity of 1.210. Boiling increases its solubility but very little.

WHAT CLASS OF EGGS TO SELECT, AND THE BEST SEASON FOR PRESERVING THEM.

It is well known to most persons who are engaged in the egg business that eggs are liable, from their susceptible nature, to absorb the flavors of many substances with which they may be kept in contact. Hence it is highly important that no preserving agent should be used which will impart any flavor or taste of a nature foreign to them.

In order to get strictly fresh eggs, they must be removed from the nests the same day they are laid, and put up immediately. This cannot be done on a large scale, as dealers in eggs usually purchase them of farmers who bring to market eggs from one day to two or three weeks old, on some of which the hens have set for a day or two, or longer, and thus many of them are stale.

At all times, and particularly during the hot summer months, great care should be taken to reject all musty or stale eggs. Eggs gathered in hot weather from damp, outdoor nests, or that have remained under a hen for a day or two, or if placed in musty grain, bran, cellar-earth, sawdust, shavings, or other substances which readily impart an unpleasant flavor, are liable to be more or less impregnated with the flavor of such articles, and are unfit to pack, though they may look clear when held before a candle.

If eggs are packed in fresh pine sawdust for a day or two, they will be flavored with turpentine; if packed in oak sawdust, they will be stained of a brown color, and are liable to become sour.

The best time to put up eggs is in March, April, or May, and again during the months of September, October and November. During the hot summer months, unless great care is taken by the farmer in gathering fresh eggs every day, they are liable to become musty. Although the farmer may gather and preserve eggs during all seasons of the year, it is not safe for persons in cities to buy eggs for preserving during the hot summer months. Such eggs are usually several days or weeks old, and, having been handled and exposed to more or less heat, they are liable to be damaged, and if put into a preserving solution when in a musty or spoiled state, their condition will not be improved.

Therefore, eggs which, though not strictly fresh, will bear inspection when candled, and have not been exposed to flavors or odors so as to affect them, form the class which is commonly used for preserving.

It is therefore, an object of importance to find a remedy for this class of eggs, which, to accommodate the egg dealers, must be kept on hand at a temperature from 50° to 80° Fahr.

TESTING AND PREPARING EGGS FOR THE PRESERVING PROCESS.

Wash the soiled eggs. Candle all the eggs carefully, rejecting those which have dark and floating spots, or that have a cloudy appearance, and all that are in the *least* cracked. Put down only those that candle perfectly clear. Reject all that swim in the water, even if they appear clear when held before a candle, as such are old eggs.

INSTRUCTIONS FOR PACKING AND SHIPPING EGGS.

In hot weather, eggs should always be shipped in old, dry, sweet oats, or coarsely powdered charcoal. In cool weather, cut rye and wheat straw will answer. Never use oat or buckwheat straw, sawdust or shavings. When packing eggs for shipment, allow at least one-half or three-quarters of an inch of packing material between the eggs and the barrels; also about one-quarter of one inch between the eggs, and about one and one-half inches between each layer. Do not put over 70 dozen into a flour barrel. There should be about two inches of packing material between the eggs and each head of the barrel. After each two or three layers are put in, they should be well settled by using a heavy plank follower, and shaking the barrel until well settled.

When heading the barrel, great caution should be used in having the head press firmly on the packing material, so that the eggs cannot work loose in the barrel by handling, and yet *not be* so tight as to break them.

GENERAL REMARKS CONCERNING EGGS IN PRESERVING SOLUTIONS.

When eggs are taken out of preserving solutions, the best plan to wash them is to put them into slotted boxes, and upon every layer or two pour cold water, and then let them become perfectly dry before packing.

Eggs should never be shipped in liquids, but should be taken out of preserving solutions and packed as directed.

Great care should be used in handling packages containing eggs in preserving solutions, as the eggs are very liable to break.

As a general rule, preserving solutions will not answer for use the second year.

Eggs should be kept in preserving solutions until they are required for use or for market.

Eggs, broken in barrels or vats, while in preserving solutions, generally spoil soon, and impair the preserving qualities of the solution. Whenever this happens, remove the unbroken eggs, wash them in cold water, cleanse the vessel and put the eggs into a new solution.

As ordinary barrels or vats are liable to leak, they should be examined every two weeks. In case of leakage, they must be supplied with additional preserving solution.

But if barrels or vats are prepared according to our process for preparing kerosene oil and other barrels and vats, all danger of leakage will be avoided.

Do not put egg-preserving solutions in vessels of iron, copper, tin, zinc, or other metal, as the chemical action of the metals upon the solutions is injurious.

THE SEX OF EGGS.

A series of experiments by an experienced poulterer in the egg-hatching business has determined, as a general rule, the following results:

Eggs containing the germ of males have wrinkles on the small ends; on the contrary, eggs which are smooth at the extremities, and nearest to roundness, produce females, while those *pointed* at one end usually engender males.

The above may be of some importance to those engaged in raising poultry.

INCUBATION.

The time required for hatching eggs when placed under fowls, or by any artificial heat, to-wit:

Hens' Eggs,..21 days.
Turkeys' Eggs,..28 "
Ducks' Eggs,...29 "
Geese Eggs,..30 "

A NEW-LAID EGG.

The large end of a new-laid egg feels *cold* when placed against the tongue, but that of a stale egg feels *warm*, because the white of a fresh egg being in contact with the shell acts as a conductor in abstracting heat from the tongue more readily than the non-conducting air bubble or cavity in the stale egg.

EGGS.

Few persons understand the magnitude of the egg trade of New York city. The receipts for nine months of 1869 averaged at least *one thousand barrels* per day. A barrel contains about 80 dozen, or 960 eggs; the aggregate, therefore, was in one day nearly a million.

Like cotton and corn, they are considered a cash article, and can be sold immediately.

One thousand barrels of eggs, at an average price of 30 cents per dozen, amounts to $24,000 *per day,* or $8,790,000 per annum.

IMPORTANT STATISTICS FOR THE YEAR 1869.

In compiling the annexed table, we are respectfully obliged to the Hon. Secretaries and other public officers of the various States; also to the Hon. Horace Capron, Commissioner of the Department of Agriculture, Washington, D. C., and to the various journals of agriculture and commerce throughout the United States, for the statistics herein set forth.

STATISTICS FOR THE YEAR 1869.

The following table shows that the total value of eggs produced in the United States exceeds fifty millions of dollars per annum:

TOTAL POPULATION OF THE UNITED STATES AND TERRITORIES:
1869.. 37,139,513
1860.. 31,443,790

Increase in nine years............................... 5,695,723

STATES AND TERRITORIES.	Population.	No. Famil's	No. Farms.	No. doz. Eggs per Annum.	Av'age Price 20 cents per dozen.
Alabama	987,461	141,131	56,139	5,414,000	$1,082,800.00
Arkansas	472,166	71,111	41,058	3,117,000	629,400.00
California	554,112	73,114	27,114	3,848,000	769,000.00
Connecticut	486,136	76,581	25,310	2,331,000	466,200.00
Delaware	140,448	18,117	6,710	818,000	169,000.00
Florida	146,390	20,113	7,134	600,000	120,000.00
Georgia	1,110,076	169,112	62,144	4,210,000	842,000.00
Illinois	2,178,766	372,882	190,523	22,648,000	4,529,604.00
Indiana	1,950,112	325,118	142,786	17,767,000	3,553,400.00
Iowa	902,040	180,408	82,596	10,898,000	2,179,000.00
Kansas	180,478	30,576	18,590	2,400,000	480,000.00
Kentucky	1,166,313	190,114	91,716	8,486,000	1,697,200.00
Louisiana	915,117	144,101	17,148	1,410,000	282,000.00
Maine	629,104	103,645	56,110	7,60,000	1,520,000.00
Maryland	704,891	117,481	108,496	12,478,000	2,49,600.00
Massachusetts	1,281,700	250,900	36,194	5,001,000	1,000,200.00
Michigan	986,724	164,454	79,511	9,766,000	1,953,000.00
Minnesota	286,478	63,583	28,148	2,400,000	480,000.00
Mississippi	847,213	104,180	42,113	2,100,000	430,000.00
Missouri	1,530,187	261,198	108,496	9,890,000	1,978,000.00
Montana, Idaho, and Wyoming Territories	52,112	5,004	850	1,000	200.00
New Hampshire	330,127	65,000	31,101	4,800,000	979,200.00
New Jersey	681,492	113,582	28,004	4,905,410	981,082.00
New York	4,885,586	780,940	212,897	28,749,000	5,779,800.00
North Carolina	1,200,315	167,118	75,361	4,111,000	822,800.00
Ohio	2,905,163	484,242	188,009	21,875,000	4,375,000.00
Oregon	121,534	19,857	8,568	900,000	180,000.00
Pennsylvania	3,297,420	544,665	176,10.	20,415,000	4,083,000.00
Rhode Island	178,231	23,615	5,438	700,500	140,010.00
South Carolina	780,412	120,171	33,241	3,014,000	6,28,00.00
Tennessee	1,106,141	163,060	83,144	7,414,300	1,492,860.00
Texas	894,147	110,04	45,19	4,567,000	913,484.00
Vermont	315,616	58,678	31,578	4,157,600	831,520.00
Virginia	1,330,528	221,730	77,216	6,150,100	1,230,020.00
West Virginia	271,800	40,466	17,113	1,645,104	325,020.00
Wisconsin	855,060	171,012	78,892	8,958,200	1,791,640.00
District of Columbia	86,120	7,485	238	13,000	2,600.00
Dakota Territory	9,312	1,127	896	15,600	3,120.00
Nebraska	78,127	3,710	6,481	600,450	120,000.00
Nevada	108,406	12,891	1,048	100,600	20,120.00
New Mexico, Arizona and Indian Territories	148,619	11,867	8,896	858,000	171,600.00
Utah Territory	81,496	7,112	9,786	1,040,000	208,000.00
Washington Territory	31,461	4,010	3,672	100,600	20,120.00
*Colorado Territory	61,181				
*Russian America	55,780				
AGGREGATE	37,139,513	6,074,253	2,371,894	258,507,860	$51,701,572.00

* The statistics of families, farms and eggs not received from Colorado and Russian America.

A French statistician estimates the total value of eggs annually produced in France at fifty-seven millions of dollars.

The total value of eggs annually produced on the globe is estimated at *five hundred and fifty millions of dollars.*

EGG—*Ovum.*

The following is a perfect chemical analysis of the egg of the common hen, (*Phasanius Gallus*), which is supposed to have been originally the jungle fowl of *India*. It is now domesticated in nearly all parts of the globe.

The egg consists of an external covering, known as the shell, (*testa ovi,* or *putamen ovi*), which is composed of—

Carbonate of Lime,	86.0 parts.
Animal Substance	3.5 "
Phosphate of Lime	1.3 "
Carbonate of Magnesia	0.9 "
Oxide of Iron	0.7 "
Sulphur	1.7 "
Gelatin	2.9 "
Water	3.0 "
Total	100

The shell, when exposed to an intense heat in the crucible, is deprived of its carbonic acid, while the other substances are either rendered inert or dissipated, leaving a residuum of nearly pure oxide of calcium. Lining the internal surface of the shell is the *membrana putaminis,* a white semi-opaque membrane, composed of—

Albumen	29.1 parts.
Gluten	36.0 "
Tannin	9.3 "
Gelatin	14.6 "
Water	11.0 "
Total	100

This lining envelopes a substance known as the white, (*albumen ovi*), a colorless, transparent, glutinous liquid, inclosed in delicate membranous cells, inodorous and tasteless. Its composition is—

Pure Albumen	13.0 parts.
Chloride of Sodium	0.2 "
Soda	0.5 "
Gluten	1.2 "
Sulphur	0.1 "
Water	85.0 "
Total	100

The white is soluble in water and alkaline solutions, coagulable by alcohol, strong acids, and by a heat of 156°F., and can be precipitated by chloride of gold, tannin, chloride of tin, corrosive sublimate, sub-acetate of lead, and sulphate of copper. Coagulation renders it insoluble.

Passing through the white to the central portion of the egg, is found the yelk (*vitellus ovi*), a thick, opaque, golden-yellow fluid, inodorous, of a bland, oily taste, and by agitation with water it forms an opaque emulsion. Its chemical composition is—

Vitellin, a peculiar albuminous principle	15.760
Margarin and Olein	21.304
Cholesterine	.938
Oleic Acid, Margaric Acid	5.462
Muriate of Ammonia	2.204
Phosphoglyceric Acid	.034
Phosphates of Lime and Magnesia	.200
Chlorides of Sodium & Potassium—Sulphate of Potassa	1.022
Gelatin	.277
Sulphur	.553
Oxide of Iron, Lactic Acid and Animal Extract	.400
Water	51.846
Total	100.000

Yelk of eggs is concrescible by heat, and becomes solid by boiling. It is employed as a medium for uniting resins and oils with water.

The white of eggs is useful as a demulcent in diseases of the intestinal mucous membrane, and as an antidote to corrosive sublimate and the soluble salts of copper, with which it forms insoluble and comparatively inert compounds.

Exposed in thin layers to a current of air, it becomes solid, retaining its transparency and solubility in water, and can be thus preserved a long time without change; in this state it may be applied in a state of solution to the same purpose as in its original condition. It soon putrefies in the fluid state, unless kept at a temperature below 50° Fahr., or *deoxygenated* and permitted to remain in its natural condition.

CLARIFICATION.

The white of the egg is used for the clarification of syrups, infusion of coffee and other liquids, which it accomplishes by undergoing coagulation, enveloping suspended impurities and undissolved particles in its flakes, and rising with them to the surface, or settling to the bottom.

ALBUMEN.

This substance, found nearly pure in the white of eggs, from which it derives its name, is also found in the serum of the blood, and in many animal and vegetable substances.

It exists in two conditions, solid and liquid—liquid in the white of eggs, humors of the eye and serum of the blood; solid, in the brain and nerves of animals, and in the seeds of plants. As found in the white of eggs, it is colorless, tasteless, odorless and soluble in alkaline solutions. It is precipitated from all of its solutions by alcohol, and by heat, which coagulates it, after which it is not again soluble in water. Like all other nitrogenized animal substances, it is very prone to decomposition. Being capable of changing in the blood into fibrin, which again becomes musculin, (the substance of muscles), albumen is justly esteemed by physiologists a most perfect article of food. Indeed, the value of meats and vegetables is largely estimated by the amount of albumen present. This accounts for the well-known fact that eggs may well be substituted for meats.

DESICCATED EGGS.

Break a number of fresh eggs into an evaporating vessel, and expose them to a heat of 125° Fahr., over a water-bath, with occasional stirring until dry. Then pack them in airtight vessels. When thus dried, the residue presents a bright orange color. When required for use, one part of dried egg should be well beaten with three times its weight of water.

Desiccated eggs may be used for making puddings, custards, etc.

DOES THE ANIMAL WARMTH OR GERMINATING HEAT RETARD OR PROMOTE THE DECOMPOSITION OF EGGS?

This is a subject of controversy among chemists. It is claimed by some that it is absolutely necessary to destroy the life of the germ in order to preserve the egg. Wherefore they recommend, for that purpose, agents which will not render the egg distasteful or injurious as an article of food. Others contend that instead of destroying the germ of the egg, it is only necessary to suspend its animal life.

When we reflect that the absorption by the egg of alkalies or acids destroys the life of the germ, and that when the egg is deprived of its vitality decomposition is the result, we see that the retention of the vital principle tends to its preservation. *An egg never decomposes so long as it has life.* Our processes, which are based upon this correct and truly philosophical theory, avoid the immediate contact with the egg of those destructive agents which are used to aid in the protection of the egg against the various influences of atmospheric gases, vapors and dust. After a lapse of twelve months, or longer, eggs preserved *by our processes* retain all their pristine beauty and freshness.

BARREN EGGS, OR EGGS WHICH ARE NOT FECUNDATED, ARE BEST FOR PRESERVING.

The hen at certain periods prepares a batch of eggs which, when sufficiently matured, she "lays," whether they are fecundated, or not, by the male bird.

As a matter of course, hatching cannot take place unless the eggs are fecundated, but they are equally good for cooking, and better for preserving, from the circumstance that they do not contain the germ-vesicle, and, as a consequence, the germinating heat, *i. e.*, the *punctum saliens* of animal life.

Experiments have proved that when unimpregnated eggs are placed under a setting hen for twenty-one days, (the usual period of incubation), both the yelk and albumen remain in their normal condition; showing conclusively that the barren are preferable to the fertile or fecundated eggs, because capable of enduring a higher temperature without change.

Poulterers should make a note of this fact, and not allow the male bird to associate with hens that are kept merely for laying eggs for preserving, and which are not designed for producing chickens.

CONCLUDING REMARKS CONCERNING LIME COMPOUNDS FOR PRESERVING EGGS.

An objection may be raised against the use of the "Cream of Lime Compound," according to formula (see page 11), as the lime, after remaining at rest a few months, "packs" about the eggs, and requires considerable labor to take them out of the mixture. This may be obviated by using the following:

Take of fresh, unslaked lime, ten pounds;

Common barrel salt, one pound;

Cold or hot water, twenty gallons.

Mix and stir occasionally for a day or two. Then allow the solution to rest for twenty-four hours, at the expiration of which time the undissolved lime will have subsided, leaving a *clear solution*, which is now ready for use, and is sufficient to cover about one hundred and fifty dozen eggs, the number required to fill a 42 to 45 gallon barrel.

Place the eggs carefully in the solution, so as not to disturb the sediment. When the barrel is filled within three inches of the top, spread over the eggs a thin cotton cloth, so that they may be entirely covered, and pour on the top of the cloth "Cream of Lime Compound" to the depth of two inches, and then pour over all a quart of paraffin oil, as directed on page 12.

Eggs put up in the lime and salt solution should be kept

at a temperature below 50° Fahr., and only in barrels prepared by the insulated process, and the solution covered with the refined paraffin oil; otherwise the barrels and the atmosphere are liable to change the character of the lime-water. (See pages 7 and 8.)

By strictly following these directions, if the eggs are kept at a temperature below 50 Fahr., they may be preserved in as good condition as if put up with the "Cream of Lime Compound."

Lime solutions or mixtures are not to be preferred for keeping eggs, but the formulas already given are the best combinations of lime for that purpose.

Fresh slaked lime may be used in the lime processes instead of the fresh, unslaked lime; but the latter is preferable.

ALL EGG-PRESERVING SOLUTIONS COOLED BEFORE USING.

All solutions and liquid mixtures designed for egg-preservatives, should be cooled to the temperature of about 40° Fahr., by the addition of ice broken into small pieces so that it will readily melt.

To each twenty gallons of solution or mixture, add from fifteen to twenty pounds (or more, if required) of finely broken ice, to reduce the temperature of the liquid to 40° by the thermometer; then put the eggs therein, as soon as the ice melts.

If the barrel is insulated, and the surface of the solution covered with the refined paraffin oil, and kept in a cool cellar, the temperature of the solution will remain below 55° for months, which will insure the preservation of eggs a much longer time.

PRESERVING EGGS, MEAT, VEGETABLES AND FRUITS BY HEAT.

The boiling of eggs and meat produces a marked change in these articles of food, by coagulating their albumen, which is the substance first involved in putrefaction and disorganization.

Cooked meat and eggs keep sweet much longer than when raw.

Air is a necessary agent in the process of decay or putrefaction. If animal or vegetable substances can be deprived of air and kept *in vacuo*, no visible change will take place for a very long time.

Boiling expels this internal air. Hence, if vegetable or animal substances be placed in a vessel and deprived of air by heat or other means, and the vessel then be hermetrically sealed, their preservation will be secured.

The application of heat, as we before remarked, coagulates the albumen, rendering it inactive and less inclined to change. By the heating process, fruits and vegetables are boiled in their own juice, whereby their albumen is coagulated. Heat has the peculiar effect not only of changing the combination of the constituent parts of vegetable and animal substances, but of retarding, at least for many years, if not altogether, the natural tendency of these bodies to decomposition. This opinion is confirmed by many important facts, which cannot be reconciled with the supposition that oxygen is the sole or even principal agent of decomposition. Thus milk which has been merely scalded will keep sweet much longer, even if freely exposed to, or purposely impregnated with oxygen gas, than milk which has not been heated.

Experiments have proved that oxygen may be present with fermentable matter without producing any effect whatever, as certain conditions cause or accelerate fermentation. So different or opposite states prevent or retard it. This is true, whatever may be the nature of the fermentation.

The well-known preserving process of Appert does not wholly depend upon the exclusion of oxygen from the provisions he preserves, after the albumen is coagulated.

Eggs, meat, vegetables and fruits put into tin cans, glass or earthenware jars, and kept for some time in boiling water, in order to completely expel their internal air and coagulate their albumen, and then sealed up while hot, may be preserved thus for winter use.

In dead animal bodies, the albumen first decomposes, serving as a ferment, or leaven, to infect the other animal constituents. Plants, which contain much vegetable albumen, as mushrooms, cabbage, etc., very soon decay when exposed to the air, particularly in warm weather.

To induce putrefactive fermentation, the same conditions are required as in the *vinous* and *acetic*, *viz*: moisture with certain degrees of temperature.

Could we deprive animal and vegetable substances of both air and moisture, no change would ever take place. The presence of air, although not always necessary, usually hastens decomposition. It is upon the foregoing laws of chemistry that most of the methods of preserving food are founded. The putrefactive fermentation, like the acetous and vinous fermentations, requires but a small amount of animal or vegetable substance in a state of decomposition for its inauguration. Even a decaying molecule inoculates others with which it may come in contact, causing them to putrefy. Even the effluvia or vapor of decaying matter will sometimes exert this destructive effect.

The inevitable change to which inanimate organic matter, whether animal or vegetable, is subject, is denominated fermentation, of which the following are the chief varieties:

First—The Vinous Fermentation.

Second—The Acetous Fermentation.

Third—The Putrefactive Fermentation.

By the first two varieties, the useful products, alcohol and acetic acid, are obtained. But the last is that complete change termed putrefactive decomposition, or rotting, by which animal and vegetable substances, particularly those containing nitrogen, are resolved into more simple and staple compounds, which, if liquids or gases, evaporate, while earthy or mineral matters remain. This change does not take place precisely in the same manner in animal as in vegetable substances; while vegetables generally pass through all the stages of fermentation, the flesh of animals passes at once into the putrefactive condition.

Animal substances contain a large proportion of nitrogen, as one of their elementary constituents, which is found only in small proportion as a constituent of vegetable matter. Many kinds of the latter contain none at all, as, for example, lignin or woody matter, gums, resins, etc., which decay much more slowly than animal matter.

The saccharine juices which many plants and fruits contain, if expressed, pass spontaneously in warm weather into the vinous and thence into the acetous fermentations, giving rise to carbonic acid, which escapes, and alcohol, which, by absorption of oxygen passes into acetic acid or vinegar. Vinous fermentation, if not arrested, as it may be by well-known means, soon changes into the acetous fermentation, of which vinegar is the product. If a considerable quantity of nitrogenized material remains in the vinegar, the acetous will soon pass into the putrefactive fermentation, which results in complete destruction of the liquid for all useful purposes. There is a time, however, though brief, when vegetables and fruits are through the vinous fermentation, before becoming positively sour and unwholesome.

When the juices of plants enter into the acetous fermentation, the acids thus generated destroy the cohesion of the ligneous fibres, and thus the whole plant is soon reduced to a pulpy state, and putrefaction follows. There is, however, very little of that remarkably disagreeable odor which exhales from putrefying animal matter, from the fact that the elements necessary to produce the offensive gases—sulphur and phosphorus—exist in vegetables in small proportions. When vegetables putrefy, their oxygen and a part of their hydrogen unite and form water, while another portion of their hydrogen combines with carbon, forming carbureted hydrogen. The chief part of the carbon, however, remains in the free and amorphous form of this element, and gives the decaying substance the black color so commonly seen in rich soils, which are the products of decaying vegetable matter.

The elementary substances which compose the animal and vegetable kingdom are held together by the laws of organic life, but when deprived of this bond, have a tendency to separate from each other and enter into new combinations. This is a universal law of nature; organic bodies come into existence, and, if permitted, live their allotted time and die. If nothing retards the usual course of things, they pass into other conditions, and the material substances of which they consist form the corporeal part of other living beings. Hence, life is death, but the grand result is *life*.

For example: When the egg commences to decay, its albumen is the base of putrefactive fermentation, and subsequently the *yelk is involved* in the same chemical change

The ultimate elements of a fresh egg are as follows:

Carbon—about ....55 parts.
Nitrogen, " 16   "
Oxygen,   " 17   "
Hydrogen, "   7   "
Sulphur, "   3   "
Phosphorus" 2   "

Which, in the progress of organic dissolution, separate from each other, and combine again as follows: The carbon unites with oxygen and forms carbonic acid; one portion of the hydrogen forms water with the oxygen; another part, uniting with the nitrogen, forms ammonia; another portion combines with the carbon, producing carbureted hydrogen gas, and the remainder unites with the phosphorus and sulphur, producing phosphoreted and sulphureted hydrogen gases, which are, in a great measure, the cause of the fetor, (so offensive to the sense of smell), evolved by the breaking of a perfectly rotten egg, which is justly entitled to the appellation of *egg ultimatum*.

NUMBER ONE PROCESS FOR INSULATING ALL WOODEN VESSELS—HOW TO PREPARE OR INSULATE CARBON OR KEROSENE OIL, LARD AND LINSEED OIL OR OTHER BARRELS, WHETHER NEW OR OLD; ALSO WOODEN VATS, FOR HOLDING EGG-PRESERVING SOLUTIONS, PORK, BEEF, BRINE, CIDER, VINEGAR, ALKALIES, ACIDS, SIRUP, BUTTER, WATER, ETC.

The simplicity, cheapness and effectiveness of the method of preparing carbon or kerosene oil barrels for containing egg-preserving solutions, render it practicable by all dealers in eggs.

Kerosene or carbon oil barrels are generally well made, iron-bound and durable, and can be obtained in almost every town or village at a reasonable price. But being completely saturated with the oil, and impregnated with the peculiar odor of kerosene, such barrels cannot be used for general purposes without preparation.

A series of chemical experiments has developed the following sure and simple method of rendering these barrels suitable for the preservation of eggs and the other purposes above named:

PROCESS AND FORMULA FOR INSULATING THE BARRELS OR VATS.

The barrel must be well hooped, water-tight, clean and dry. It is then charred in the following manner, viz.: Build a fire inside the barrel with shavings, so that the blaze may char the whole interior surface.

In the case of kerosene oil barrels, the inner surface will readily burn after the ignition of a few shavings. Other barrels may also be readily charred by the use of about a pint of kerosene oil spread over their inner surface and allowed to remain a few minutes, in order that the wood may absorb a portion of it. Ignite it by some shavings, and in a short time the entire interior will become well charred. The combustion should be maintained until the wood is charred about one-eighth of an inch in depth, after which the ashes must be emptied out.

To extinguish the fire after the barrel is sufficiently charred, put a damp cloth over it, or turn the barrel on the other end, but do not extinguish it by water, as it would render the barrel damp and unsuitable for receiving the insulating composition.

By the inversion of the barrel on its opposite end, the ashes are emptied and the fire extinguished in a few moments. As soon as this is effected, reverse the position of the barrel, and allow the smoke and hot air to escape for a minute or two. Immediately, while the barrel is still hot, apply, as rapidly as possible, a thorough coating of the following insulating composition:

White Resin (pulverized)..6 lbs.
Paraffin Wax... .... 1 lb.

Melt these articles together, and when combined apply while hot with a clean brush or swab, spreading the composition, *before it cools*, evenly over the entire interior surface of the barrel. If this composition be thoroughly applied while it is liquid and the barrel hot, it will penetrate the pores of the wood from one-fourth to half an inch. After allowing the barrel thus prepared to remain about an hour, make another application of hot melted paraffin as a finishing coat, to completely cover any remaining air holes.

In one or two hours after this application, the barrel will be ready for use. It will be proper to use six or seven pounds of the insulating composition for each barrel, and for the last coating about a pound of paraffin will be required. When barrels thus prepared require cleaning, use only lukewarm soap-suds, as hot water will melt the paraffin.

[NOTE—TO PREVENT THE SHRINKAGE AND SWELLING OF BARRELS.—In addition to the inside coating, make a hot application of the insulating composition to the entire outside and bottom of the barrel. Barrels thus prepared may be kept in water or in damp cellars, or in a dry atmosphere, without swelling or shrinking, and with careful usage will last for years without decay.]

Do not put hot water, or mix *hot lime compounds*, in barrels which have been prepared with the insulating materials, as paraffin wax melts at 120°.

When lime compounds are used, mix them in a barrel which has not been insulated, and, when the mixture is cold, pour it in the insulated barrel.

NUMBER TWO PROCESS FOR CLEANSING AND PREPARING BARRELS AND VATS.

The following process is not so complete as that described as the No. 1, or Insulating Process, but is far preferable to the ordinary methods of preparing barrels, and may be preferred by some on account of its cheapness, being about one half as expensive:

One pound of sal soda (common washing soda), or one-half-pound of potash or concentrated lye, and one pound of fresh, unslaked lime. Put these into the kerosene or carbon oil barrel to be cleaned, and pour upon them a pail full of boiling water. Stir thoroughly about fifteen minutes; then wash, or scrub with a clean broom or long-handled scrubbing brush, the inside of the barrel over its entire surface with this caustic mixture; after which let the mixture remain during the day, occasionally scrubbing until the inside is thoroughly cleansed. Frequent scrubbings may be necessary in some hard cases.

On the following day, pour off the mixture, and immediately rinse the barrel with clean water. Then, before the barrel dries, place in it eight pounds of fresh, unslaked lime and two gallons of cold water. Let this mixture stand half a day, stirring occasionally. It will then be of the consistence of cream.

Then, with a brush, give the entire inner surface a coating of about one-eighth of an inch in thickness, and the bottom should have half an inch or more in thickness, all of which allow to remain and partly dry.

In about an hour after this application, or when the coating is half dry, apply liquid silicate of soda, of the consistence of 25° Baume, with a clean brush, or carefully pour it into the barrel to the extent of half a gallon, and then carefully roll the barrel, so that the liquid silicate may come in contact with the entire interior surface of the barrel.

This immediately combines with the lime, forming an insoluble compound of silicate of lime and soda.

A second application should be made of the liquid silicate of soda in about six hours.

A third application should be made in twenty-four hours after the first, which will dry in a few hours, forming a hard and tenacious vitreous coating or lining of the barrel.

After a barrel thus prepared has dried one day, it is ready for the reception of any egg-preservative that may be desired.

No salt, glue, grease, oil, or other substances, should ever be mixed with the lime or silicate of soda, as such substances prevent the chemical union of the silicate with the lime.

Never apply the silicate of soda to the barrel before the lime, as the lime will not afterwards properly adhere.

Neither mix the silicate with the lime mixture, but use them separately, as above directed. It is much better to apply the silicate while the limed surface is somewhat damp, or half dry, than to defer its application longer.

If the above directions are strictly followed, a barrel will be produced having an interior surface hard and similar to glazed earthenware.

This process (No. 2) may be used for cleaning all barrels, either new or old, for the preservation of eggs, etc., such as those which have contained molasses, vinegar, alcohol, wine, whisky, or other liquors. The wood of such barrels, although apparently clean, contains substances which, on exposure to the air, enter into fermentation, the results of which are acids that act upon the egg-preserving solutions, and may seriously modify them.

Many suppose that NEW OAK BARRELS are well adapted to hold egg-preserving solutions. On the contrary, they are the most unsuitable barrels that can be selected, as the sap or juice of the wood contains coloring matters and acids, which crystalize in the pores on drying. The acid (principally tannic) is readily dissolved when in contact with water, especially of an alkaline nature, thus changing the solution so that its action upon the carbonate of lime of the egg-shell stains it brown.

It also changes the alkaline character of the lime-water, or other alkaline preparations, sometimes even wholly neutralizing them and destroying all their effectiveness upon the eggs, which then soon spoil. These facts are sufficient evidence of the *unfitness* of new oak barrels for containing egg-preserving solutions, unless previously prepared for the purpose. Pine barrels are the best that can be used. Vats should *always be constructed of pine lumber*.

The application of soda or potash, as above described, converts the grease or oil of the kerosene, lard or linseed, absorbed by or adhering to the barrel, into soap, which is subsequently removed by water. In case the impurity of the barrels is an acid, it is neutralized by the alkalies employed.

The combination of lime and silicate of soda produces a hard, vitreous coating, which prevents the contents of the barrel from receiving any odor or other impurities that might be imparted by the wood.

The principal objection to this process is, that the coating is liable to crack and peel off, especially when the wood swells and shrinks.

With proper care, however, to prevent the undue drying of the vessels, the coating may last several seasons. But to render barrels or vats very durable and wholly unobjectionable, the No. 1 Insulating Process is decidedly preferable, as it entirely prevents the barrels from shrinking or swelling.

No wooden vessel should be used for preserving eggs which has not been prepared by one of these processes.

VATS FOR KEEPING EGGS.

Vats may be made in the earth three or four feet deep, under cover, or in cellars. Let the earth be excavated to the required dimensions, and the vat may be constructed of one and a half inch seasoned pine plank, and insulated, as directed for kerosene oil barrels, or the charring may be omitted, and the composition put on hot.

Or the vats may be constructed of stone or brick, and laid in water-lime (hydraulic cement). If plastered thoroughly, no insulating composition will be necessary. The cement will harden sufficiently in a few days.

When these vats are ready for the eggs, pour in the egg-preserving solution till the vat is half filled. The eggs may be placed in the solution at any convenient time thereafter, and should be deoxygenated and insulated by the No. 1 process, or by the cold insulating process. When the vat is filled, the solution should cover the eggs at least two inches in depth, and there should then be poured over all a proper quantity of refined paraffin oil to make it about one-fourth of an inch in depth. Lastly, cover the vat with a strong board cover.

REFINED RESINOUS LINSEED OIL—MODE OF REFINING AND BLEACHING.

To each gallon of raw linseed oil add four ounces of diluted sulphuric acid, (prepared by gradually adding two and a half ounces of commercial sulphuric acid to one and a half ounces of cold water, in a thin glass vessel). Mix the oil and acid well together by agitation, which should be repeated occasionally for two days; then allow it to rest two or three days, in which time the albuminous and mucilaginous matters contained in the oil will have subsided. The oil must then be carefully decanted, leaving the precipitate behind.

Then to each gallon of oil thus prepared add animal charcoal, in coarse powder, two pounds; chloride of lime, fine, dry powder, one ounce. Mix well together, and for two or three days occasionally shake the mixture; then heat it in a water-bath at boiling point for five or six hours, stirring with a glass rod or stick two or three times an hour. Then remove the vessel from the water-bath; allow it to stand two days, or even a week, agitating occasionally. Let it remain at rest at least twenty-four hours, when the oil should be carefully decanted and passed through filtering paper.

Finally, add to each gallon of the oil two ounces of slippery elm bark, pulverized. After thorough admixture by agitation, heat the mixture in a water-bath for one or two hours, with occasional stirring during the first hour. Then allow it to stand undisturbed one hour; after which pour off the clear oil, and while hot add to it one-half pound of the best white resin, pulverized; stir the mixture a few minutes, or until the resin is dissolved; then let the solution stand twenty-four hours, with occasional stirring, when it will be ready for use. Do not add more resin than recommended, as an excess retards the drying of the oil, while the proportion named accelerates the operation.

The diluted sulphuric acid carbonizes the albuminous and mucilaginous matters contained in the raw oil. The animal charcoal and chloride of lime neutralize any acid remaining, and at the same time deodorize, purify and bleach the oil. The slippery elm imparts an agreeable odor, and absorbs any water which may remain in the oil, and when heated to 200° subsides within an hour, leaving a pure, refined oil.

Raw linseed oil, prepared in this way, will keep in any climate without change; and, when applied to eggs, forms over the shell a firm, elastic, transparent coating, which materially aids in their preservation by excluding air from their substance and by preventing evaporation. The refined resinous linseed oil must not be used except for eggs which are to be kept in dry packing, as charcoal, oats, etc. If eggs coated with linseed oil are placed in alkaline solutions, the oil coating will saponify, and thus become destroyed. (See directions for using this oil for eggs on page 38.) Never use boiled linseed oil for coating eggs. Aside from its deleterious character, owing to the litharge, sugar of lead, sulphate of zinc, and other poisonous chemicals contained in it, its color darkens the egg-shell, which damages the sale of the eggs.

RAW LINSEED OIL

We have used as a coating for eggs, but find the following objections: It does not dry readily; it slightly stains the egg-shell; the egg sometimes absorbs the offensive crude odor of the oil, and it does not form as perfect a coating as when refined and combined with resin in the proportion above directed. Hence we do not recommend the raw linseed oil for coating eggs.

REFINED PARAFFIN OIL.—MODE OF REFINING AND BLEACHING IT.

Treat paraffin oil of a light color in the same manner as recommended for refining raw linseed oil, except that for the resin substitute paraffin wax, four ounces to each gallon of oil. The whole must be heated in a water-bath until the paraffin wax is dissolved.

This prepared oil may be used for the No. 1 hot deoxygenating and insulating process (see page 33), or for the cold insulating process, (see page 37.)

[NOTE.—Do not use more than four ounces of paraffin wax to each gallon of paraffin oil, when intended for the cold insulating process, as an excess of wax will leave a visible coating on the egg-shells, which is an objectionable feature when eggs are offered for sale.]

The special attention of the reader is directed to the fact that resin must not be combined with paraffin oil, as it saponifies when in alkaline solutions. Also, that PARAFFIN WAX must not be dissolved in linseed oil when used for a *cold application* for eggs, as the combination will not dry readily.

OTHER OILS FOR EGGS.

We have experimented with many oils and oleaginous substances for the purpose of producing a suitable coating for eggs, viz.: Olive, Cotton Seed, Castor, Poppy, Sperm and Lard Oils; also Tallow, Lard, Butter, etc., separately, and in combination with Beeswax, Paraffin, Caoutchouc, Resin, etc., but, thus far in our investigations, we have found nothing equal to the Refined Linseed and Paraffin Oils.

BUTTER.

Butter consists of fat globules (known as cream), each of which is inclosed in an envelope or coating of an albuminous nature, termed *casein*. This envelope is ruptured by the process of churning, and oxygen being absorbed from the air the cream becomes sour, while its temperature is increased. The fat globules coalesce into masses and form butter, while the remaining watery liquid, containing lactic acid and some butter, is expelled from between the globules in the form of buttermilk.

The process of churning may be expedited by having the cream, at the commencement, indicate a temperature of 55° Fahr. An increase of caloric results chiefly from friction, and to a small extent from an absorption of oxygen, which, combining with the constituents of milk, gives rise to a species of invisible combustion, by which heat is evolved. From these causes the temperature rises to 60° or more. Great care should be taken *not to exceed 65° Fahr., as thereby the quantity of butter will be lessened* and its quality more or less impaired.

If the temperature of cream, when put into the churn, is below 50° Fahr., a great increase of labor is necessary to separate the butter, without the least advantage. In winter the temperature of the cream should be the same as in summer.

Never add boiling water to the cream, as it melts the fat globules, which thus become oily, and if the general temperature of the cream be raised to 70° or 80° Fahr., which is often the case, a white, oily butter is produced. The bursting of the globules of *margarine*, or fatty matter, gives rise to a greasy, sticky, unpalatable butter, liable to become strong and unfit for any other purpose than cooking, and sometimes not even for that.

It will therefore be seen how very important a knowledge of the foregoing details is to the butter maker.

Butter and cream are not changed in winter, except through neglect. The pernicious custom of keeping milk in the same room occupied by the family, subject to variations of temperature from 60° to 90° Fahr. during the day and down to the freezing point at night, should never be practiced. Indeed, it is, under such circumstances, impossible to get sweet, palatable cream or good butter. There is also an absorption of the animal effluvia constantly exhaled from the bodies of persons inhabiting the room, as well as of the odorous principles of smoke from the atmosphere, which causes the smoky taste so often found in winter butter.

Cleanliness is indispensable in butter making. Clean vessels, clean milkers, pure air, and a uniform temperature of 55° to 60° Fahr., are necessary conditions for the production of good butter.

If the feed of the cow is good, consisting of young and tender hay, with some bran or odorless food in winter, and care is taken not to break the globules of the butter by working it too much, and if the buttermilk be well expressed, good butter will be the inevitable result.

When milk and cream are churned together, a higher temperature is required than for cream alone, ranging from

70° to 75° Fahr., before butter can be obtained. If the butter is unusually slow in forming, the addition of a little vinegar, or cream of tartar, or rennet solution, will cause the formation of butter almost immediately.

The acidity of the milk is caused by the conversion of a portion of the sugar contained in it into lactic acid; and if this change is not sufficient, the addition of the vinegar or cream of tartar supplies the want of acid, and the butter forms.

THE CAUSE OF SOUR AND RANCID BUTTER.

Fresh butter contains more or less buttermilk — the less the better for the butter, and the more certain its preservation. It should be worked out with a ladle or proper butter machine. The hands ought not to be used, on account of their high temperature (blood heat is 98°), which melts the globules, thus causing the butter to become greasy and sticky. Butter properly made, salted and packed in jars or firkins, if kept at or below a temperature of 50°, will remain in a perfectly sweet condition for a very long time.

Butter containing much buttermilk, if kept at a temperature of from 75° to 90°, soon sours; lactic acid is formed; and if kept for some time at a temperature of from 90° to 110°, butyric fermentation sets in, giving it a rancid odor and strong taste, owing to the presence of butyric acid, which characterize the incipient or first stages of its decay. *Butyric acid* is very volatile, and possesses a very powerful and disagreeable odor. It is the product of the decomposition of the *butyrine*, to which principle good butter owes its excellent flavor. At a temperature of 315° Fahr., butyric acid is completely converted into vapor; and to restore rancid butter it is only necessary to raise the temperature to this degree, when the butyric acid escapes, leaving the remainder perfectly sweet. Therefore rancid butter may be used in cooking, by raising its temperature to 315° Fahr., which deprives it of all this acid, the cause of its offensive odor. But this heat also destroys the globules, and renders the butter unpalatable for the table.

HOW TO RESTORE SOUR AND RANCID BUTTER.

Butter dealers, as well as consumers, feel the importance of a reliable and practical process for the purification and refining of poor butter; and it is from the want of a proper knowledge of butter making, and sometimes from carelessness, that a large proportion of the butter offered for sale is not suitable for table use.

We shall proceed to show that butter, however imperfectly made, may be rendered quite palatable and but little, if any, inferior to good dairy butter, and also how, even after the destruction of the *butyrine*, which imparts the peculiarly appetizing flavor and grass-like taste to fresh butter, it may be restored by a cheap and simple process.

The discoveries of science have enabled the chemist and manufacturer to convert extremely repugnant compounds into wholesome articles of food. Among the most important discoveries on the list, may be classed those relating to sour and rancid butter.

We confidently hope that since the immortal Blot has lectured upon, and taught the science of cookery, the day is not far distant when missionaries of health shall spread the gospel of knowledge to butter makers, who, from no fault of their own, have quite generally been excluded from the light of science.

Butter may be restored by neutralizing the lactic and butyric acids of sour and strong butter, thus destroying the causes of both its unpleasant taste and odor.

We will now give several processes, hot and cold, for the restoration of butter.

NUMBER ONE—COLD PROCESS.

Place two or three pounds of fresh, unslaked lime in a clean barrel, and pour over it twenty gallons of pure cold water, which allow to remain, with occasional stirring, for one day, and afterwards at rest ten or twelve hours, or until clear. Then carefully pour or draw off the clear liquid, and strain it through two or three thicknesses of fine muslin or linen into a clean, odorless barrel, of the capacity of forty to forty-five gallons.

It is now ready for the reception of the rancid butter, which must be cut with a broad, sharp knife into thin slices, not exceeding one-fourth of an inch in thickness—the thinner the better. Put in one hundred pounds, or as much as the lime-water will cover, and finally over all, inside of the barrel, place a clean and floating cover, to prevent the butter on the surface from being exposed to the air.

Remove the cover several times each day and stir the butter well with a long, clean stick. At the expiration of thirty-six or forty-eight hours, the rancidity of the butter will be entirely removed.

The chemical action of this butter restorative is to cause the mass of butter to resume its original globular condition, thus imparting the appearance of new butter just churned and ready to be gathered.

The solution should now be drawn off and thrown away;

after which thoroughly rinse the butter with cold water, fill up the barrel with pure water, and let it stand half a day. Then remove the butter, and let it drain several hours. It will then be ready for salting (or the butter preservative), and will answer the same purpose as new butter, if a good cooking butter only is wanted. This process removes much of the salt from the butter, and bleaches it quite white. To give the desired color, use the butter coloring.

HOW TO RENDER THIS BUTTER OF SUPERIOR QUALITY FOR TABLE USE.

Previous to salting or coloring the butter, a fresh grass taste may be imparted to it by putting it into a revolving churn with new milk, and keeping the churn in motion for fifteen or twenty minutes.

For example: Take fifty pounds of butter, thus prepared, and five or six gallons of new milk, to which add the strained juice of three medium-sized raw carrots. Churn the butter in the new milk and carrot juice, which impart to it not only the butyrine, upon which depends the rich flavor of good table butter, and which was lost when it became rancid, but also a delicate yellow color, and equal in flavor to good June butter.

The foregoing process converts the most rancid butter into a good saleable article, at a reasonable expense.

This butter is now ready to be worked and salted in the same manner as new butter, or the butter preservative may be used instead of salt, and if the carrot juice in the milk has not sufficiently colored the butter, the butter coloring may be used to give the desired "June tint."

OTHER AGENTS USED FOR REFINING BUTTER.

For restoring rancid butter we have experimented with the chlorides of soda and of lime, but find them objectionable, for the reason that while they remove rancidity from the butter, they impart to it a flavor of chlorine, which is quite as disagreeable.

We have also used butyric ether to restore the natural odor to butter which has been deprived of its rancidity, but find that it does not answer the purpose, and is not to be compared with new milk and carrot juice, when used for the same purpose.

ANIMAL CHARCOAL FOR REFINING BUTTER.

Sour and rancid butter may be restored sufficiently for all culinary purposes by filtering it at a temperature of 200° Fahr., through animal charcoal, which at once removes from it all odor and color. But butter wholly free from flavor is as unpalatable for table use as that in which the opposite condition prevails.

HOW TO PREPARE BUTTER FOR HOT CLIMATES.

All butter designed for shipment to hot climates should be prepared by clarifying it in a water-bath, at a temperature of 200° Fahr. If butter be thus melted and allowed to remain at rest, the albumen and casein, or *cheesy* portion, will coagulate and settle to the bottom, leaving the butter pure and transparent, like oil. Then immediately draw off the butter into ice-cold water, without disturbing the sediment, in order that it may rapidly cool, and so prevent the crystallization of the *stearin* and the separation of the *olein*, which results would injure the flavor and appearance of the butter.

When cold, pack it down with the preservative, in as solid a manner as possible.

Butter thus prepared will be paler than before, and may, if necessary, be properly colored.

It will have a firmer consistence than before, and if put into close vessels and kept in a cool place, will remain sweet for months, even without salt.

Butter, like oils, is liable to the change called rancidity, which proceeds from the casein and albumen found in it, as well as the water which is not entirely expelled.

By the application of salt, or the preservative, this rancidity is in a degree retarded.

HOW TO COLOR BUTTER.

Nearly all lovers of butter prefer that which is of a light, rich, golden color. The following original process is a wholesome and simple method of bringing white or "streaked" butter to this fine tint without giving it the least appearance of having been colored. Good butter, if white or streaked, may be rendered more saleable by properly coloring it—a fact admitted by all produce dealers.

The following is a formula for a

NUMBER ONE BUTTER COLORING—YELK OF EGGS AND ANNATTO.

Take the yelks of sixty-four fresh eggs, which will be equivalent to one quart of yelk. The eggs may be broken into a large, convenient dish, and the yelks carefully separated from the whites. Add to the yelks thus obtained six ounces of pure glycerin, which will dissolve them, and beat together thoroughly with a spoon or egg-beater. Then pour this solution into a half-gallon bottle or jug, and agitate occasionally during five or six hours; then add twenty-four ounces of pure *sulphuric ether*, and shake well together for a few minutes. The jug must be tightly corked, to prevent the evaporation of the ether.

Shake, without removing the cork, a few times during three or four hours, and then let it remain at rest twenty-four hours. During this time the ether will have extracted the rich, yellowish-red coloring substance of the yelks, and if a glass vessel is used, it will be seen to have risen to the surface, owing to its light specific gravity.

Carefully pour, or draw off with a syphon, into an evaporating pan or other convenient vessel, all that portion of the liquid of a yellowish-red color. There will be about twenty-four fluid-ounces in quantity, or about the same in bulk as of the ether used. This must be evaporated carefully to sixteen ounces, which should be done by setting the vessel containing it into a water-bath, or a pail of water, at a temperature *not exceeding* 140° *Fahr.* Water boils at 212°, and ether at 96° Fahr.; therefore the ether will rapidly evaporate, leaving a residue, which is the desired coloring, and which may be appropriately termed "*oleum vitellus ovi*," or oil of egg-yelks.

It should not be forgotten that while evaporating the ether, there must be no fire or lighted lamp in the room, or fire in adjoining rooms where a draft can possibly convey the vapor of the ether, which is as inflammable and explosive as gunpowder. Ethereal vapors, which are heavier than air, flow thirty or forty feet distant and take fire, instantly conducting the flame the entire length and breadth of the ethereal volume of vapor, and wrapping the contents of the room in one vast sheet of flame in a moment. On a large scale, the ether may be recovered by distillation, by means of suitable apparatus, and again used for the same purpose.

The oil of egg-yelks should not be evaporated below one-third of the quantity of the ether used—that is, to sixteen ounces—as it would become too thick for use.

The sediment which is left may be treated with half the former quantity of ether in the same manner, and with a similar result, except that less color will be obtained.

Having shown how to obtain one of the products used for coloring butter, we will now explain how to combine it with another to obtain the requisite color.

The process, which is quite simple, is as follows:

Pure Extract of Annatto—one-fourth pound;

Alcohol, 95 per cent.—one quart.

Cut the annatto into small pieces, put them into a bottle or jug containing the alcohol, and cover the mouth of the vessel by tying a piece of paper over it; then set it into a water-bath or kettle of water heated to 175° or 200° Fahr., for two or three hours, agitating its contents occasionally. It must then be removed and allowed to rest twenty-four hours, and afterwards strained through filtering paper. The liquid thus obtained must then be evaporated in an open vessel, in a water-bath, to one pint. (On a large scale, the alcohol may be recovered by distillation.) This we may properly term the concentrated tincture of annatto.

Concentrated Tincture of Annatto—one pint;

Oil of Egg-yelk—two pints.

Mix in a bottle, and shake well together.

This quantity will color one hundred and fifty, or more, pounds of butter, according to the tint desired.

Before using, this mixture should be well shaken. Then sprinkle over and work into the butter thoroughly; or, if preferable and more convenient, the requisite quantity of salt or butter preservative needed for the butter may be saturated with the color and incorporated in the same manner. By this operation the butter is both salted and colored.

This butter coloring imparts to butter and cheese a perfectly natural color.

[NOTE.—The glycerin, after dissolving the oily portion of the yelks, owing to its great density (1.270), settles to the bottom, together with the yellowish-white remainder of the yelk. More ether may be added to this residue until all of the coloring matter is extracted, leaving the mass colorless; but after the first maceration the subsequent additions of ether do not produce a saturated solution of the coloring substance, and therefore the secondary tincture should be used with a fresh quantity of yelks.]

The above coloring, instead of being used in a liquid state, may be mixed with equal parts of *oil of butter* and digested for about an hour in a water-bath, at a temperature of about 120° Fahr., or until the ether is evaporated. Work it into butter in the same manner as if it were salt. One ounce of this preparation is sufficient for five or six pounds of butter, according to the shade desired.

BUTTER COLORING—THE USE OF ANNATTO.

It is the custom of those who use annatto for coloring butter and cheese, to dissolve it in solutions of soda, saleratus, etc., to extract its coloring substance. These alkaline solutions of annatto produce a dull brown, nankeen color, unsuitable for the purpose, and to a certain extent saponify, or convert into soap, the butter thus colored.

When annatto is used for coloring, it should be first cut into small pieces, which must then be covered with deodorized alcohol, 95 per cent., in a suitable vessel placed in a water-bath, the heat of which ranges from 175° to 180° Fahr. The coloring substance of the annatto will be chiefly extracted in three or four hours, which may be known by the dark appearance of the alcohol. Remove the vessel, and let the liquid settle a few hours. Then pass the tincture through filtering paper, and evaporate in an open vessel to one-half. On a large scale, the alcohol should be recovered by distillation.

This is a good method for obtaining a preparation of annatto for coloring butter or cheese.

When using the tincture of annatto for coloring butter, it may be sprinkled over and worked into the butter, or the salt may be colored with the tincture before being incorporated with the butter.

As a large proportion of the annatto of commerce is adulterated, care should be taken that an inferior article is not used. Pure annatto is worth at this time from $1.50 to $2.00 per pound, at wholesale.

Another method of using annatto for coloring butter is, to melt butter in a water-bath at about 200° Fahr., until the albuminous and cheesy matter separates and subsides; then pour off carefully the pure *oil of butter*.

Take three ounces of annatto, cut into fine pieces, and macerate it for one week in four ounces of deodorized alcohol (95 per cent). Or a similar result may be obtained by digesting the annatto and alcohol for two or three hours in a water-bath heated to 180° Fahr.

This is sufficient for one quart of the *oil of butter*, to which add both the tincture and sediment of annatto. Digest the whole in a water-bath, at a temperature of about 180° Fahr. for two or three hours, stirring occasionally. By that time the oil of butter will be of a dark orange color. Then carefully strain through a fine cloth, when it will be ready for use. It should be warmed to a temperature of about 70° when used. Work it into butter in the same manner as salt—an ounce of this preparation to five or six pounds of butter, which may be varied according to the shade desired.

BUTTER COLORING—THE CARROT.

It is often asked why the juice of carrots cannot be used for coloring butter. The answer is, because the colored juice of the carrot will not combine with butter or any other oleaginous compound, unless churned with milk or cream, as described below; and to extract the color from the juice, and to reduce it to a form for use, requires a long and expensive process, thus rendering it too costly for utility.

But a fine color may be imparted in the process of making winter butter, by incorporating with it the juice of the common orange, garden carrot.

Grate or bruise well a carrot of ordinary size, and squeeze its juice through cloth. Put the juice thus obtained into three gallons of cream, and churn. In color and taste winter butter thus obtained is little, if any, inferior to the best May or June butter.

More or less of the juice may be used according to the color required; but a proper proportion will give it the true color.

Just before grating the carrots, wash them thoroughly in warm water with a stiff brush, so as to perfectly remove all the dirt from the indentations on the surface. Then scrape off the outside skin with a dull knife, throwing it away. Cut off half an inch of the top, and two or three inches of the bottom of the carrot. This will remove all earthy or foreign deposits, which, if left, would communicate an unpleasant taste to the butter. All the coloring properties of the carrot are contained in the rind, which is usually about half an inch in thickness; hence it is unnecessary to grate the core, or central portion of the carrot.

OTHER AGENTS FOR COLORING BUTTER.

Fresh egg-yelks may be used to impart color, in making winter butter, by mixing them with the cream before churning, but we greatly prefer the use of the carrot.

Of the various coloring agents with which we have experimented, with a view of obtaining an innocuous and proper color for butter, we mention Saffron, Turmeric, Marygold, Fustic, etc., but we do not find any of them equal to the preparations of egg-yelk and annatto.

BUTTER PRESERVATIVE.

HOW TO KEEP BUTTER SWEET.

To keep butter sweet and to give it a wax-like consistence, instead of using dairy salt, use the butter preservative, which arrests any tendency to sourness and the consequent destruction of its *butyrin*, to which is due that delicious flavor only found in good, new, or well-preserved butter.

HOW TO PREPARE THE BUTTER PRESERVATIVE.

Ashton's Fine Liverpool Salt..................................11 pounds
Powdered White Sugar.................................... 3 pounds
Powdered Saltpetre (chemically pure)............... ¾ pound.

Mix well together, and use according to the following

DIRECTIONS:

Immediately after the butter is made, work it thoroughly with pure cold water, thereby removing all the buttermilk, which is, in a measure, the first cause of rancid butter.

Then into each twelve pounds of the butter work one pound of butter preservative, instead of salt; let the butter stand over night, and in the morning work it over; then pack it down solid, and spread a cold, wet cotton or linen cloth over the butter, and finally cover it with salt at least one-half inch deep. Keep it in a cool place.

Butter thus prepared is better after standing two or three weeks.

HONEY-BUTTER.

Instead of using salt or the preservative, thoroughly incorporate with twelve pounds of butter one pound of strained honey. This process will not only improve the flavor of the butter, but extend its preservation for an indefinite period.

GLYCERIN FOR BUTTER.

After restoring rancid butter, and when coloring and salting it, add one ounce of *pure glycerin* to each three pounds of butter. The glycerin combines readily with the butter and gives it a smooth and lustrous surface, which is characteristic of good butter.

Glycerin is not in the least unwholesome. It communicates a sweet, fresh taste, and materially assists in the preservation of all substances with which it may be incorporated.

CHEMICAL COMPOSITION OF BUTTER.

Carbon 65.60
Hydrogen 17.60
Oxygen 16.80

Butter consists of two distinct proximate principles— *Stearin*, a tasteless, odorless and colorless substance, which melts at 100° Fahr., and *Olein*, the oily portion of butter, which melts at 50° Fahr.

Butter softens as the temperature rises from 40° to 96° Fahr., at which point it becomes completely liquid.

	Olein.	Stearin.
Butter made in winter contains	37	63
Butter made in summer contains	60	40

This difference in constitution accounts for the difference between hard and soft butter.

BUTTER FIRKINS, PAILS, ETC., INSULATED.

All vessels, whether earthen, stone or wood, when used for containing butter, should be insulated with pure refined paraffin wax.

This should be melted in a tin vessel, and applied *hot*, with a brush, to the inside surface of the vessel, covering it with a coating one-eighth of an inch thick.

This coating will prevent the vessels absorbing salt from the butter, and from communicating any flavor to it. The paraffin wax is a bad conductor of heat, and thus prevents, in a great degree, injurious effects to the butter from the external changes of temperature.

After butter is packed in vessels prepared in the above manner, a white cotton cloth (new muslin), saturated in salt water, should be carefully spread over and pressed firmly on the butter, leaving no edges, and a layer, one-quarter of an inch thick, of hot paraffin wax should be poured over this cloth, so that the union by contact of the wax with the sides of the vessel shall be complete. Afterwards spread a layer of dampened salt, one inch deep, over all, and then a cloth and substantial cover. Keep the package in a cool place, and if the butter was sweet when packed, it will remain in the same condition for years.

[NOTE.—It is best, a few minutes before packing butter as above, to work into every hundred pounds ten pounds of powdered ice, which must be as small as wheat grains. This will reduce the temperature of the butter to 35° or 40° Fahr.; and if packed in the insulated vessel, and kept in a cool cellar, it will not rise to a temperature above 55° Fahr. for months.]

This process will insure cold, hard, sweet butter at all times. The addition of the ice will add to the profit of the butter packer in two ways, viz.: By the additional weight of the ice, and the improved quality of the butter when offered for sale.

The purchaser, although he may pay for ten per cent. of ice, obtains sweet, hard butter, and is the gainer in the end.

By insulating butter in this manner, and with the free use of finely pulverized ice, the great question, how to preserve butter without failure, must be decided.

Butter packers who have no ice-crusher can place the ice in a barrel, and by means of a wooden pounder reduce it to the fineness required, although the finer the better. A good butter-working machine is a most valuable auxiliary to the butter packer, and when the ice is added, it should immediately be worked into the butter before it chills, as the ice mixes more readily at first, and the butter should be packed without delay, before the ice can melt.

To prevent the shrinking or swelling of butter firkins, make a *hot* application of the insulating composition to the entire outside and bottom of the vessels; and when they are coated, both outside and inside, there will be no material change in the wood for a long time.

NUMBER TWO PROCESS FOR PREPARING BUTTER FIRKINS.

When it is not convenient to insulate the wooden vessels designed for butter packing, they should be filled with salt water (three pounds of salt to each gallon of water), and allowed to remain for four or five days or more. The wood becomes saturated with salt, and will not therefore absorb any from the butter. This will also prevent the wood from imparting any of its flavor to the butter.

After the salt water is poured out, rinse with cold water; let the firkin drain well for half a day, and then apply a heavy coating of glycerin over its entire inner surface.

Butter may be packed immediately, or at any convenient time, after applying the glycerin.

New oak firkins are frequently found to have an injurious effect upon the butter, from the presence of tannic acid contained in the oak wood; but if prepared by the above, or the No. 1 process, this objection is removed.

CREAM.

When milk is allowed to remain at rest from twelve to twenty-four hours, according to the temperature of the air, a large proportion of its fat globules, by virtue of their low specific gravity, (being lighter than milk), rise and form a thin stratum or layer upon the surface, which is known as cream.

When milk is kept in a room at a temperature from 50° to 60° Fahr., the cream will rise with the greatest rapidity and regularity. More cream will rise if the depth of the milk does not exceed three or four inches. It is essential that the milk should be kept cool in warm weather, to prevent acidity. But if the temperature is lower than 40° Fahr., the cream rises slowly and imperfectly.

CREAM—ITS CHEMICAL COMPOSITION.

Cream is a yellowish-white, opaque, smooth, unctious fluid, and possesses an agreeable flavor. Its chemical composition is as follows:

Whey (or serum)	92.0
Curd (or caseous matter)	3.4
Butter	4.6
	100

CREAM—ITS PRESERVATION.

Cream may be preserved a long time if prepared as follows:

White Sugar	4 pounds
Dissolve in Boiling Water	1 quart
Add, while hot, Sweet Cream	2 quarts.

Stir the mixture well, and when cold put it into jugs or bottles, and keep it in a cool place.

This preparation will be found convenient for coffee, tea, and other purposes, where sugar and cream are both required.

If five quarts of cream are reduced to four quarts by boiling in a water-bath, and when cool placed in jugs or bottles well corked, it will keep for months.

MILK.

ITS COMPOSITION AND PRESERVATION.

Milk is obtained from the class of animals called *Mammalia*, and is intended by nature for the nourishment of their young.

Pure Cows' Milk is an aqueous fluid of a yellowish-white color, being most yellow at the beginning of the period of lactation, and is marked by an agreeable, slightly saccharine taste.

The specific gravity of new milk averages.............. 1030
The specific gravity of skimmed milk averages......... 1035
The specific gravity of cream averages................... 1024
The specific gravity of water distilled is................. 1000

An analysis of new milk exhibits the following composition:

Water 873.00
Casein.. 48.20
Butter (fat)......... .... 30.00
Milk Sugar.. 43.90
Phosphate of Lime.. 2.31
Phosphate of Magnesia....................................... 0.42
Phosphate of Iron.. 0.07
Chloride of Potassium... 1.44
Chloride of Sodium.. 0.24
Soda, in combination with Casein........................ 0.42

Total...1000.00

The average weight of a gallon of good, rich, new milk is 8¼ lbs.; a gallon of pure water weighs 8 lbs.

PRESERVING MILK.

In order to preserve milk sweet for years, put it into strong bottles, which place in a water-bath, and gradually raise it to the boiling point, by which means the small quantity of air contained in it is expelled. While the bottles are boiling hot, cork them securely, using wire to retain the corks, and finally cover with good sealing-wax.

Milk, if boiled for a few minutes, will keep sweet a long time in warm weather, even when freely exposed to the atmosphere.

If three pounds of sugar be added to each gallon of milk before boiling, and it afterwards be placed in suitable bottles or jugs for use, it will keep still longer.

New milk, reduced by boiling to one-half its original volume, will keep sweet much longer than the usual time.

Milk heated to 212° will remain sweet for a few days. If heated to 220°, under pressure, it will remain sweet for two or three weeks, but if heated to 250°, under pressure, it will keep almost indefinitely.

TO DETECT WATERED MILK.

The usual method of adulterating milk is by the addition of water. The extent of its adulteration may be determined by the following plan. If a tube of glass, of convenient size, be divided into one hundred equal parts, and then filled with milk and allowed to stand twenty-four hours, the cream will rise to the upper part of the tube and occupy from eleven to thirteen parts of the tube, if the milk be genuine; otherwise, the cream will occupy less space in proportion to the amount of adulteration.

EFFECTS OF HEAT AND AGITATION.

If cream is kept warm for some days, it becomes thicker and partially coagulated, in consequence of the lactic acid, which precipitates the caseous matter contained in the small portion of milk with which the cream is mixed.

If cream in this state be violently shaken, as in the operation of churning, the oily portion, or butter, quickly separates, leaving a liquid called buttermilk.

SKIMMED MILK

Consists of—

Water	92.9	parts.
Curd	2.8	"
Sugar of Milk	3.4	"
Lactic Acid	.3	"
Lactate of Potassa	.2	"
Lactate of Iron	.1	"
Chloride of Potassium	.1	"
Phosphate of Potassa	.1	"
Phosphate of Lime	.1	"
Total	100	"

MISCELLANEOUS FACTS.

As a general average, three gallons of good milk yield one pound of good butter; although chemical analysis shows but three-fourths of a pound of *pure* butter in this quantity of milk. Hence one-fourth of each pound of butter made in the ordinary way consists of the various other substances enumerated in the foregoing analysis.

The white, almost opaque appearance of milk is an optical illusion; for when examined by a microscope of moderate power, it is seen to consist of a perfectly transparent liquid, in which are suspended numerous lucid globules of fat (known as butter), surrounded by albuminous envelopes.

By agitation, these envelopes are broken mechanically, as in churning, and the butter collects in masses.

Milk boils at 199° Fahr., and in boiling a curd of caseous matter, partially coagulated, rises to the surface, forming a pellicle or thin skin, which, if removed, will soon be succeeded by another. This action will continue until the residuum becomes watery and incapable of producing any more such pellicles.

Milk should never be put into zinc or lead vessels, as it speedily dissolves a portion of these metals and becomes poisonous.

TO PREVENT MILK FROM SOURING.

New milk is very slightly alkaline in character, and the cause of its becoming sour is the warm temperature of the atmosphere and the absorption of oxygen, which produce lactic acid.

So long as the alkaline character of milk is maintained, it cannot sour. As the result of many experiments, we propose the following as the best method for preserving milk in a sweet condition:

Calcined Magnesia.. 1 ounce.
Phosphate of Soda (pulv.)................................. 3 "

Mix well together, and thoroughly stir one ounce of this mixture into three gallons of milk. This quantity will keep milk, during quite warm weather, at least twenty-four hours longer than if not used. By its addition from time to time, in small quantities, milk may be preserved sweet almost an indefinite time. Care should be taken, in using this preservative, not to add too great a quantity at one time, as when used in excess it communicates a perceptibly alkaline taste.

WHY LIGHTNING CAUSES MILK TO SOUR.

Oxygen and nitrogen gases, which constitute atmospheric air in the proportion (by weight) of 23 parts of the former to 77 of the latter, are mixed, but not combined. By the action of lightning, these gases, through which it passes, are caused to combine, and thus are produced nitrous oxide, nitric oxide, hyponitrous, nitrous and nitric acids, according to the proportion of each gas in the combination. The acids thus produced in the atmosphere become diffused, and the slightest quantity of them absorbed by milk causes lactic fermentation and sourness. We might further consider the slight proportion of ammonia also produced, but deem it unnecessary to do so in this connection.

WHY STALE MILK CURDLES WHEN BOILED.

In stale milk, fermentation has already commenced, which the heat of the fire greatly accelerates. The lactic acid formed during this fermentation, acting upon the casein of the milk, coagulates it.

Milk contains soda and potash, which are combined with the casein. These compounds (caseate of soda and caseate of potassa) are soluble in water, and the milk is sweet; but when any acid deprives the casein of these alkalies by combining with them, then the casein is no longer soluble in water, but is precipitated in the form of curd.

BOIL MILK IN A WATER-BATH.

It should always be boiled in a water-bath. Otherwise the organic substances of the milk will sink to the bottom in the form of coagulated casein and adhere to the kettle.

CHEESE.

THE COMPOSITION OF CHEESE.

The best cheese is obtained from new milk, and is a mixture, in various proportions, of coagulated casein and butter.

Casein is found in milk, and in the blood; also in peas, beans, and other leguminous plants. It is soluble in alkaline solutions, and its solution in milk is due to the alkali (soda) present; but if the latter be neutralized by an acid, as lactic acid, the casein coagulates, forming the curd. The same effect is produced by a calf's stomach, dried, which is called *rennet* (and contains muriatic and lactic acids), and by other acids. The degree of heat most favorable for the coagulation of milk by rennet (or other suitable acids), is about 90° Fahr., its natural heat when obtained from the cow.

By analysis, cheese is found to consist of:

Carbon	59.781
Hydrogen	7.429
Oxygen	11.409
Nitrogen	21.381
	100.000

The large quantity of nitrogen it contains sufficiently explains its tendency to decomposition, and at the same time accounts for its well known histogenetic (flesh-making) properties.

Its wonderful power of exciting fermentation, of which digestion is a variety, by its own internal changes, is recognized in the following couplet:

> " Cheese itself is a peevish elf—
> It digests all things but itself."

Centuries have elapsed since the author of this couplet (which is attributed to Galen) lived; yet the truth conveyed is unchanged. The moderate use of cheese is highly beneficial, not only as food itself, but as a promoter of digestion.

The carbonaceous matter of cheese, or other food, is fuel for the body, and produces, by respiration, animal heat.

The nitrogenized portion of cheese produces muscle and other similar structures of the body.

Professor Liebig has very ingeniously classified what he terms the plastic elements of nutrition, to which belong—

Vegetable Fibrin,	Vegetable Casein,
Vegetable Albumen,	Animal Flesh,
Blood.	

And, the elements of respiration, to which belong—

Fat,	Grape Sugar,
Starch,	Milk Sugar,
Gum,	Pectin,
Cane Sugar,	Alcohol.

Other modern investigators, after comparing the fat-forming and flesh-forming values of cheese with that of flour and meat, have arrived at the following statement:

	FLESH-MAKING PROPERTIES. Per Cent.	FAT-MAKING PROPERTIES. Per Cent.
Cheese contains	24	31
Flour contains	6	36
Meat contains	15	30

Food taken into the body varies in its effects in different individuals. Some persons are inclined to obesity, while others are constitutionally lean, and all the feeding or abstinence possible will not wholly change these conditions.

In the business of life, obesity generally characterizes persons constitutionally inactive, and who require strong motives to impel them to violent physical exertion. Such individuals possess more of the lymphatic or watery temperament, and are apt to preserve their equilibrium of temper while others do not. Hence it is better for judges, child-bearing women, and all persons whose duties require little muscular activity, to be inclined to obesity. In accordance with the unerring wisdom displayed in nature, we discover the presence and exemplification of these conditions in the animal organization in exactly those cases where it is most required, e. g., in females, judicial officers, etc.

Inferior kinds of cheese are not very digestible, nor will they assist digestion so much as good old cheese. The lives of persons who eat to a surfeit of rich food may often be prolonged by means of a little old cheese of the best quality, used as a condiment, and which, when taken into the stomach, causes the rapid disintegration of the mass of food by exciting a copious flow of saliva and a greatly increased secretion of the gastric juice, all of which are the most important agents in the process of digestion.

Cheese should be well masticated. This is the principal secret of its agreeing so well with some persons, while others who do not sufficiently masticate their cheese complain of its disagreeing with them. Poor cheese, with which the market is flooded, is unfit to be eaten except by ostriches or other animals possessing the strongest digestive powers.

In the process of cheese-making, much care is required,

especially in the cooling and stirring of the milk as soon as taken from the cow, and in preserving it free from all impurities.

THE PROCESS OF CHEESE-MAKING.

The materials used in making cheese are milk, rennet, salt, and coloring matter.

Rennet is the stomach of a calf, and may be used either fresh or after being salted and dried.

It is generally kept in the latter state, for the sake of its better preservation. The stomach is taken from the calf as soon as killed, and after being cleaned of the curd of milk always found in it, is well salted on both sides, and, after draining well, is stretched on a bent stick and dried.

In the preparation of cheese, the milk may be of any kind, from the poorest skimmed to that rich in cream, according to the quality of cheese required.

The present high price of cheese will incite great competition in its manufacture, whereby we hope that it will become both cheaper and better than that generally found in market.

The process of cheese-making is very simple; but to make good cheese, even with the best materials, pure air and cleanliness are indispensable.

The materials being ready, the greater portion of the milk is put into a large tub, and the remainder sufficiently heated to raise the temperature of the whole to 90° Fahr., the heat of new milk. The whole having been well mixed, the rennet is added, and the tub covered.

[NOTE.—If the milk be not warm enough when the rennet is put into it, the curd will be tender, and the cheese will never be firm, but will bulge out at the sides; but if it be hot, it will cause the cheese to swell, "heave," and become spongy, hard, dry and unpalatable, because most of the "richness" will go off with the whey. In hot weather, care should be taken, if the cows are pastured in unshaded grounds or where water is not within their reach, to add cold spring water to the milk as soon as it is brought into the dairy, until it arrives at the proper degree of heat, which is from 85° to 90° Fahr.]

Allow the tub to stand until the milk is turned, when the curd should be struck down with the skimming-dish a few times; after which allow it to subside.

The vat, covered with the cheese cloth, is next placed on a "horse" or "ladder" over the tub, and filled with curds by means of the skimmer. The curd is pressed down with the hands, and more is added as it sinks. This process is continued until the curd stands about two inches above the edge of the vat. The cheese, thus partially separated from the whey, should be now placed in a cheese tub, and a proper quantity of salt added, without removing it from the vat; after which a board should be placed over and under it, and pressure applied for two or three hours.

The cheese should now be turned out and surrounded by a fresh cheese cloth, and then subjected to pressure for ten or twelve hours. It is then commonly removed from the press, salted all over, and pressed again fifteen or twenty hours.

The quality of the cheese largely depends on this part of the process, as if any of the whey has been left in the cheese it will not keep, but will rapidly become ill-flavored. Before placing the cheese in the press the last time, the edges should be pared smoothly and neatly.

It now only remains to wash the outside of the cheese in warm whey or water, wipe dry, and color with annatto, as is usually done.

In gathering the curd, preparatory to making cheese, collect it with the hands, very gently pressing it towards the sides of the tub, letting the whey run off through the fingers, and ladling it out as it collects.

The cheese being made, it should be placed in a cool, damp cellar, at a temperature not above 50°; a few degrees less will be better. Any place subject to great changes of temperature is unfit for storing cheese.

It will be seen that very slight differences in the materials, preparation and storing of the cheese essentially influence its quality and flavor.

The proper season for manufacturing cheese, which in this country has become a very staple article and is the source of a large revenue, is between the first of May and the last of September. Under favorable circumstances, the business may be continued at earlier or later periods of the year.

The process of cheese making should not be commenced before the rennet and the coloring material have been properly prepared. The rennet is first soaked in water, to which may be added a few simple aromatics, as cloves, etc., which serve to destroy any offensive odor of the rennet, and to give an agreeable flavor to the cheese. The rennet may remain in the water any reasonable length of time, with the result of increasing the strength of the fluid the longer it is left in it. An average amount of this fluid for coagulating fifty gallons of milk is estimated at half a pint. The proper quantity is, however, best learned by care and daily experience. A handful or two of salt, properly used, will aid materially in producing a proper coagulation.

Instead of rennet, the Hollanders sometimes use a small

quantity of muriatic acid, which is said to cause the peculiar flavor of "Dutch" cheese.

Should the whey be of a slightly greenish color, it is evident that the curd has been properly formed; but if it be white, it is equally certain that the coagulation is imperfect. If much caseous matter be wasted in the whey, the cheese will have a poor flavor.

The vat used is simply a strong, circular wooden tub, similar to a half-bushel measure in shape. Hard wood is preferable in its construction. If turned out of a solid block, it will be better for service. The bottom is not tightly inserted, and, as well as the sides, is perforated, in order to permit the free egress of whey when the curd is subjected to pressure. The press is a combination of mechanical powers, such as the lever and screw, and is too well known to require any further description here.

Before the cheese is placed in the press, it should be enveloped in a piece of thin, open linen.

To harden the skin of the cheese, after its removal from the vat, it is put into a vessel of warm or hot whey for an hour. After being taken from this whey, the cheese is again subjected to pressure for half an hour, and then turned in the vat, and so alternately turned and pressed for forty-eight hours.

To salt a cheese properly, the salt should be thoroughly mixed with the curd previous to its being put in the vat. The amount of salt used must be graduated by the size of the cheese, as too much will make it unpleasant, and if there is too little the cheese will not keep.

COLORING CHEESE.

Coloring cheese is a very general custom, for which purpose annatto is considered preferable. The usual manner of coloring milk for cheese is to dip a piece of the annatto into a bowl of milk, and then rub it on a smooth stone until the milk assumes a deep red color. This infusion, freed from the sediment which separates by standing a short time, is to be added to the milk of which cheese is to be made. It imparts to the milk a reddish, nankeen color, which becomes deeper in proportion to the age of the cheese. Annatto, dissolved in solutions of soda or saleratus, is also used to color cheese.

But the most suitable coloring for cheese is the butter coloring heretofore described: either the egg yelk and annatto (see page 85), or the oil of butter and annatto (see page 87). Add a sufficient quantity to the milk while warm, and stir well together before the rennet is added. These butter colorings impart to the "cheese milk" a rich, mellow, light-orange tint, far superior to the water or alkaline solutions of annatto. After the cheese is made, its exterior surface may be slightly tinged with the butter coloring.

HOW TO PRESERVE CHEESE.

By immersing the cheese in hot paraffin wax two or three minutes, or by applying the wax with a brush, the cheese will be preserved from flies, dust, etc., and rendered proof against maggots or "skippers," whereby the cheese dealer will be saved much annoyance and loss.

MEAT.

PRESERVING MEATS.

Animal food is rendered harder and less digestible by being salted for preservation.

In the process of salting, besides common salt, several other antiseptics are frequently employed to improve the meat, among which are Nitrate of Potassa, Sugar, Vinegar, Spices, etc.

The theory of the preservation of meat by alkaline or neutral salts is, that they abstract water from the flesh, the existence of which in meat is necessary to its decomposition. When applied, the salts become dissolved in the water they withdraw from the meat, and at the same time a small quantity of the solution penetrates the meat by a species of endosmosis.

The albumen and fibrin being thus deprived of their water, are concentrated and less prone to putrefaction. Hence, salted meats are more readily dried in the air than fresh meats.

Salting greatly impairs the nutritious qualities of the meat, and, if long continued, will corrugate and harden the fibrin, rendering it less easily digestible; but the action of salt for a few days does not materially impair the nutritious qualities of meat.

When kept very long in salt, meat becomes so disagreeably and strongly saline that it is difficult, by soaking in water, to sufficiently deprive it of this objectionable character. Even boiling salted meat is not sufficient to extract the salt from the middle of the meat, for so much boiling is requisite that its quality is thereby greatly injured, and many of its nutritive properties are lost.

Salting is performed in two ways, viz.: Dry-salting and pickling.

Dry-salting consists in packing meat in dry salt, and sometimes rubbing its surface over with salt. Meat thus salted will keep longer, but is deprived of a greater proportion of its nutritive properties than when cured by pickling. For exportation, or for keeping in hot climates, dry-salting is necessary, for obvious reasons, to preserve beef and pork.

The pieces of meat most suitable for salting are those which have the fewest large blood-vessels, and are most solid.

Very little salt penetrates meat, except through the cut surfaces, to which it should always chiefly be applied. All openings or cavities in the meat should be well filled with salt.

For each hundred weight of meat, about eight pounds of salt will be requisite. It should be rubbed into every part, moulding and turning the meat very often, to "open the grain."

The meat is then to be put into tubs, with a layer of coarse rock salt between the pieces. The juices of the meat dissolve the salt, forming a strong solution called "brine." In about a week, it is usual to take out the meat, and re-pack it in smaller vessels, with the addition of more coarse salt, in which condition it should remain at least one month before it can be relied on to preserve through winter or during transportation. Cutting out the bones of meat to be salted in this manner is advantageous to its preservation.

If the salting is performed immediately after the animal is slaughtered, and while the flesh is still warm, and before the fluids are coagulated, the salt penetrates rapidly, by means of the blood-vessels and capillaries, throughout the entire substance of the meat.

Tainted meat does not readily absorb curative agents.

DRY-SALTING FOR BEEF, PORK OR OTHER MEATS.

Rock, or Turk's Island Salt..............................6 pounds.
Sugar (light-brown or white).............................2 pounds.

Mix together, and rub thoroughly over the meat.

In packing, apply a layer of the mixture over each piece of meat.

The time required for this compound to penetrate the pores of the meat varies from one and one-half to two weeks, according to the size and compactness of the meat. The sugar is not only a preservative, but renders meat more juicy and "mellow."

PICKLE FOR BEEF, PORK OR MUTTON.

Coarse Salt..8 pounds.
Sugar-house Sirup..2 quarts.
Nitrate of Potassa.. ½ ounce.
Bicarbonate of Potassa....................................... ½ "
Soft Water...8 gallons.

Mix, boil and skim well, and when cold pour over the meat.

This makes sufficient pickle to cover one hundred pounds of meat.

When salt is used alone in curing meat, it is apt to communicate a greenish tinge.

Nitrate of Potassa has a sharp, bitterish, cooling taste, possesses about four times greater antiseptic power than common salt, and imparts to meat a fine red color; but it has also the effect of hardening the meat and of giving it a harsh taste; hence but a very small quantity of it should be used.

Sugar-house Sirup of a pleasant flavor imparts a mild and delicious taste, gives the meat a natural red appearance, and is a good antiseptic.

Bicarbonate of Potassa (saleratus) has a tendency to preserve the juices and tenderness of the meat by preventing the coagulation of its albumen.

Cochineal is sometimes used to impart to meat a red color, but we do not advise its use.

Notwithstanding the antiseptic powers of salt, brine is very liable to putrefaction, as the blood and juices of the meat which it contains are more liable to decomposition than the flesh.

Pork can be preserved by a smaller quantity of salt than beef or mutton, as it takes up less salt and contains less water in the form of juice.

When pork and beef are equally salted, the former will be properly cured in ninety days, while the beef will have such an excess of salt as to be almost unfit for food.

The fatty portions of salted meat absorb less salt than the lean parts. Pork contains much fat, which is the cause of the effect above mentioned.

The fat of fresh pork is too gross to be much relished in this climate, especially in hot weather, but when salted becomes firmer, more agreeable to the palate, and much more digestible.

Fat, in general, has less tendency to putrefaction than lean meat, which is illustrated by the preservation of lard, tallow, oils, etc.

THE PRESERVATION OF MEAT BY SMOKING.

The smoke of burning wood, as hickory, beech and maple, as also of bark, corn-cobs, etc., is generally supposed to communicate the finest flavor to meat.

The preservation of meat by smoking is due to the acid vapor in the smoke, termed *pyroligneous acid.*

By adding a quart of pyroligneous acid to a barrel of meat, much less salt is required in pickling. Pyroligneous acid coagulates the albumen of the meat, but does not act upon the fibrin. Its antiseptic properties are well established.

HAMS AND SHOULDERS, BACON, DRIED BEEF, MUTTON, ETC.

These meats, after being salted and immersed in hot paraffin wax for two or three minutes, will have a thin coating of paraffin, which renders them impervious to air, moisture, flies, dust, mould, etc.; and thus prepared they will keep much longer than if not subjected to the paraffin process.

The paraffin can readily be removed by peeling it off with a knife, or by dipping the meat into boiling water a few minutes, which will melt and save it, as the paraffin may be collected on the surface of the water when it becomes cold.

The above may be applied to fresh beef and other meats.

APPLES AND CIDER.

The apple-tree (*Pyrus Malus*) is indigenous to the soil of Europe, but naturalized in this country.

The apple-tree is supposed to have been introduced into England by the Romans.

Homer describes the apple as one of the precious fruits of his time; and it was cultivated and highly esteemed among the Romans, who brought it from the East and set a high price upon fine bearing trees.

It was cultivated in the gardens of monasteries during the Middle Ages, to which source the greater number of our cultivated varieties trace their origin. All varieties of the apple are said to be derived from the Wild Crab, which is the type of the fruit if left to degenerate, and to which it speedily does if uncared for.

By culture, crossing and grafting, improved varieties are produced.

The apple-tree, if favored by a good soil and climate, lives to a great age. Reports show that apple-trees yield fruit for two centuries, and that there are orchards now in Asia five hundred years old.

It is estimated that there are about fifteen hundred varieties cultivated in the United States.

Apple-trees do not yield fruit in tropical countries, but, like the oak, extend from the tropics to the latitude of 60°. The apple is, therefore, the growth of temperate and rather cold climates.

The fruit, or apple, contains both *malic* and *acetic* acids, has a pleasant and refreshing flavor, and is a useful and healthy article of diet, when perfectly ripe, which may be eaten either raw, roasted, stewed, or boiled.

However, apples should not be eaten raw by dyspeptics or patients afflicted with gout, rheumatism, etc.

Raw apples should always be well masticated before being swallowed.

An apple tea may be made for fever patients, by boiling a tart apple in half a pint of water, and sweetening the tea with sugar.

CIDER—(*Sicera.*)

Cider is a fermentable liquor, consisting of the juice of apples. It was known to antiquity, and is mentioned by Pliny, who called it the "*wine of apples*," as made by the Romans in Italy.

Cider is made in nearly all the temperate climates of the world. The process of making it is too well known to require more than a brief description.

The apples are crushed or ground in a mill, the pulp or pomace placed in a cider press, and the juice expressed. This, when first made, is known as *sweet cider*, which if kept at a temperature below 45°, will remain the same condition.

But if the cider is kept at a temperature above 45°, fermentation takes place. The best plan is to place the barrels of cider in the shade, and allow it to ferment at a temperature between 45° and 55°. This is a slow process of fermentation, but for domestic use is the only proper one, as at a low temperature nearly all of the saccharine matter is converted into alcohol, which remains in the liquor instead of undergoing the process of acetification.

The saccharine juice of apples, or any other fruit, should be kept at a temperature between 45° and 55°, but not to exceed 60°, when undergoing the vinous fermentation, by which the loss of the spirit resulting from the transformation of the alcohol into acetic acid, is prevented. The retention of the spirit in an unaltered state in the cider greatly enhances its quality, and by its conservative and chemical action precipitates the nitrogenous substances.

Many persons, after making cider, leave it exposed to the sun, or in a temperature, ranging from 70° to 100° Fahr., which soon converts the alcohol formed by the decomposition of the sugar into *vinegar*, by the absorption of atmospheric oxygen, and thus the *cider* acquires that peculiar and unwholesome acidity known as "rough" or "hard" cider.

In practice, it has been found that *sour* apples produce the best cider. This arises from the fact that they contain less sugar and more *malic acid*, which acid impedes the conversion of alcohol into vinegar. But cider made from sour apples is not equal in quality to that prepared at a low temperature from sweet or sub-acid apples, which are rich in sugar.

In Worcestershire and Herefordshire, England, the best cider-makers prepare cider by fermenting it, at a low temperature, from selected, ripe, sub-acid apples. This cider remains in an unchanged condition for twenty-five years, and is frequently sold for champagne.

In America much of the cider offered for sale is prepared from "*selected cider apples*," which are usually the half-rotten, small and unripe apples; hence we have a diversity of flavored cider. Unripe and rotten apples do not contain sufficient sugar to undergo the proper vinous fermentation, and cider made from them becomes bitter and unpalatable, and frequently even putrefies.

THE PRESERVATION AND FLAVORING OF CIDER.

Cider made from sound, ripe apples, and having undergone the vinous fermentation (in a cellar), at a temperature of from 45° to 55° Fahr., is in the half-hard or pleasantly acidulated state.

Carefully rack or draw it off, so as not to disturb the sediment, and strain through fine flannel into a clean barrel. When the barrel is half-filled, add

Sulphite of Lime......................................4 ounces.
Fresh-laid Eggs..8 in number.

Beat up shells and all in a pint of the cider, stir into half a pailful of the cider for a few moments, and pour all into the half-barrel of cider. Then add

Oil of Wintergreen....................................1 ounce.
Oil of Sassafras..½ ounce.
Alcohol (95 per cent.)................................1 pint.

Mix. Shake well together for a few moments; then pour it into the cider. Lastly, add five pounds of good raisins (bruised), and fill up the barrel with cider. (The reason for putting these articles in the cider when the barrel is half-filled is, that they may be evenly mixed.)

The barrel should then be bunged up tightly. In two or three weeks' time the cider will settle clear, have a fine flavor, and constitute a most wholesome beverage.

The addition of the above cider-flavoring preservatives will not convert poor cider into good; neither will it change sour into sweet cider, but it *will arrest and prevent any further fermentation*.

For the ordinary cider of commerce, the above process will give entire satisfaction.

If flavoring be not desired, the essential oils of wintergreen and sassafras may be omitted.

Cider, the specific gravity of which is about 1.060, consists of water, mucilage, sugar, malic acid, tartaric acid, tannic acid, etc.

Cider is not valued principally for the alcohol it contains, but for its agreeable mixture of sugar and acid, forming a pleasant sub-acid, and when it reaches that state of fermentation which generates sufficient carbonic acid gas to saturate the water of the apple-juice, it is in the most wholesome and palatable state for a beverage.

When cider has reached this state, it is ready for bottling; after which cork securely, place the bottles in a cool cellar, and it will keep for years.

In making cider, the following rules should be observed:

Slight fermentation will leave the cider thick and unpalatable; rapid fermentation will impair both its strength and durability; excessive fermentation will make it sour, hard and thin. See that the fermentation proceeds at a temperature between 45° and 55°, and it will not be confounded with acetous.

100 lbs of apples will usually make eight gallons of cider.

Good cider yields about nine per cent. of alcohol; ordinary cider about four per cent.

[NOTE.—SULPHUROUS ACID GAS, as developed by burning brimstone in the air, has long been known and used as a preservative agent. It is composed of one equivalent of sulphur (16) and two equivalents of oxygen (16), and therefore is represented by the chemical formula SO_2. It is characterized by a strong affinity for an additional equivalent of oxygen, with which it combines, forming sulphuric acid, SO_3. The process of fermentation, decay and putrefaction are all dependent upon oxydation. Therefore, if a substance be deprived of free oxygen, or if the free oxygen in proximity to it be monopolized by some other substance having a stronger affinity for it, its decay will be retarded, if not wholly prevented, while these conditions are maintained.

Cider contains not only sugar, but nitrogenous matter in abundance, the decay or oxydation of which causes the sugar, as it were by sympathy, to decompose into carbonic acid gas, which partly escapes and partly remains, imparting its pungent prickling taste to the liquor, and into alcohol, which, being a liquid, remains dissolved in the water, and gives to the cider its intoxicating properties. The amount of oxygen necessary to effect the decomposition of the nitrogenized matter of the cider being very small, it always is present dissolved in the cider, so that filling vessels full and hermetrically sealing them is of no avail as a means of preventing fermentation. By boiling, this oxygen is temporarily expelled, but soon returns, unless its access is prevented. The addition of sulphurous acid, which is best effected by adding one of its compounds, effectually monopolizes and removes the oxygen which would otherwise cause fermentation. For this purpose sulphite of soda or sulphite of lime is added to the cider, which is not thereby injured in flavor or rendered in any respect unwholesome.]

CHAMPAGNE CIDER.

Good Clear Cider, (slightly sour)..........................36 galls.
Proof Spirit.. 2 "
Strained Honey...10 lbs.

Stir well together, and keep tightly bunged, allowing it to remain in a cool cellar for thirty days; then add

Skimmed Milk..1 quart.
Old, Rich Cheese (in small pieces)........................1 lb.
Raisins, bruised to a pulp ....8 lbs.

After standing three or four weeks, it may be decanted into champagne bottles. Wire and cover the cork with tinfoil. It is far more wholesome than the genuine champagne.

The bottle will open with a brisk report, and its contents pass for a good imitation of "imported" champagne.

CIDER WINE.

Take new cider and boil it down one-half; add five pounds of bruised raisins to each barrel, and keep in a cool cellar. After it is one year old it will have the taste of Rhenish wine, and its flavor will continue to improve by age. When it is two years old it may be bottled, and will then pass for a good article of "imported wine."

ARTIFICIAL CIDER.

Take a barrel from which sugar-house sirup has just been been drawn out, and put into it

Good Sugar-house Sirup	3 gallons.
Hot Water	5 gallons.

Stir well together, and let it stand one hour. Then add

Tartaric Acid	12 ounces.
Dried Sour Apples	7 lbs.

Before adding the apples, pour on three gallons of hot water and let them stand two or three hours. Finally add

Cold Water	30 gallons.

Keep the barrel (with the bung out, and covered with gauze to keep out flies, etc.,) where the thermometer ranges from 60° to 70° for two or three days, or until the cider becomes pleasantly acidulated. Then add

Oil of Wintergreen	1 ounce.
Oil of Sassafras	$\frac{1}{2}$ "
Alcohol	$\frac{1}{2}$ pint.

Mix, shake well together, and pour into the barrel, which bung up and roll about until its contents are well mixed.

Keep it in a cool cellar.

This makes a wholesome summer beverage.

If it should, in the course of time, become too sour to drink, it will make good vinegar.

But by adding the sulphite of lime and eggs, as recommended for the preservation of cider, it will keep a long time.

CIDER—WITHOUT APPLES.

Take a sirup barrel, as above directed, and pour into it

Good Sugar-house Sirup ....3 gallons.
Hot Water..5 "

Stir well, and let stand one hour. Then add

Cold Water...32 gallons.
Tartaric Acid..12 ounces.
Brewers' or Hop Yeast......................................2 quarts.

Stir well together, or roll the barrel about until well mixed. If kept with the bung out, at a temperature between 60° and 70°, it will be good cider in forty-eight hours.

Then keep in a cool place.

This cider will remain good but a short time unless kept at a temperature below 45°.

All the above preparations constitute perfectly wholesome summer beverages.

SWEET CIDER—(*Imitation.*)

Water (warm)...35 gallons.
Honey (strained)...20 pounds.
Catechu Gum (powdered)...................................1 ounce.
Alum (powdered)..2 ounces.
Yeast (Brewers' or Hop)..................................1 pint.

Ferment for two weeks, at a temperature from 60° to 75°. Then add

Nutmeg (powdered)..1 ounce.
Cloves (powdered)..1 ounce.

If too sweet, add good cider vinegar to suit the taste. If too sour, add more honey.

CIDER—(*Imitation.*)

Water (warm) .... 35 gallons.
Sulphuric Acid .... ½ pound.
   (Or, sufficient to make the water pleasantly sour.)
Sugar-house Sirup .... 6 gallons.

Stir well together, and let stand twelve hours.

Boil in one gallon of water one hour:

Alum (pulverized) .... 3 ounces.
Cloves (pulverized) .... 4 ounces.
Ginger (pulverized) .... 4 ounces.
Bitter Almonds (pulverized) .... 4 ounces.

Add to the first, when nearly cool. It will be ready to use in twenty-four hours.

BOTTLING OR CANNING SWEET CIDER.

Boil sweet cider about ten minutes, in tin cans or bottles. Immediately cork, and hermetrically seal while hot.

Cider thus prepared will keep fresh and sweet for years, if the vessels are kept air-tight.

The juices of grapes, currants, blackberries, etc., may be preserved in the same manner, and are considered more wholesome than wine.

PERRY.

This beverage—"*wine of pears*"—is prepared from pears in a manner similar to the manufacture of cider from apples, and is a wholesome and pleasant drink.

MEAD.

Mead is a liquor prepared from honey diluted with water, and fermented. It is the Hydromel of the Romans. Pliny records, and Virgil celebrates this drink, made of honey mixed with fruits.

(*Our Improved Process.*)

Strained Honey .... 100 pounds.
Hot Water .... 30 gallons.

Stir thoroughly and simmer for one hour. Remove the scum, and when about cool, add

Fresh Hops...1¼ pounds.

Put all together in a *sugar-house sirup barrel*. Stir well, and allow the barrel to remain, with the bung out, at a temperature of from 55° to 65° for three or four weeks, or until fermentation takes place. Then add:

Cinnamon Bark, pulverized........................... ½ ounce.
Cloves, pulverized.................................... ½   "
Ginger-root, pulverized...............................2   "
Mace, pulverized..................................... ½   "
Nutmegs, pulverized..................................1   "
Dried Cherries, pulverized............................4   "
Dried Raspberries, pulverized.........................8   "

Stir all together; bung up the barrel, and keep it in a cool cellar for six months or a year. Then it may be bottled for use.

SIRUP.

Sirup is a thick solution of sugar in water, and when only sugar and water are employed it is called *Simple Sirup*, which forms the basis of Flavored or Medicated Sirups.

In the preparation of sirups, only the refined sugar should be used, as they will then be less liable to spontaneous decomposition, and if the water is pure, the sirup will be perfectly transparent, without the trouble of clarification. If too small a proportion of sugar is employed, the sirup is liable to ferment; but if too great a quantity is used, crystals of sugar will be deposited.

The following is the best formula:

Pure White Sugar..8 pounds.
Pure Cold Water...2 quarts.

Mix together, in a tin or porcelain vessel, occasionally stirring, for one or two hours; then place the vessel in a hot water-bath, and allow it to remain about one hour, or until the sugar is all dissolved. The sirup should then be removed, and, when cool, bottled or put in jugs for use. When preparing sirup, do not allow it to boil, but it may simmer for a minute or two. Remove from the fire as soon as made, because a long continued heat will impair its efficiency.

The proper degree of concentration is 30°, Baume's saccharometer, when boiling, and 35° when cold; or, specific gravity when boiling 1,261, and when cold 1,320. Its boiling point is 221°. A gallon of this sirup weighs 12 pounds.

Sirups, when kept at a high temperature, sometimes undergo the *vinous fermentation*, but they may be restored by boiling for a few moments, which expels the alcohol and carbonic acid. Sirups thus recovered are less liable to subsequent changes, as the fermenting principles have been decreased or consumed.

Simple sirup, prepared as above directed, is a choice and delicious article for the table, more wholesome than molasses or sugar-house sirup, and far preferable in flavor.

"SODA," OR FLAVORED SIRUPS.

LEMON SIRUP—(*Imitation.*)

Citric Acid, pulverized	1 ounce.
Oil of Lemon	20 drops.
Simple Sirup	1 gallon.

Rub the citric acid and oil of lemon with four ounces of the sirup in a mortar; then add the mixture to the remainder of the sirup, and dissolve by a moderate heat over a water-bath.

When cool, bottle for use.

A table-spoonful of this sirup, added to a glass of cold water, forms an agreeable extemporaneous lemonade and refrigerant beverage.

When water is charged with carbonic acid gas it constitutes what is known as "soda-water," to which this and other flavored sirups are added.

[NOTE—Carbonic acid gas is obtained from powdered marble by means of diluted sulphuric acid. See process for manufacturing carbonic acid gas.]

LEMON SIRUP—(*Genuine.*)

Cut off the ends of lemons and squeeze out the juice	1 quart.
Add Pure White Sugar	3 lbs.

Cut up and add the rinds of two lemons. Simmer a few minutes in a porcelain vessel; then strain, and when cool put into bottles or jugs for use, and keep in a cool cellar. To be used in the same manner and for the same purpose as the imitation "lemon sirup."

CREAM SIRUP.

Simple Sirup.. ....2 quarts.
Sweet, Rich Cream................................ ....1 "

Heat gradually together in a water-bath for half an hour. When cool, bottle for use. To flavor cream sirup, add

Fluid Extract of Vanilla................................1 ounce.
Fluid Extract of Nutmeg............................... ½ "

Used with carbonic acid water, commonly known as soda-water.

GINGER SIRUP.

Simple Sirup........... .... 1 gallon.
Fluid Extract of Jamaica Ginger.......................1 ounce.

Mix. Heat, and stir half an hour over a water-bath. When cool, bottle for use.

ORANGE SIRUP.

Simple Sirup........... ....1 gallon.
Essence ("Extract") of Orange....................... ½ ounce.

Mix, and proceed as for ginger sirup.

SARSAPARILLA SIRUP.

Simple Sirup... 1 gallon.
Oil of Wintergreen.......................................40 drops.
Oil of Sassafras...40 "
Dissolve the Oils in Deodorized Alcohol............ 2 ounces.

Mix, and shake well together.

STRAWBERRY SIRUP—(*Genuine.*)

Expressed Juice of Ripe Strawberries.................1 quart.
White Sugar...4 pounds.

Mix, and simmer a few minutes, or until the sugar is dissolved, in a porcelain kettle. Strain, and when cool put in bottles or jugs for use. Keep in a cool cellar.

STRAWBERRY SIRUP—(*Imitation.*)

Tincture of Orris Root	½ ounce.
Acetic Ether	40 drops.
Simple Sirup	1 gallon.

Stir well together, and it will be ready for use.

RASPBERRY SIRUP—(*Genuine.*)

Expressed Juice of Ripe Raspberries	1 quart.
White Sugar	4 pounds.

Simmer a few minutes in a porcelain kettle, until the sugar is dissolved. Strain, and when cool put in bottles or jugs, and keep in a cool cellar.

RASPBERRY SIRUP—(*Imitation.*)

Tincture of Orris Root	½ ounce.
Simple Sirup	1 gallon.

Stir well together, and it will be ready for use.

PINE-APPLE SIRUP—(*Genuine.*)

Expressed Juice of the ripest and best flavored Pine-apples	1 quart.
White Sugar	4 pounds.

Simmer a few minutes in a porcelain kettle until the sugar is dissolved; strain, and when cool put into bottles or jugs, and keep in a cool cellar.

PINE-APPLE SIRUP—(*Imitation.*)

Butyric Ether (called "Pine-apple Oil")	50 drops.
Dissolve in Deodorized Alcohol, 95 per cent	1 ounce.
Simple Sirup	1 gallon.

Stir well together, and it will be ready for use.

BLACKBERRY SIRUP.

Expressed Juice of ripe Blackberries	1 quart.
White Sugar	4 pounds.

Simmer a few minutes in a porcelain kettle, until the sugar is dissolved; strain, and when cool put in bottles or jugs, and keep in a cool cellar.

VANILLA SIRUP.

Essence of Vanilla.................................1 ounce.
Simple Sirup......................................1 gallon.

Stir well together, and it will be ready for use.

ROSE SIRUP.

Essence ("Extract") of Roses......................1 ounce.
Simple Sirup......................................1 gallon.

Stir well together, and it will be ready for use.

PEACH SIRUP.

Expressed Juice of ripe, good Peaches.............1 quart.
White Sugar.......................................4 pounds.

Simmer a few minutes in a porcelain kettle, until the sugar is dissolved; strain, and when cool put in bottles or jugs, and keep in a cool cellar.

COFFEE SIRUP.

Essence ("Extract") of Coffee.....................1 ounce.
Simple Sirup......................................1 gallon.

Stir well together, and it will be ready for use.

WINTERGREEN SIRUP.

Essence ("Extract") of Wintergreen................1 ounce.
Simple Sirup......................................1 gallon.

Stir well together, and it will be ready for use.

ORGEAT SIRUP.

Essence ("Extract") of Orgeat.....................1 ounce.
Simple Sirup......................................1 gallon.

Stir well together, and it will be ready for use.

NUTMEG SIRUP.

Essence ("Extract") of Nutmeg..........................1 ounce.
Simple Sirup..1 gallon.

Stir well together, and it will be ready for use.

MACE SIRUP.

Essence ("Extract") of Mace............................1 ounce.
Simple Sirup..1 gallon.

Stir well together, and it will be ready for use.

CINNAMON SIRUP.

Essence ("Extract") of Cinnamon......................1 ounce.
Simple Sirup..1 gallon.

Stir well together, and it will be ready for use.

COLORING FOR SIRUPS.

Cochineal is used to color the strawberry imitation sirup, and gives it a beautiful red tint. Wintergreen, raspberry and sarsaparilla sirups are usually colored with tincture of camwood; lemon and ginger sirups with tincture of turmeric; pine-apple requires no coloring. Various shades may be produced in the sirups, according to the quantity of the above tinctures added.

COCHINEAL FOR COLORING.

Powdered Cochineal......................................2 ounces.
Water..1 quart.

Boil together for a few minutes in a porcelain kettle. While boiling, add

Cream of Tartar...$\frac{1}{4}$ ounce.
Alum, in Powder..$\frac{1}{8}$ "

When the coloring matter is all extracted from the cochineal, strain and bottle for use.

Most of the sirups used for soda-water are imitations of the genuine, because they are less expensive. The fruit sirups should all be made from expressed juices, as directed in the foregoing formulas. A glass of the ordinary soda-water contains about two table-spoonsful of flavored sirup—the remainder of the beverage being water charged with carbonic acid gas, drawn from the fountain.

When the fountain is charged with a solution of carbonate of soda in water, each gallon of the flavored sirups should have added to it three-fourths of an ounce of tartaric acid, dissolved in a little water. But in most of the fountains, at the present time, neither soda nor tartaric acid is used.

PORTABLE LEMONADE.

Citric Acid, in powder................................... 3 ounces.
Pure White Sugar, powdered........................ 2 pounds.
Oil of Lemon..15 drops.

Mix well together, and keep in a closely corked bottle.

A tea-spoonful of this, added to a tumbler-ful of cold water, forms a wholesome and agreeable beverage. Travelers will find this a convenient way of procuring a pleasant and refreshing drink, at any time or place.

VEGETABLE AND ROOT BEERS.

SPRUCE BEER.

Essence of Spruce	1 pint.
Bruised Ginger	8 ounces.
Allspice, bruised	1 "
Hops	8 "
Cold Water	5 gallons.

Mix and stir occasionally for five or six hours. Then boil for fifteen minutes. Strain, and pour into a clean barrel, and add

Warm Water	20 gallons.
Sugar-house Sirup	$1\frac{1}{2}$ "
Brewers' Yeast, or good Hop Yeast	1 quart.

Mix altogether, and allow it to remain, for fermentation, in a room where the temperature is between 60° and 70°. If the bung be left out of the barrel for six hours, the beer will have fermented; bung up, and it will be ready for use in twenty-four hours. It forms a wholesome and medicinal beverage. Keep the beer in a cool cellar.

[NOTE.—To prepare the *essence* or *extract of spruce*, mentioned above, simmer one pound of young spruce twigs in half a gallon of water, for twenty or thirty minutes. Then strain and bottle for use. It should be used immediately, or within a few hours, unless it is kept in a very cool place.]

SARSAPARILLA COMPOUND ROOT BEER.

Hops	1 ounce.
Sassafras Bark	$\frac{1}{2}$ "
Burdock Root	1 "
Dandelion Root	1 "
Sarsaparilla Root	2 ounces
Spikenard Root	1 ounce.

All these roots should be crushed or cut into small pieces, and may be either green or dry. Place them in suitable vessels, and add

Cold Water..2 gallons.

Stir occasionally for six hours, and then simmer altogether for one hour. Strain, while warm, and add

Brewers', or Hop Yeast, half a tea-cupful.
Sugar-house Sirup...1 pint.

Mix altogether in a jug and shake thoroughly. Let the jug remain in a warm room, for six hours, uncorked. Then cork and keep it in a cool place.

This is a delightful spring beverage, alterative in its effects, and may prevent attacks of illness.

LEMON BEER.

Four Lemons, cut into thin slices.
Ginger, ground...4 ounces.
Sugar-house Sirup... ½ gallon.
Brewers' or Hop Yeast......................................1 pint.

Mix the lemons and ginger in half a gallon of warm water. Let the mixture stand in a warm place for six hours, and then simmer for about one hour. It is then to be put into a barrel and the sirup and yeast added. Then add

Warm Water..12 gallons.

Ferment in a warm place, with the bung out, for six hours, then bung up tightly; after which remove the beer to a cool place.

GINGER BEER.

Ground Ginger...3 ounces.

Simmer it in two quarts of water for half an hour. Add

Honey, strained..4 ounces.
Juice of...2 lemons.

Stir well together, and strain while warm. Add

Warm Water..2½ gallons.
Sugar-house Sirup..3 pints.

Put all into a jug and shake well together. Keep the jug, uncorked, in a warm room, for twenty-four hours, or until it ferments. Then cork and keep in a cool cellar.

CORN BEER.

Warm Water..2 gallons.
Sound Corn...1 pint.
Sugar-house Sirup..1 quart.

Put altogether in a jug, which must be tightly corked and kept in a warm room. It will be in a condition for drinking in about three or four days.

ROOT BEER.

American Sarsaparilla Root (powdered)............1 pound.
Guaiac Chips..8 ounces.
Birch Bark...3 ounces.
Sassafras Bark..2 ounces.
Prickly Ash Bark..¼ ounce.
Spice Wood..4 ounces.
Hops..8 ounces.
Water, warm...3 gallons.

Stir well together, and let it stand six hours; then simmer for three hours, stirring occasionally. Strain while warm. Then add

Tincture of Ginger..4 ounces.
Oil of Wintergreen..½ ounce.
Dissolved in Alcohol.......................................1 pint.

Shake well together. Then add

Warm Water..28 gallons.
Sugar-house Sirup..2 gallons.
Yeast...3 quarts.

Bung up the cask, and if kept at a temperature of from 60° to 75° for twenty-four hours, it will be in good state for a beverage.

This, if properly fermented, may be used in *fountains*, as there will be a sufficient pressure of carbonic acid to force up the beer in the manner of soda-water.

WINES.

CURRANT WINE.

Expressed Juice of Currants, strained............ 30 gallons.
White Sugar................................105 pounds.

Mix, and pour into a barrel, with the bung out, which place in a cool cellar where the thermometer indicates a temperature of about 50° Fahr. Cover the bung-hole with gauze, to exclude flies and dust. Let it remain undisturbed for four or five weeks. Then put in the bung. It may be left in the barrel, or bottled, and will improve by age. No spirits are required to increase its strength.

RHUBARB WINE.

Expressed Juice of Rhubarb, or Pie-plant,
    strained.................................... 20 gallons.
White Sugar................................150 pounds.
Warm Water................................ 10 gallons.

Mix altogether in a barrel, put into a cool cellar, and let it ferment for five or six weeks, covering the bung-hole with gauze, to keep out flies and dust. Then put in the bung, and at the end of two or three months it should be bottled. It will be fit for use, however, as soon as fermentation has fully ceased.

TOMATO WINE.

Expressed Juice of the garden Tomato, strained. 30 gallons.
White Sugar................................120 pounds.

Mix, and put into a barrel, which place in a cool cellar, leaving the bung-hole open, but covered with gauze, to exclude insects and dust. Let it remain undisturbed for five or six weeks. Then put in the bung. Whether left in the barrel or bottled, it will improve by age, and be ready for use at any time. It is a very excellent and healthful beverage.

BLACKBERRY WINE.

Expressed Juice of Blackberries, strained	30 gallons.
White Sugar	80 pounds.

Mix in a barrel, which must be bunged, and place in a cool cellar. In two or three months it will become splendid wine.

PORT WINE—(*Imitation.*)

Wild Grapes (bruised to a pulp, without breaking the seeds)	50 pounds.
Elder Berries (bruised to a pulp, without breaking the seeds)	10 pounds.
White Sugar	50 pounds.
Warm Water	30 gallons.

Mix together in a barrel, which must be placed in a cool cellar. Leave it undisturbed for five or six weeks, to ferment, keeping out dust and flies by covering the bung-hole with gauze. Then put in the bung, and bottle at convenience, leaving the sediment in the barrel. Add no spirits. This is better than much of the "superior port" of the shops.

PORT WINE—(*Genuine.*)

Cider (sweet)	30 gallons.
Alcohol, 95 per cent	6 gallons.

Into another vessel put

Extract of Logwood (pulverized)	1¾ pounds.

Simmer in four gallons of water one hour, and add to the cider and alcohol while warm. Then add

Alum (pulverized)	1½ pounds.
Cream of Tartar	1 pound.
White Sugar	24 pounds.

Stir well together, and roll the cask occasionally for one day. Allow it to settle for a few days, and it is ready for use.

This makes a *native* wine extensively used in America as an "imported" wine.

ISABELLA OR CATAWBA WINE.

Ripe Grapes (bruised to a pulp in a barrel,
    without breaking the seeds).....................100 pounds.
Warm Water.. 3 gallons.

Stir well together, and let stand for three or four days in a cool cellar. Then express the juice, strain, and add

White Sugar...60 pounds.

After standing thirty days, or until fermentation ceases, it should be drawn or racked off and strained. It may be kept in bottles or in casks.

APPLE WINE.

Cider, fresh from the press...........................30 gallons.
White Sugar...40 pounds.

Proceed as directed in the process for making currant wine.

STRAWBERRY WINE.

Expressed Juice of Strawberries, strained......... 30 gallons.
White Sugar...120 pounds.

Proceed, in all respects, as prescribed in the formula for making currant wine.

RASPBERRY WINE.

Expressed Juice of Raspberries, strained............30 gallons.
White Sugar...70 pounds.

Mix together in a barrel, and continue the process as directed for currant wine.

ELDERBERRY WINE.

Expressed Juice of Elderberries, strained...........30 gallons.
White Sugar...70 pounds.

After mixing the materials in a barrel, proceed in all particulars as in the process for making currant wine.

GINGER WINE.

Ginger (ground)	1 pound.
Hot Water	10 gallons.

Simmer gently for one hour; then add

White Sugar	20 pounds.
Lemons, sliced	2 pounds.

Continue to simmer for thirty minutes longer, and then remove from the fire.

When nearly cold, add

Yeast	$\frac{1}{2}$ pint.

Put all together in a barrel, and ferment as directed in the preparation of other wines. When fermentation ceases, rack off the wine, and bottle when clear.

VINEGAR.

(*Acetum.*)

Vinegar has been known for thousands of years. It is mentioned by Moses, and was in common use among the Israelites. In that age it was made from wine. Vinegar was also in common use among the Greeks and Romans, who employed it in their cookery, and as medicine.

ITS PROPERTIES.

As a condiment, vinegar is refreshing, and, if used *moderately*, is wholesome. It appears to render fatty and gelatinous food more digestible; but if used in excess is injurious to the stomach.

HOW VINEGAR IS FORMED.

Sugar and water, and all saccharine vegetable juices, infusions of malt, wine, cider, and all liquors susceptible of vinous fermentation, may be converted into vinegar by exposure to a temperature between 75° and 90° Fahr., with access of air. They undergo an action called acetous fermentation, and which is developed under the influence of a microscopic fungus termed *torula aceti*. The several changes which occur during this fermentation are included in the term *acetification*, during the progress of which heat is disengaged, the liquid becomes turbid, and filaments are formed, which move in numerous directions, and, finally, the liquid becomes transparent, with a pultaceous deposit of the filaments; its alcohol has disappeared, and vinegar now occupies its place.

This change is supposed to take place in consequence of the formation of a new substance called *Aldehyd*, the result of the loss of a part of the hydrogen of the alcohol. Alcohol consists of four equivalents of carbon, six of hydrogen, and two of oxygen. Through the action of the atmosphere it loses two equivalents of hydrogen, and becomes *aldehyd*.

Hydrated acetic acid consists of four equivalents, each, of carbon, hydrogen and oxygen. One equivalent of water is basic, and may be replaced by any metalic oxyd.

Aldehyd is an ethereal fluid, very inflammable and colorless, with a pungent taste and smell; its density is 0.79. It absorbs oxygen with avidity.

Its name has reference to its character—alcohol *dehydrogenized*.

Aldehyd Resin, a soft, light-brown mass, giving a nauseous, soapy smell when heated to 212°, is formed by decomposing the aqueous solution of *aldehyd* with caustic potassa.

CIDER VINEGAR.

The cider is placed in barrels with the bung-holes open, and exposed to a temperature between 75° and 90° Fahr. The acetification is perfected in about two months. This fermentation must be watched during its progress, and as soon as vinegar is formed it must be racked off into clean barrels; otherwise it will become spoiled by running into the putrefactive fermentation.

Vinegar is also made by various other methods, many of which require a comparatively short time for its formation. A pint of boiling *milk* added to forty gallons of vinegar, and stirred into it, will clarify it without injuring its aroma, and will also render red vinegar pale.

MANUFACTURE OF VINEGAR.

The true nature of the process of making vinegar quickly consists in the mere oxydation of alcohol in contact with organic matter, which is effected by exposing the largest surface of a vinegar-making fluid of proper temperature to atmospheric air, by means of a perforated vinegar generator, in which are placed beech, maple or basswood shavings, or corn cobs, through which the fluid passes and slowly drips into a vessel beneath. As the fluid passes slowly through the shavings, there is exposed a large surface of it to the air, oxygen is absorbed, and the temperature of the fluid rises to 104° Fahr., remaining stationary at that point, while the action goes on favorably.

The fluid may be passed through the generator two or three times, if it should not prove of sufficient strength at first; and thus vinegar may be made in from twenty-four to forty-eight hours.

MANUFACTURE OF VINEGAR—(QUICK PROCESSES.)

Number One.

Alcohol, 95 per cent	1 gallon.
Good Vinegar	1 quart.
Soft Water, warmed to 75°	15 gallons.
Yeast	1 pint.

Mix and pass through a vinegar generator.

Number Two.

Pure Cider	2 gallons.
Water, warmed to 75°	1 gallon.

Mix and pass through a vinegar generator.

Number Three.

Alcohol, 95 per cent	1 gallon.
Molasses	1 quart.
Soft Water, warmed to 75°	14 gallons.
Good Vinegar	1 quart.

Mix and pass through a vinegar generator.

MANUFACTURE OF VINEGAR—(SLOW PROCESSES.)

Number One.

Good Molasses	3 gallons.
Soft Water, warmed to 75°	30 gallons.
Yeast	1 quart.

Mix well together, and keep in a warm temperature in a barrel, with its bung out and the hole covered over with gauze, to keep out flies.

Number Two.

Acetic Acid, pure	4 pounds.
Molasses	1 gallon.
Warm Water, soft	35 gallons.

Mix, and keep at from 75° to 90° Fahr., and it will become vinegar in about twenty days.

INSTANTANEOUS PROCESS.

Acetic Acid, pure	1 pound.
Pure Water	6 pints.

Mix.

HOW TO CONSTRUCT A VINEGAR GENERATOR.

To construct a vinegar generator, or graduation vessel, simply prepare an oaken tub, narrower at the bottom than at the top, and furnished with a loose lid or cover. The tub may be of any convenient size, from six feet to ten or twenty feet high, and from two to four or five feet in diameter. The higher and more capacious the tub, the greater the quantity of vinegar which can be generated in a given time.

Below the lid, or cover, is placed a perforated shelf, or false bottom, having a number of small holes filled with pack-threads, extending down six inches and prevented from falling through by knots at their upper ends. The shelf is also perforated with four open glass tubes, as air vents, each having its ends projecting above and below the shelf. The tub, at its lower part, is pierced with a horizontal row of eight or ten equidistant, round holes, to admit atmospheric air. One inch above the bottom is a syphon discharge-pipe, whose upper curvature stands one inch below the level of the air-holes in the side of the tub. The body of the tub being filled with beech-wood shavings, the alcoholic liquor, which should be at a temperature of from 75° to 80° Fahr, is placed on the shelf. It trickles slowly down through the holes by means of the pack-threads, diffuses itself over the shavings, and runs off by the syphon-pipe. The air enters by the circumferential holes, circulates freely through the tub, and escapes through the glass tubes. As the oxygen is absorbed, the temperature of the liquid rises from 100° to 104° Fahr., and remains stationary at that point, while the operation goes on favorably.

It will be necessary to pass the liquor through three or four times before acetification is complete, which generally requires twenty-four hours.

A cheap, extemporaneous vinegar generator may also be constructed by placing new oak barrels (the heads being removed) one above the other, until the pile is five or six barrels high, or less. Have them securely fastened, by nailing strips of boards on the outside of the barrels. Perforate the barrels, and arrange as described above. To secure the joints against leakage, where the barrels rest upon each other, make a thorough application of paraffin wax, applied while hot.

ANOTHER MODE OF CONSTRUCTING A GENERATOR.

Take six new oak barrels, or those which have been used for vinegar or molasses, respectively numbering them from one to six. Remove one head from each. With a three-quarter inch auger, then bore fifteen holes through the sides of each barrel, an equal distance apart, all slanting towards the bottom of the barrel, (to prevent the vinegar from running out on the side). These holes should be about twelve inches above the lower end of the barrel. Set the barrels side by side, and insert a faucet in each, near the bottom. Fill up the barrels with thick beech, maple, or basswood shavings, which must be new and planed from the edges of inch-boards. They should be each about two feet long, and formed into rolls. Clean corn-cobs, however, will serve the same purpose for a few months, but for permanent and continued manufacture the shavings are preferable. When cobs are used, they should be put in the barrels in layers, crossing each other, to prevent their becoming too closely packed, and over all, when the barrel is nearly filled with cobs, should be laid shavings, to the depth of about six inches. Pine shavings must be avoided in making vinegar. Cover over the top of the shavings or cobs a flannel cloth, for the purpose of retaining the heat generated in the barrel by oxydation during the chemical transformation. Then gradually pour all over the cloth, in each barrel, one gallon of good vinegar, for the purpose of *souring* the shavings or cobs. Let the barrels stand unmolested one day, when the vinegar must be drawn from them by means of the faucet in each. The next day pour on the alcohol, vinegar and water, as recommended in either number one, number two, or number three process.

For example: Heat two gallons, prepared according to the number one formula, to 80° Fahr., and pour it carefully over the cloth in barrel number one. Repeat this process every hour during the day. After six hours have elapsed, draw off all that has settled in the bottom and pour it over the cloth in barrel number two, at the rate of one gallon every half-hour. It will drip slowly through the shavings, and, as fast as it drips through, pass the same liquor into all the remaining barrels in rotation, and in the same manner. Continue to pour the fluid through barrel number one, as before described, and so on through each other barrel. When the liquid has passed through all the barrels, as it will within thirty-six hours from the commencement, if the barrels have been kept in a room where the temperature ranges between 75° and 90° Fahr., the vinegar will be found good, sharp, pure and wholesome. If stronger vinegar is required, it can be passed again through one, two, or more of the barrels, until the desired strength is obtained. It is essential that the temperature of the room in which the vinegar is made should be neither less than 75° nor more than 90°.

TO DECOLORIZE VINEGAR.

When a colorless vinegar is required, add to each gallon of vinegar one pound of coarsely-powdered animal charcoal, and stir occasionally for two or three days. Allow the mixture to rest three or four days; then draw off and strain the vinegar, which, if well prepared charcoal has been used, will be colorless, and similar to white wine vinegar.

FRUIT VINEGARS.

Various fruits yield saccharine juices, which, at a temperature ranging from 60° to 100°, spontaneously pass first through vinous and then acetous fermentation, resulting in vinegar, the odor and flavor of which, in some degree, correspond to the fruit from which the juice was expressed. But currants, gooseberries, pie-plant (rhubarb), and various other excessively acid substances, are deficient in sugar, which must be added to secure fermentation.

Vinegar may be strengthened by freezing it and removing the ice which forms on the surface. It is only the water of the vinegar which freezes, leaving the acetic acid in solution in the remaining water.

VINEGAR REFINED BY BOILING.

If vinegar be boiled a few seconds in a covered porcelain or glass vessel, the heat will congulate the albuminous and mucilaginous substances contained in it. If it be then strained through flannel, and put into bottles, which should be kept well corked, it will remain in a good condition for a long time.

VINEGAR REFINED BY DISTILLATION.

Distill vinegar until about two-thirds of it has passed over. The impurities, not being volatile, are left behind. The part distilled is nearly pure acetic acid. Dilute this with water to the proper strength for vinegar. This is known as distilled vinegar.

GOOSEBERRY VINEGAR.

Reduce eight gallons of ripe gooseberries to a pulp, and, having placed them in a suitable barrel, add twenty-five gallons of warm water. Stir occasionally during one day. Then strain through coarse flannel, and add either six gallons of sugar-house sirup, or forty-eight pounds of brown sugar, or, if preferred, fifty pounds of strained honey. Mix well together, and keep at a warm temperature, leaving the bung-hole of the barrel open, but covered with fine gauze to keep out flies, dust, etc.

RHUBARB VINEGAR.

Rhubarb (pie-plant) vinegar may be formed from the juice of the stalk of the rhubarb plant, by adding of warm water four times the weight of the juice, and one and a half pounds of brown sugar to each gallon of the juice thus diluted. Ferment in the manner previously described.

But the quantity of sugar required to produce the vinous fermentation renders the juices of fruits and vegetables a very expensive material for making vinegar. Furthermore, they do not produce any better vinegar than that made from three gallons of molasses and thirty gallons of water.

THE ADULTERATIONS OF VINEGAR.

Sulphuric, nitric and muriatic acids are sometimes used to impart acidity to vinegar. Burnt sugar is often added for coloring, and acetic ether to give it a pleasant flavor. Vinegar not containing more than one-thousandth part of mineral acid is not injurious, and preserves better than pure vinegar. Still we do not advise the adulteration of vinegar with any of the mineral acids.

TO DETECT SULPHURIC ACID IN VINEGAR.

Take of the Suspected Vinegar.......................4 ounces.
Starch (common)............................... ....1 drachm.

Agitate, and add

Iodine............... ....5 grains.

Shake well together.

If the vinegar is pure, the presence of iodine will change its color to a blue tint; but if sulphuric acid is present, no such reaction will take place, for the resultant of starch in its presence is glucose, a substance not affected by iodine.

WINE VINEGAR.

When wine passes through the acetous fermentation, it is denominated "wine vinegar," and contains not only acetic, but also citric and tartaric acids, together with a small quantity of acetic ether, which gives it an agreeable flavor, and is in no respect injurious.

MISCELLANEOUS.

No attempt should be made to run the solution of sugar or diluted sirup through the generator, during the process of making vinegar, as a mucilaginous substance, called "mother," forms, which soon fills up the apertures of the generator, and arrests the operation. Sirup, however much diluted, should always be converted into vinegar by the slow processes, in barrels. Use only the alcoholic preparation in the generator, as set forth in the quick processes.

THE STRENGTH OF VINEGAR.

The pleasant and refreshing odor of vinegar is derived from acetic acid and acetic ether.

The strength of vinegar is designated by the manufacturer

by numbers, as follows: 18, 20, 22, and 24—the latter number representing the strongest, which contains about five per cent. of anhydrous acetic acid, and is known as "*proof vinegar.*" In order that these numbers may be more fully understood, the following tables are introduced to indicate the saturative power and specific gravity of vinegar, as well as to explain the technical terms employed by manufacturers:

1 oz. No. 18 vinegar requires 18 grs. pure, dry carbonate of soda for complete neutralization.
1 oz. " 20 " " 20 " " " " " " " " "
1 oz. " 22 " " 22 " " " " " " " " "
1 oz. " 24 " " 24 " " " " " " " " "

The ounce of vinegar is liquid measure.

The specific gravity of No. 18 Vinegar is..................1006
The specific gravity of No. 20 Vinegar is..................1012
The specific gravity of No. 22 Vinegar is..................1019
The specific gravity of No. 24 Vinegar is..................1035

Vinegar No. 24 is "Proof," 5° by the acetometre, or "1 Vinegar."
5° Overproof (or O. P.), is 10°, or "2 Vinegars."
10° Overproof (or O. P.), is 15°, or "3 Vinegars," etc.

One fluid-ounce of vinegar termed "extra strength" will saturate 32 grains of pure, dry carbonate of soda.

TINCTURES.

[Tinctures are solutions of medicinal substances in diluted or strong alcohol.]

TINCTURE OF CAMPHOR.
(*Spirits of Camphor.*)

Camphor Gum	4 ounces.
Alcohol, 95 per cent	1 quart.

Agitate until the camphor is dissolved.

TINCTURE OF MYRRH.

Gum Myrrh	4 ounces.
Alcohol, 76 per cent	1 quart.

Macerate for fourteen days, and filter through paper.

TINCTURE OF CATECHU.

Gum Catechu, cut fine	4 ounces.
Alcohol, 76 per cent	1 quart.

Macerate for fourteen days, and filter through paper.

TINCTURE OF GUAIACUM.

Gum Guaiacum, pulverized	4 ounces.
Alcohol, 95 per cent	1 quart.

Macerate for fourteen days, and filter through paper.

TINCTURE OF OPIUM.
(*Laudanum.*)

Gum Opium, sliced	3 ounces.
Boiling Water	10 fluid-oz.

Reduce the opium to an emulsion in a wedgwood mortar. Then add

Alcohol, 76 per cent	20 ounces.

Put altogether in a bottle, and agitate occasionally for one day. At the end of twenty-four hours it will be of full strength. Filter through paper.

TINCTURE OF RHUBARB.

Rhubarb Root, bruised..................................4 ounces.
Alcohol, 76 per cent....................................1 quart.

Macerate for fourteen days, express, and filter through paper.

TINCTURE OF BLOODROOT.

Bloodroot, powdered...................................6 ounces.
Alcohol, 76 per cent....................................1 quart.

Macerate for fourteen days, express, and filter through paper.

TINCTURE OF GINGER.

Ginger Root, powdered................................8 ounces.
Alcohol, 95 per cent....................................1 quart.

Macerate for fourteen days, express, and filter through paper.

TINCTURE OF SENNA.

Senna Leaves (Alexandria).............................4 ounces.
Alcohol, diluted...1 quart.

Macerate for fourteen days, express, and filter through paper.

COMPOUND TINCTURE OF SENNA.

(Elixir Salutis.)

Senna Leaves (Alexandria).............................2 ounces.
Jalap, in powder.......................................1 ounce.
Fennel Seeds, bruised.................................. $\frac{1}{2}$ "
Alcohol, 76 per cent....................................1 quart.

Macerate for fourteen days, express, and filter through paper.

TINCTURE OF CAPSICUM.

Cayenne Pepper..1 ounce.
Alcohol, 76 per cent....................................1 quart.

Macerate for fourteen days, express, and filter through paper.

TINCTURE OF COLUMBO.

Columbo Root, bruised....................................4 ounces.
Alcohol, 76 per cent.......................................1 quart.

Macerate for fourteen days, express, and filter through paper.

TINCTURE OF PERUVIAN BARK.

Peruvian Bark, powdered...............................6 ounces.
Alcohol, 76 per cent.......................................1 quart.

Macerate for fourteen days, express, and filter through paper.

TINCTURE OF BLACK COHOSH.

Black Cohosh Root (in powder).......................4 ounces.
Alcohol, 76 per cent.......................................1 quart.

Macerate for fourteen days, express, and filter through paper.

TINCTURE OF GOLDEN-SEAL.

Golden-Seal Root, in powder...........................6 ounces.
Alcohol, 76 per cent.......................................1 quart.

Macerate for fourteen days, express, and filter through paper.

TINCTURE OF LOBELIA.

Lobelia Herb, in powder.................................4 ounces.
Alcohol, 76 per cent.......................................1 quart.

Macerate for fourteen days, express, and filter through paper.

TINCTURE OF PRICKLY ASH.

Prickly Ash Berries, in powder........................8 ounces.
Alcohol, 76 per cent.......................................1 quart.

Macerate for fourteen days, express, and filter through paper.

TINCTURE OF SPEARMINT.
(*Spirits of Mint.*)

Spearmint Leaves, fresh, sufficient to fill a glass jar.
Holland Gin, sufficient to cover the Spearmint Leaves.

Macerate for seven days, express, and filter through paper.

TINCTURE OF OIL OF PEPPERMINT.
(*Essence of Peppermint.*)

Oil of Peppermint...1 ounce.
Alcohol, 95 per cent...1 pint.

Agitate in a bottle for a few minutes, and it will be ready for use. The alcohol will readily dissolve the oil, and a strong essence will be the result. The same process will apply to nearly all tinctures (or essences) made from the essential oils.

TINCTURE OF OIL OF SASSAFRAS.
(*Essence of Sassafras.*)

Oil of Sassafras...1 ounce.
Alcohol, 95 per cent...1 pint.

Dissolve the oil in the alcohol.

TINCTURE OF OIL OF CINNAMON.
(*Essence of Cinnamon.*)

Oil of Cinnamon..1 ounce.
Alcohol, 95 per cent...1 pint.

Dissolve the oil in the alcohol.

TINCTURE OF OIL OF WINTERGREEN.
(*Essence of Wintergreen.*)

Oil of Wintergreen..1 ounce.
Alcohol, 95 per cent...1 pint.

Dissolve the oil in the alcohol.

In making other tinctures of oils (essences), viz., Anise,

Lavender, Spearmint, etc., dissolve the essential oils of either in alcohol, 95 per cent., in the proportion of one ounce of the oil to one pint of the alcohol.

COLORING TINCTURES.

The tinctures of essential oils, as peppermint, etc., are sometimes colored—those of a red tint with tincture of red sanders wood, and those of a yellow color with tincture of turmeric. But we do not recommend the coloring of tinctures. A few green leaves of peppermint are sometimes added to the tincture of peppermint, to give it a greenish tint, and to this there can be no objection.

PREPARING TINCTURES.

In the preparation of tinctures, the roots, leaves, barks, etc., used are generally dry, and should be pulverized. Alcohol stronger than 76 per cent. should never be used in the manufacture of tinctures from roots, leaves and barks.

EXTRACTS.

HYDRO-ALCOHOLIC EXTRACT OF GOLDEN-SEAL ROOT.

Golden-Seal Root, in powder.........................2 pounds.
Alcohol, 95 per cent............................ ....1 quart.

Let this mixture stand twenty-four hours; then transfer to a percolator, and gradually add alcohol (95 per cent.) until it passes off without the taste of the root.

To the powder in the percolator add
Warm Water...... ....3 pints.

Let the mixture stand twenty-four hours. Then gradually add a sufficient quantity of water, until the liquid passes only slightly impregnated with the properties of the golden-seal. Strain the alcoholic and aqueous liquids together, and evaporate to the proper consistence.

This extract possesses all the tonic virtues of the root, and may be used in all cases where that is indicated.

This same process may be used for making the hydro-alcoholic extracts of yellow-dock root, bloodroot, etc.

TO PREPARE FLUID EXTRACTS.

These preparations contain all the virtues of the drugs from which they are made, in a liquid form, and are uniformly of such strength that a pint of extract is equal to a pound of the drug, or a drop equal to one grain.

The following is a general process for their manufacture, to be varied according to the nature of the active principles of the drugs operated upon:

Take of the Drug, finely powdered................16 pounds.
Alcohol, 76 per cent........................a sufficient quantity.

Moisten the drug with the alcohol, and pack it well into a conical percolator. Add alcohol, from time to time, until fourteen pints of tincture have been obtained and set aside.

Continue the percolation with alcohol until the tincture passes through nearly colorless.

Then add water, in the same manner, until the alcohol is washed out of the drug.

Distill the alcohol from all the tincture, except that set aside, and evaporate the residuary liquor down to the measure of two pints, by a water-bath.

Finally, mix the residuary liquor with the reserved tincture, and filter through Swedish filtering paper.

This is an extremely convenient and reliable form for the administration of many remedies. Over three hundred different extracts are now made by Messrs. Garrison & Murray, druggists and chemists, of this city.

PERFUMERY.

SPIRIT OF BERGAMOT.

Fresh Bergamot Leaves, bruised......................2 pounds.
Alcohol, 95 per cent., deodorized......................1 gallon.
Distilled Water...$1\frac{1}{2}$ gallons.

Digest over a water-bath for five or six hours, in a closely covered vessel, at a heat not exceeding 125° Fahr.

The same process will serve for producing spirits of lavender, rosemary, etc.

A more refined article may be made from the foregoing preparation, by drawing off six quarts by distillation.

SPIRITUOUS HUNGARY WATER.

Rosemary Flowers, fresh, and bruised ....$1\frac{1}{2}$ pounds.
Lavender Flowers, fresh, and bruised................ $\frac{1}{2}$ pound.
Alcohol, 95 per cent., deodorized......................3 quarts.
Distilled Water..1 gallon.

Digest over a water-bath for five or six hours, and proceed as in the formula for spirit of bergamot, distilling in the same manner for a refined article.

SPIRITUOUS COLOGNES.

NUMBER ONE COLOGNE.

Oil of Bergamot	½ ounce.
Oil of Rosemary	½ ounce.
Oil of Neroli	¼ ounce.
Oil of Lavender	¼ ounce.
Alcohol, deodorized (known as cologne spirits), 95 per cent	1 quart.
Rosewater	8 ounces.

Shake well together, and it will be ready for use.

NUMBER TWO COLOGNE.

Oil of Rosemary	2 drachms.
Oil of Lavender	2½ drachms.
Oil of Lemon	½ ounce.
Oil of Bergamot	½ ounce.
Oil of Neroli	½ drachm.
Alcohol, 95 per cent. (cologne spirits)	3 pints.
Orange-flower Water	1 pint.

Shake well together, and it will be ready for use.

OINTMENTS.

Ointments comprise a class of medicines which contain certain vegetable or mineral substances. Their consistence is softer than that of salves or plasters, the heat of the body being sufficient to melt them. Butter, lard, or oil, with wax, are the usual vehicles for combining their virtues.

VENICE TURPENTINE OINTMENT.

Venice Turpentine............1 pound.
Common Tar............6 ounces.
Fresh Butter............2¼ pounds.

Simmer until they are united.

USE.—This ointment may be employed in the treatment of scald-head (*tinea capitis*). Wash the parts thoroughly with soap-suds, and apply twice or three times a day.

GREEN OINTMENT.

Leaves of the Double Tansy............2 ounces.
Catnip............2 ounces.
Wormwood............3 ounces.
Hops............1 ounce.

Bruise these herbs, put them into a jug, and cover with

Alcohol, 76 per cent............1 quart.

Allow it to stand two weeks. Then pour into a kettle or basin, and add

Lard............3 pounds.

Simmer one hour, and strain. Then add

Gum Turpentine............4 ounces.

Simmer for fifteen or twenty minutes, stirring occasionally. When nearly cool, pour into bottles or boxes for use.

USE.—This ointment is very cooling and relaxing. It is useful in sprains, swellings, contracted sinews, etc.

STRAMONIUM OINTMENT.

Fresh Stramonium Leaves, bruised to a pulp........½ pound.

Put them into a bottle, and add

Alcohol, 76 per cent............... ....1 quart.

Let it stand two or three days. Then pour into a kettle or basin, and add

Lard............... ....3 pounds.

Simmer together, and strain. Pour into boxes or bottles before it has entirely cooled.

USE.—This is a good application for scalds, burns, sores, piles and cutaneous eruptions.

BITTERSWEET OINTMENT.

Bark of Bittersweet Root............... ....½ pound.
Alcohol, 76 per cent... ....½ pint.

Macerate for two weeks. Then pour into a kettle or basin, and add

Fresh Butter............... ....1½ pounds.

Simmer one hour, and strain.

USE.—Excellent for sores of various kinds.

YELLOW-DOCK OINTMENT.

Yellow-Dock Roots, bruised........................1 pound.
Alcohol, 76 per cent.....................................½ pint.

Macerate for two days. Then pour into a kettle or basin, and add

Fresh Butter............ ....1½ pounds.

Simmer one hour, and strain.

Use.—This ointment is used for salt-rheum, scrofulous humors, etc.; and by combining it with the bittersweet ointment, it will be excellent for tumors, etc.

COMPOUND POKE-ROOT OINTMENT.

Poke-Root, bruised..4 ounces.
Bark of Bittersweet Root, bruised......................2 ounces.
Yellow-Dock Root, bruised.................................3 ounces.
Stramonium Leaves...1 ounce.
Alcohol, 76 per cent..8 ounces.

Macerate for two weeks. Then pour into a kettle or basin, and add

Fresh Butter..2 pounds.

Simmer one hour, and strain.

Use.—This is an excellent ointment for salt-rheum, scald-head, itch, and other cutaneous diseases, and is invaluable for scrofulous and fever-sores.

[Note.—Instead of macerating the materials for two weeks, the bottle or jug containing them may be placed in a water-bath, heated to about 150° Fahr., for ten or twelve hours, by which process the same result is obtained.]

PLASTERS.

ADHESIVE AND STRENGTHENING PLASTER.

White Resin	2½ pounds.
Burgundy Pitch	3 ounces.
Beeswax	3 ounces.
Mutton Tallow	4 ounces.

Melt together, and add

Oil of Sassafras	½ ounce.
Oil of Hemlock	½ ounce.
Camphor Gum	½ ounce.

Dissolve the sassafras, hemlock and camphor together in

Alcohol, 95 per cent	4 ounces.

Then add

Tincture of Myrrh	2 ounces.
Tincture of Guaiacum	2 ounces.

Incorporate all the articles, by stirring well together. Then pour the whole into a vessel of water, and work it with the hands until cold. It may then be made into rolls for use.

This plaster can be made softer or harder, as the season may require, by using more or less resin.

USE.—This is a valuable preparation for wounds, sores, cuts, boils, bruises, felons, etc., and is unequaled as a rheumatic and strengthening plaster for pains in the sides, back and limbs. When warm, spread on cloth or leather.

IRRITATING PLASTER.

Tar	¾ pound.
Gum Turpentine	½ pound.
Beeswax	6 ounces.
Burgundy Pitch	½ pound.

Melt together, and strain. As it cools, stir in

Poke-root,
Bloodroot, } Finely pulverized............each 2 ounces.
Indian Turnip,

When the whole mass is well incorporated, spread on soft leather, and place over the part affected.

USE.—This may be used as a counter-irritant in the case of deep-seated pain in any part of the body. Keep on the plaster until eruptions are produced.

TANNING.

The skin of animals is composed of two parts or layers. The external one, which is thin, is called the cuticle, or *epidermis*. The inner one, called the *cutis vera*, or true skin, consists of minute fibres, composed chiefly of gelatin, or glue.

When a solution of gelatin, or glue, is mixed with an infusion of oak or hemlock bark, gum catechu, or any other vegetable astringent, a precipitate is formed consisting of the tannin of the astringent matter and the gelatin. This compound, which is insoluble in water, and not subject to putrefaction, is the substantial basis of leather.

Skin may be converted into leather by three methods. The simplest, and probably the first that was invented, consists in soaking the skin in water, and then forcing grease or oil into its pores by hard rubbing; the oil, which is thus introduced in the place of water, preserves the suppleness or pliability of the skin as long as it remains. In this manner the Indians prepare their deer and buffalo skins. Sometimes they soak the skins in a mixture of the fat and brains of the animal; after which this mixture is well rubbed with the hands. The skins are then hung up to dry in the smoke, which, by its antiseptic properties, aids in preventing putrefaction.

Tanning is the process by which animal skins are converted into leather—a product possessing certain properties that differ from the raw hide, skin or pelt, and which adapt it to the purposes for which it is generally employed.

Chemically considered, leather is a compound of gelatin and tannin, possessing the desirable qualities of durability, pliability, insolubility, and a great indifference to the action of chemical re-agents. Tanning essentially consists in saturating the skin with a diluted solution of tannic acid, with which the cellular and elastic tissues gradually combine as it penetrates inward, forming an insoluble compound that resists putrefaction completely. This is leather.

The principal steps necessary in the manufacture of good leather in an expeditious manner are as follows:

First.—Soaking and washing the hides or skins in pure water, for the purpose of cleansing and softening them.

Second.—The removal of the hair, to effect which three or four pounds of unslaked lime are added to a barrel of water, in which mixture the hide or skin should be soaked a day or two. By this treatment the albumen surrounding the bulbous roots of the hair is dissolved, which facilitates its removal by scraping with the blunt edge of a knife or other instrument used for that purpose.

Third—The thorough cleaning of the hides or skins. This is effected by the copious use of water, and afterwards scraping them on a beam, with the "fleshing-knife," to remove all superfluous fat, etc.; and, lastly, by soaking them for a day or two in cold water, to which bran, in the proportion of a peck to a barrel of water, has been added.

Finally.—Take them out and rinse thoroughly, when they are prepared for tanning.

The following is the formula for the decoction now to be used:

Sumach Bark, powdered, or cut into small pieces... ¾ pound.
Cold Water..1 gallon.

Mix, and let the bark soak for about twelve hours. Then simmer the whole for three or four hours in a well tinned or copper vessel, (iron vessels should not be used), gradually adding hot water, from time to time, to make up the quantity lost by evaporation. Then pour off, and strain through muslin; and while hot add to each gallon of this decoction the following:

Sulphuric Acid (Oil of Vitriol)........................ 1 ounce.
Common Salt...16 ounces.

Mix all well together, in a convenient-sized wooden vessel, in which, when cooled to about 98° Fahr., immerse the skins, as previously prepared, for about thirty minutes. Then remove and hang them up. When nearly dry, they should be pulled and rubbed until thoroughly dry; and this completes the process of tanning.

To keep leather in a pliable condition, and to render it water-proof, we suggest the following, which may be called the

COMPOUND LEATHER DRESSING.

Good Sperm Oil...1 quart.
Paraffin Oil...1½ pints.
Castor Oil...6 ounces.
Tallow... ¾ pound.
Light Colored Resin, powdered......................... ¼ pound.
Paraffin Wax..2 ounces.

Melt together by means of a water-bath, and when cold apply to the leather as long as it is absorbed.

This composition is far superior to the ordinary dressing

for leather, as it not only makes it pliable, but, possessing antiseptic properties, preserves it a much longer time.

The castor and paraffin oils protect the leather from the ravages of rats, mice, and other vermin.

HOW TO TAN THE SKINS OF ANIMALS WITH THE HAIR OR FUR ON THEM.

Whether the hides or pelts are dry or green, put them into lukewarm water, and let them soak over night, or longer if necessary, until they are soft; then wash them thoroughly in warm soap-suds; after which remove all fat and fleshy substances, wash in clear, cold water, and hang them in the air to dry. When nearly dry, work and rub them until they are soft and dry. Then take a sponge or brush, and thoroughly saturate the flesh side with the sumach and salt compound, which should be at about blood-heat, or 98°, as given in the process for tanning leather. This application should be repeated two or three times during the day, the repetition being governed by the thickness of the skin, which, when thoroughly saturated with this compound, and dried, is thoroughly tanned. When the hide or pelt is nearly dry, after the last application, it should be worked and rubbed until dry and soft.

When it becomes soft, apply the compound leather dressing, and work it well into the pores of the skin.

A little care will be necessary to avoid greasing the hair or fur.

The following is an excellent and cheap method of

RENOVATING FURS.

Rub warm wheat bran thoroughly with the hands into the fur or hair of the skin, which can be done conveniently by laying the fur on a table or bench. Then brush out the bran, and the fur will present a clean, bright appearance.

HOW TO TAN SHEEPSKINS, DOG, SQUIRREL, COON OR OTHER PELTS, WITH THE HAIR ON.

Wash the skins in strong soap-suds, made by using hot water, carefully squeezing out and cleansing the wool, or fur, from all dirt and grease. Then wash in cold water until the soap is all removed. Next, dissolve half a pound of salt and one-fourth pound of alum in half a gallon of warm water, and put into a tub containing one and a half gallons of cold water, in which immerse the skins. Let them soak twelve hours, and then hang them over a pole to drain. When well drained, stretch them carefully on a board to dry. Stretch them several times while drying. Before they are entirely dry, sprinkle on the flesh side one ounce each of powdered alum and saltpetre, rubbing in the mixture well. Then lay the flesh sides together, and hang them in the shade for two or three days, turning them over every day until they are dry.

Finish by scraping the flesh side with a blunt knife, to remove any remaining scraps of flesh, and then rub (the flesh side) with pumice or rotten-stone and the hands. Very beautiful mats, mittens, etc., can be made of skins tanned as above.

TO COLOR FURS OR HAIR PELTS.

Carbonate of Soda..4 ounces.
Hot Water..1 gallon.

Dissolve. Then add

Acetate of Lead (pulverized)....................................$\frac{1}{4}$ ounce.
Sulphate of Iron...$\frac{1}{2}$ ounce.
Litharge...$\frac{1}{2}$ ounce.

Stir together for five minutes. Then allow the liquid to cool to 100° Fahr. The furs (having previously been washed in soap-suds, to remove from them all grease, and then dried,) should now be immersed in the coloring bath and slowly moved about in it for five minutes. Then air the furs for five minutes. Repeat this process three or four times, or until the desired dark shade is produced.

This dye may be made stronger by adding double the quantity of acetate of lead, sulphate of iron and litharge, while warm, to the carbonate of soda solution. Apply this dye to the furs by means of a brush. Light or dark shades may thus be produced, according to the strength of the dye and the number of applications that the furs receive.

ANOTHER MODE OF TANNING.

Put the skins into soft soap. Let them remain from one to two days, or until the hair can be readily removed. Scrape off the hair with a dull knife, and rinse the skin in warm water. Then apply equal parts of pulverized alum and fine salt to all portions of the skin, on both sides. Roll and pack away for twenty days. Then unroll, and with the hands pull and stretch the skin until it is soft and pliable. This is a good method of tanning skins of deer, squirrels, dogs, etc., with the hair off.

SOAP.

(*Sapo.*)

According to history, the Gauls are supposed to have been the originators of soap made from tallow and wood-ashes. All the alkalies employed in washing were known to the ancient Greeks and Egyptians, and used by them.

Soaps embrace all those compounds which result from the re-action of salifiable bases with oils and fats. The theory of soap-making is very simple, depending on the affinity existing between the alkalies and fat acids; on the solubility in water of the alkaline stearates, margarates, oleates, etc.; and, finally, on the power of a certain amount of free alkali, or common salt, to coagulate the soap and render it insoluble in the liquid in which it swims, and which, in fact, runs off its surface as water does off the surface of fat, while yet the soap retains its solubility in pure water.

There are two principal varieties of soap—*hard* and *soft*. Hard soap is made of soda and tallow, or oil; soft soap, of potash and grease, or oil.

When soda and tallow alone are employed, the soap s white.

Common yellow, or resin soap derives its peculiarities from an admixture of resin and a small quantity of palm-oil with the tallow employed—the palm-oil being used to improve the color of the soap.

The following constitutes what we consider the best practical process for making soap for family use, without the employment of expensive apparatus.

TRANSPARENT HARD SOAP, PERFUMED.

White Bar Soap, cut into thin slices..................25 pounds.
Alcohol, 95 per cent................................... 2 gallons.

Heat gradually in a tin or copper kettle, stirring until the soap is all dissolved. Remove the kettle from the fire, and when partially cool, add

Essence of Sassafras.......................................4 ounces.

Stir well together. Then pour into pans one inch deep. When cold, cut into square bars, or it may be run into cakes, or rolled into balls.

This is a superior toilet soap.

WHITE BAR SOAP, PERFUMED.

Carbonate of Soda..20 pounds.
Soft Water, hot..10 gallons.

Stir until the soda is dissolved. Then add

Freshly-slaked Lime......................................20 pounds.

Stir occasionally for five hours. Allow it to settle for twelve or fifteen hours; then pour off the clear solution into another kettle, and add

Tallow...20 pounds.

Boil, with repeated stirrings, until all is dissolved. Then pour off, to cool, into a shallow box, and when partially cooled, add

Essence of Sassafras......................................1 pint.

Stir well together. Then pour into pans or tight boxes two or three inches in depth. When cold, cut into bars or cakes.

Other essences may be used to perfume the soap, if preferred.

To make "almond" soap, omit the essence of sassafras and use the essence of almonds, which is prepared thus:

Oil of Bitter Almonds.................................... 2 ounces.
Alcohol, 95 per cent..................................... 12 ounces.

Agitate for a few minutes, until the oil is dissolved. Incorporate with the soap, when partially cooled, as above directed.

SOFT SOAP FROM HARD SOAP—QUICK PROCESS.

Soft Water, hot... 20 gallons.
Carbonate of Soda (Sal Soda)............................ 6 pounds.

Stir, keeping up the heat, until dissolved. Then add

White Bar Soap, in thin slices .... 20 pounds.

Stir altogether, over the fire, until the soap is dissolved. When partially cooled, pour into a barrel for use.

This forms an excellent soft soap.

IMPROVED SOFT SOAP.

Soft Water, hot... 20 gallons.
Liquid Silicate of Soda (30° Baume)..................... 1 gallon.

Stir well together a few minutes. Then add

Common Bar Soap, cut in thin slices..................... 20 pounds.

Stir well together until dissolved. When partially cooled, pour into a barrel for use.

This we consider a superior soft soap.

SOFT SOAP—COMMON.

Concentrated Lye.. 2 pounds.
Soft Water.. 5 gallons.

Boil together until the lye is dissolved. Then add either

Lard, Oil, Tallow, or "Soap-grease"..................... 8 pounds.

Boil for thirty minutes, stirring occasionally. Then add Soft Water, boiling..................................25 gallons.

Stir well together, and when cool put into barrels for use.

It is cheaper to purchase the concentrated lye for making soap than to employ lye made by the slow process of leaching wood-ashes in barrels, it being much cleaner, less troublesome, and quite as efficient.

WASHING COMPOUNDS.

The materials in common use for preparing washing compounds are sal-soda and borax. The principal objections to their employment are, that borax is too expensive, and that sal-soda is liable to stain and rot the fibres of cloth, if used in excess. A very good washing compound may be made as follows:

Carbonate of Soda (Sal-Soda).........................2 pounds.
Fresh, Unslaked Lime....................................1 pound.
Water, hot...2 gallons.

Boil for thirty minutes, stirring occasionally. Allow it to settle a few hours, until it becomes clear; then carefully pour off and strain. It may be kept in jugs or bottles for use.

Add half a pint of this solution to ten gallons of water, and allow the clothes to soak in it for ten or twelve hours; then boil and wash the clothes. The labor of washing will be greatly lessened, and the boiling will not require many minutes.

IMPROVED WASHING COMPOUND.

Liquid Silicate of Soda (30° Baume)..........1 pint.
Water, (warm or cold), four or five pails
    full, or.......................................10 or 12 gallons.

Stir together for a few minutes, and the water will be perfectly soft and excellent for washing.

Soak the clothes in this water all night before washing them. In the morning boil the clothes in the water fifteen minutes; then wash them. Very little soap will be required.

Silicate of soda, for washing, is superior to sal-soda, borax, etc.

Do not use spirits of turpentine, alcohol, or ammonia, etc., as they are expensive and inferior to the foregoing preparations.

HARD WATER MADE SOFT FOR WASHING.

Rain or soft water is better adapted than any other for washing and cleaning, but it cannot always be readily obtained. When water is hard—which is the condition of most of the well water—and will not readily unite with soap, it indicates the presence of earthy salts, usually carbonate or sulphate of lime. Hard water curdles soap, imparting to the water a milky appearance, which is caused by the formation of an insoluble compound between the oil or alkali of the soap and the salts of lime. This prevents, in a measure, the formation of a lather or soap-suds. If the hardness is caused by carbonate of lime, held in solution by an excess of carbonic acid, it may be detected by boiling the water for a few hours in an open vessel; the carbonic acid passes off in the form of gas, by evaporation, and the lime precipitates to the bottom, leaving the water soft, which may then be carefully poured off and used for washing. In most cases, however, the hardness is caused by the presence of sulphate of lime, but boiling will not remove sulphuric acid. Therefore it is necessary to decompose the sulphate of lime by using an alkali—either carbonate of soda (known as sal-soda,) potash, pearlash, or their equivalents. *Wood ashes* will answer the purpose, by mixing a quart or two in a barrel of water and letting it settle a few hours; or a piece of sal-soda of the size of a hen's egg, dissolved in a quart of hot water, poured into a barrel of hard water, and stirred thoroughly, will render it soft. A small piece of quick-lime or borax will also produce the same result; sal-soda is preferable, but should not be used in excess, or it will cause the clothes to appear yellow, and also by its caustic action injure the fabrics.

The above amount is sufficient to soften a barrel of common hard water. And in washing do not add any more sal-soda, *using only good soap* with this prepared soft water, and the clothes will be white and pure.

TO SETTLE AND PURIFY MUDDY WATER.

Dissolve a piece of alum, the size of a hickory nut, in a pint of hot water; pour it into a barrel of water, and stir it thoroughly for a few minutes. It will purify and precipitate all the mud and impurities to the bottom in a few hours. When the water is very muddy, double the above quantity of alum may be required.

TO PREVENT PRINTS FADING.

Wash in cold rain-water, adding a handful of salt to a pail of water. Do not expose them to the sun to dry, but roll the articles tightly in a coarse cloth until dry enough to iron.

TO REMOVE STAINS FROM SILK, COTTON, LINEN, AND OTHER GOODS, RESTORING THE COLOR.

Silk, cotton, linen, and other fabrics are liable to be stained by the action of vinegar, lemon juice, cream of tartar, tartaric, sulphuric, and other acids, or by wine and various kinds of fruits and vegetables, which contain more or less acid, as, for instance, currants, strawberries, cherries, pie-plant, apples, oranges, etc. The acid changes the color of the fabrics to a reddish and brownish appearance. It is a well established chemical fact that an alkali will neutralize an acid, and a very appropriate alkali is ammonia.

Apply a few drops to the stained parts of the fabrics, and the original color will soon be restored. Sometimes several applications may be required to fully neutralize the acid.

CLOTH RENOVATOR.

Soft Water... ½ gallon.
Transparent Soap, cut into thin slices............2 ounces.

Heat together in a water-bath, until the soap dissolves. Into a bottle or jug put

Cold Soft Water.. ½ gallon.
Liquor Ammonia, concentrated. ....8 ounces.
(Or Aqua Ammonia....................................1 quart.)

Agitate, and keep it tightly corked.

When the solution of soap and water has cooled, add it to the solution of ammonia. Agitate thoroughly, and it will be ready for use. Shake thoroughly, also, before using, at any time.

By following the subjoined directions carefully, this renovator will remove grease, oil, paint, tar, wax, varnish, etc., from all kinds of clothing, silks, satins, ribbons, cottons, woolens, table-covers, carpets, etc., without shrinking or injuring the cloth or color.

Directions for Use.—Lay the cloth or garment on a clean board or table. Then pour upon the soiled part a little of the renovator, and rub thoroughly with a brush or firm sponge for a few moments. Make a second application, if necessary. Then rinse the sponge in clean cold or warm water; squeeze it nearly dry, and rub the cloth (with the nap) for a short time, in order to produce a polish. Dry the garment, and it will have the appearance of being new. By chemical action, the renovator converts grease and oil into a harmless soap, which, with the dust, paint, varnish, resin, pitch, etc., is immediately loosened by the friction of the sponge or brush.

Stained garments are restored from the effects of vinegar, lemon-juice, cream of tartar, or other acids, and brought to their original color, by the use of the renovator, one or two applications of which will remove most stains of fruit.

Should the renovator not pour freely from the bottle, add a little water.

BAKING POWDER.

Bicarbonate of Soda, dry........................1 pound.
Cream of Tartar, dry..........................1¼ pounds.

 These materials should be thoroughly dried by exposure to the sun or in an oven; then carefully mixed and put into bottles, which must be tightly corked. If mixed when dampness is present, effervescence will ensue, and the virtue of the compound be lost.

 One teaspoon-ful of this powder should be added to each quart of flour used. Mix with cold water, or milk, as desired, and bake immediately.

 This powder, being mixed with flour, as above directed, constitutes a good "self-rising" flour.

 Use as a substitute for yeast or sour milk, in making biscuit, tea-cakes, rolls, or other pastry.

YEAST CAKES.

Brewers', or Hop Yeast................................1 quart.
Wheat Flour...................sufficient to form a thick batter.
Fine Salt...1 tablespoon-ful.

 Stir well together, and, after it has risen, knead it thoroughly in sufficient corn-meal to make a stiff dough. Roll it into sheets about one inch thick, and let it stand one hour. Then roll it again into sheets, about one-fourth of an inch in thickness; then cut into cakes about two inches square, and dry them in the shade or an oven. They must not be dried in the sun, or they will ferment and spoil.

 Directions for Use.—Dissolve one yeast-cake in one pint of warm water, and add three tablespoons-ful of flour. Set it near the fire, and allow it to rise. Then knead it into the bread. As soon as it is light, bake it in a hot oven.

LIQUID GLUE.

White Glue..10 pounds.
Gum Arabic.. 1 pound.
Warm Water.. 3 quarts.

Let the mixture stand twelve hours, in a glass or porcelain vessel. Then place it over a water-bath, stirring occasionally until dissolved. Then add

Acetic Acid..2 quarts.

Or sufficient to give the glue the required consistence.

Have the temperature of the water about 100° Fahr. Keep the vessel closely covered. Stir occasionally for two or three hours. When partially cool, bottle for use.

This is a superior and convenient glue for joining wood, etc.

INDIA RUBBER COMPOUND LIQUID GLUE.

India Rubber, thinly sliced............................ ½ ounce.
Gutta Percha.. ¾ ounce.
Naphtha..1 pint.

Mix, cork tightly, keep in a warm room, and shake occasionally during one day. In two or three days the rubber will have dissolved. (It may be sooner dissolved by placing the mixture over a water-bath, heated to 100° Fahr.) Then add

Gum Shellac, finely powdered.....................1¾ pounds.

Heat together until all are dissolved. Then pour upon plates of metal to cool and harden in sheets, like glue.

When used, melt it in a glue-pot until soft.

For joining pieces of wood, leather, etc., this preparation has no equal.

CANDLES.

Tallow, refined..10 pounds.
Paraffin Wax, refined................................... 1 pound.

Melt together, and run into moulds, or dip wicking in the mixture, as for ordinary candles. These candles will be found superior to any made from tallow only.

Tallow, before being used for candles, should always be refined. The following process is a good one for the purpose:

Alum, pulverized...3 pounds.
Hot Water...6 gallons.

Boil together until the alum is dissolved. Then add

Tallow, cut into slices...10 pounds.

Stir well together, and boil for about one and a half hours, often stirring, and removing the scum that rises to the surface. Then strain through two thicknesses of flannel.

When cold, the tallow may be removed from the solution of alum.

This process will effectually purify and bleach tallow, preparatory to making candles.

PARAFFIN CANDLES.

Paraffin wax, melted and run into moulds, or dipped, as preferred, makes the most perfect candle known. It gives a clear, brilliant light, requires no snuffing, and one pound of paraffin candles will burn as long as two and a half pounds of candles made from tallow.

Paraffin candles require wicks only half the size of those used in tallow candles.

THE HAIR.

For ages chemists have endeavored to find substances capable of changing the color of the hair to an imitation of its natural appearance. Innumerable compounds, also, have been devised with a view of restoring hair to bald heads; and hair-dressings, in abundance, may be found in the form of "oils," "bears' grease," "pomades," "lustrals," etc.

Most of the hair "restoratives" in use at the present time are injurious to the scalp. Those which have been in use for the past fifteen years are based principally upon the prescription made for an affection of the scalp of General Twiggs, during the Mexican war, which, in his case, partially restored gray hair to its natural color.

The following is the prescription referred to:

Rosewater............1 pint.
Acetate of Lead............2 drachms.
Lac Sulphur............2½ drachms.
Glycerin............1 ounce.

Mix. Shake before using, as all the lead and sulphur do not dissolve in the rosewater, but precipitate to the bottom of the bottle. As numerous cases of lead-poisoning have resulted from its use, all preparations for the hair which contain lead should be avoided.

HAIR OILS.

NUMBER ONE HAIR OIL.

Castor Oil, deodorized	3 ounces.
Oil of Citronella	1 drachm.
Oil of Lavender	1 drachm.
Oil of Neroli	20 drops.
Cologne Spirits, 95 per cent	1 pint.

Agitate thoroughly in a bottle for a few minutes, and the solution will at once become clear and beautiful. When a greater proportion of castor oil is used, it renders the hair gummy.

NUMBER TWO HAIR OIL.

Glycerin	4 ounces.
Rosewater	1 pint.

Agitate together in a bottle for a few moments, and it will be ready for use.

Hair oils are sometimes colored a beautiful red with the tincture of alkanet root; but coloring adds nothing to their value.

Olive oil should never be used for the hair, as it is very liable to become rancid, and does not leave the hair in as good condition as castor oil.

Cocoanut oil is sometimes used for dressing the hair, but for this purpose is also inferior to castor oil.

HAIR INVIGORATOR AND "RESTORATIVE."
(To Prevent the Loss of Hair.)

Castor Oil, deodorized	¾ ounce.
Carbonate of Ammonia	⅛ ounce.
Tincture of Cantharides	⅛ ounce.
Rosewater	8 ounces.
Bay Rum	8 ounces.
Alcohol, deodorized, 95 per cent	12 ounces.

Agitate well together in a bottle, and it will be ready for use. Shake the bottle thoroughly just before using, and apply to the hair once a day. We consider this, for an external stimulus, equal to anything that can be used for a "hair restorative."

INSTANTANEOUS HAIR DYE.

Nitrate of Silver, in crystals	½ ounce.
Distilled, or Soft Water	3 ounces.

Agitate in a bottle until the silver is dissolved. Then add, gradually, liquor ammonia (about two ounces), until the solution becomes *cloudy* from the formation of the oxyd of silver. Continue to add ammonia until it becomes clear again from the re-dissolving of the oxyd of silver. This constitutes the hair dye.

Before applying the dye, the following No. 1 preparation must be used:

Pyrogallic Acid	1 drachm.
Rosewater	8 ounces.
Alcohol	2 ounces.

Agitate until dissolved, and it will be ready for use.

Directions for Use.—Wash the hair or whiskers with warm soap-suds, to which a little carbonate of potassa, or the shampooing compound, may be added, until all oil or grease has been removed. Then rinse with clear water, and thoroughly rub with a towel until the hair is nearly dry. Then, with a brush, apply the No. 1, or pyrogallic solution to every part of the hair or whiskers designed to be colored. Within a few minutes, with another brush, apply the dye, and the hair or whiskers will instantaneously become dark or black. When the hair is quite dry, wash it with weak soap-suds, rinsing, afterwards, with clear water. If the hair is free from grease when the dye is applied, the color will remain good until the new growth requires another application.

SHAMPOOING COMPOUND.

Carbonate of Potassa (Salts of Tartar)	¾ ounce.
Soft Water	1 quart.
Aqua Ammonia	1 ounce.
Oil of Bergamot	10 drops.
Oil of Lavender	15 drops.
Transparent Soap (cut into thin shavings)	1 drachm.

Agitate in a bottle, and when the soap is dissolved the solution is ready for use. Apply a little to the head, washing the hair thoroughly with the hands. Then rinse with soft water, and dry with a coarse towel. This is also an excellent substitute for soap while taking a bath.

HAIR CURLING LIQUIDINE.

Borax	2 ounces.
Gum Arabic (pulverized)	1 drachm.
Scalding Hot Water	1 quart.

Stir while dissolving. Remove from the fire as soon as dissolved, and when but luke-warm add

Spirits of Camphor	2 ounces.

In which has been mixed

Oil of Rosemary	30 drops.
Oil of Lavender	30 drops.

Put altogether in a bottle; then add a handful of rose leaves, and shake well just before using. On retiring to rest wet the hair with the liquid, and roll it on twists of paper. In the morning unwrap and form into beautiful ringlets. Keep the bottle corked.

PEARL WASH FOR REMOVING TAN, FRECKLES, AND SUN-
BURNS; FOR CURING CHAPPED HANDS AND LIPS, AND
FOR BEAUTIFYING THE COMPLEXION.

Borax (pulverized)	1 ounce.
Hot Water	1 pint.

Dissolve the borax in the water, and when it has cooled add

Rosewater	4 ounces.
Oil of Bergamot	10 drops.
Oil of Lavender	7 drops.
Oil of Lemon	7 drops.
Glycerin	$\frac{1}{2}$ ounce.

Mix altogether in a tightly corked bottle. Just before using, agitate the bottle. Twice a day, morning and evening, (and oftener if desired), moisten the skin with it. A few weeks' application is generally sufficient.

INKS.

BLUE-BLACK WRITING INK.

Extract of Logwood, pulverized...2 ounces.
Hot Water...1 gallon.

    Simmer over a water-bath one hour, or until the logwood is dissolved. Into a bottle put

Bichromate of Potassa...100 grains.
Prussiate of Potassa...40 grains.
Warm Water..4 ounces.

    Agitate until dissolved; then add to the logwood solution. Stir well together; strain through flannel, and when cold add

Corrosive Sublimate..10 grains.
Warm Water..1 ounce.

    Agitate until dissolved. Lastly, add

Carbolic Acid, in crystals...1 drachm.
Cloves..1 dozen.

    This ink exhibits a jet black when first spread upon paper, does not corrode, and costs about five cents a gallon.

    To make a good copying ink, add one ounce of pure white sugar and one ounce of glycerin to one gallon of the above.

BLUE WRITING INK.

Prussian Blue (best)...4 ounces.
Oxalic Acid...½ ounce.

    Grind together finely in a mortar, and add

Cold Water..8 ounces.

    Continue grinding for a few moments. Then add

Mucilage of Gum Arabic...8 ounces.

    [This mucilage is made by dissolving gum arabic in its weight of warm water.]

    Renew the grinding for a few moments; then pour the mixture into a bottle. Rinse the mortar with

Cold Water..8 ounces.

    And pour that also into the bottle. Shake altogether thoroughly, and allow it to stand twenty-four hours. Then add

Cold Water..7¼ quarts.

    Shake well. This makes two gallons of good writing ink, of a fine blue tint.

MARKING INKS.

    By using one-half the quantity of water in either of the foregoing formulas, a superior ink for marking boxes and barrels will be produced—black or blue, as preferred.

BLACK INK—WRITING OR COPYING.

Soft Water, in an iron kettle..1 gallon.
Nut-galls, pulverized..8 ounces.
  Simmer for four or five hours in a water-bath; then add
Sulphate of Copper...½ ounce.
Sulphate of Iron..2½ ounces.
  Dissolve in
Warm Water...8 ounces.
  Add this to the decoction of galls, stir well together, and add
Pure White Sugar..2 ounces.
Gum Arabic, in powder...2 ounces.

Simmer altogether for three or four hours, stirring occasionally. Then strain while hot through two or three thicknesses of cloth. When cool, bottle for use.

If this ink is not to be used for copying, one-half of the quantity of sugar and gum arabic named will be sufficient. An excess of gum arabic and sugar prevents the ink from flowing freely.

BLACK INK—POWDER.

Extract of Logwood, pulverized..2 ounces.
Nut-galls, pulverized...2 ounces.
Sulphate of Iron, pulverized...¾ ounce.
Sulphate of Copper, pulverized..1 drachm.
Gum Arabic, pulverized..2 drachms.

Finely pulverized and evenly mixed, these make an excellent ink-powder for the rapid production of black ink, as follows:

To three-fourths of an ounce of this powder add one pint of boiling water. Stir occasionally for an hour, strain, and it will be ready for use.

GREEN WRITING INK.

Bichromate of Potassa..1 ounce.
Soft Water, warm...4 ounces.
  Agitate until dissolved. Add to this solution, while warm,
Alcohol, 95 per cent..1½ ounces.
  Shake well together. Then add, gradually,
Strong Sulphuric Acid..............................until it assumes a brown color.

Evaporate the liquor to one-half. When cool, dilute with half a pint of soft water. Filter it; then add

Alcohol..2 ounces.
Strong Sulphuric Acid..20 drops.

After remaining at rest for a few days, this ink assumes a beautiful green color. Then add

Gum Arabic, in powder..2 drachms.
  Which completes the process, and it is ready for use.

RED WRITING INK.

Brazil Wood..1 pound.
Diluted Acetic Acid...2 quarts.
Distilled Water..2 quarts.

Simmer for three or four hours in a water-bath, or until about one quart is evaporated. Strain through cloth, and add

Alum, in powder..4 ounces.

Continue to simmer until only two quarts are left. Then add

Gum Arabic, in powder..2 ounces.

When the mixture has become cold, add

Proto-chloride of Tin...½ ounce.

Shake well together, and it is ready for use.

This ink is cheaper and better than the "carmine" ink, as it is free from the bluish tint, and of a more permanent character.

RED (CARMINE) INK.

Aqua Ammonia..2 ounces.
Pure Carmine..2 drachms.

Shake well until the carmine is dissolved, and add

Soft Water..14 ounces.
Gum Arabic, in powder... 2 drachms.

Agitate altogether, and as soon as the gum arabic is dissolved it is ready for use.

GOLD WRITING INK.

Chloride of Gold...1 drachm.
Gum Arabic, pure white, in powder... ½ drachm.

Dissolve the gum in one ounce of pure soft water.

Rub well together with a pestle in a wedgewood mortar, and it is ready for use.

When gold ink is used, it should be shaken immediately before writing.

SILVER INK.

Chloride of Silver..1 drachm.

Proceed throughout exactly as in the formula for gold ink, and use in the same manner.

BRONZE INK.

Bronze, in powder, of any color..1 drachm.

Proceed, in all respects, as in preparing gold and silver inks.

VIOLET INK.

Extract of Logwood...2 ounces.
Hot Water...1 gallon.

Simmer until dissolved, strain, and add

Chloride of Tin..2 ounces.

Stir well together.

This is a good violet ink.

CRIMSON INK.

Violet ink, combined with equal parts of red ink, produces a fine crimson ink. Mix the two in a bottle, and agitate thoroughly.

INDIA INK.

Lampblack, extra fine..½ ounce.
Nut Oil...¼ ounce.

Mix in a wedgewood or porcelain mortar, and grind together with the pestle until thoroughly combined.

White Glue...1 ounce.
Cold Water..3 ounces.

Soak the glue in the water for four or five hours; then dissolve over a water-bath, at a temperature of 200°. Keep up the heat, and add to the solution of glue the mixture of lampblack and oil, stirring and kneading them together, until the ingredients are perfectly incorporated. Remove from the water-bath, and, when sufficiently cool, form into small cakes, or press into moulds, and leave them to dry in the open air.

The peculiar odor of the Chinese india ink may be produced by adding a few grains of camphor gum or musk to the ink while kneading it.

SYMPATHETIC, (OR, "INVISIBLE") INKS.

BLUE SYMPATHETIC INK.

Chloride of Cobalt..½ ounce.
Distilled Water..1 pint.

Shake well together until dissolved, and it is ready for use.

Characters written on paper with this liquid are invisible, from their paleness of color, until the ink has been dried by exposure to heat; then the letters appear of a blue color. When cooled for a short time, moisture is absorbed, and the writing once more disappears.

GREEN SYMPATHETIC INK.

Add to eight ounces of the blue sympathetic ink two drachms of chloride of nickel. Agitate together until dissolved, and it is ready for use.

ANOTHER GREEN SYMPATHETIC INK.

Nitro-Muriate of Cobalt..2 drachms.
Soft Water..1 pint.

Agitate together, and it is ready for use.

This fluid, when applied to paper, and heated. gives a green tint, which disappears on cooling.

YELLOW SYMPATHETIC INK.

Sulphate of Copper..2 drachms.
Muriate of Ammonia...2 drachms.
Water, soft..1 pint.

Agitate together until dissolved, and it is ready for use.

This ink is colorless when used, but turns yellow upon exposure to heat.

BLACK SYMPATHETIC INK.

Sulphuric Acid.. ½ ounce.
Soft Water... 1 pint.

Agitate together, and it is ready for use.

ROSE-PURPLE SYMPATHETIC INK.

Acetate of Cobalt.. ½ ounce.
Nitrate of Potassa... 1 drachm.
Soft Water... 1 pint.

Agitate together until dissolved, and it is ready for use.

Heat developes the color, which disappears again when cooled.

BLACK INDELIBLE INK.

Nitrate of Silver, in crystals.. 8 ounces.
Distilled Water.. 8 ounces.

Mix, and agitate in a perfectly clean one-quart bottle, having a glass stopper, until the silver is dissolved.

Into another bottle put

Carbonate of Soda, in crystals... 12 ounces.
Distilled Water, (warm).. 12 ounces.

By placing the bottle in a vessel of warm water, and agitating, the soda will readily dissolve.

After the contents of both bottles are dissolved, mix the two solutions, by adding the *second* to the *first*, in the following manner: Filter the solution of soda through a clean cotton or linen cloth, and as it passes through the cloth, which should be placed in a glass funnel, let it drip directly into the solution of silver. After both solutions are in one bottle, agitate occasionally for thirty minutes, during which time a precipitate, of the color and consistence of cream, will have formed. This must be collected and washed on a filter, to wit: In a wide-mouthed, clean bottle that holds two quarts, place a large glass funnel, into which insert a sheet of white filtering paper. Upon the paper then pour about one-fourth of the precipitate, at one time. Repeat every ten minutes, pouring out the same quantity each time, until the entire mixture has been poured into the funnel. The liquid portion will pass or drain through the filtering paper in about one hour, leaving the precipitate on the paper. After remaining forty minutes to drain, pour upon the precipitate that remains in the funnel four ounces of distilled water. In about ten minutes pour upon the precipitate four ounces more of distilled water, and repeat this washing or filtering process five times in all, with an interval of ten minutes between each. After the last addition of water to the precipitate, leave it undisturbed for one hour and a half. Then remove the filtering paper, with the precipitate, (as they cannot easily be separated), into a clean, wide-mouthed bottle that holds two quarts. Throw away the filtrated liquid.

Then add the following solution, which must be prepared the day previous:

Sub-acetate of Copper, (chemically pure)...........12 drachms and 48 grains.
Strong Liquor Ammonia...3 ounces.
Diluted with Distilled Water..2 ounces.

Agitate occasionally for 24 hours. Filter this solution of copper through *two* thicknesses of filtering paper, in a glass funnel, into a bottle by itself. Then add it to the washed precipitate in the wide-mouthed bottle. Stir with a glass rod occasionally, for half an hour. Then add Tartaric Acid, pure and finely powdered..........2 ounces and 320 grains.

Constantly stirring the mixture with a glass rod for ten or fifteen minutes, or until effervescence has ceased. Then let it stand about fifteen minutes, when the following is to be added:
Strong Liquor of Ammonia...8 ounces.

Or a sufficient quantity to dissolve the tartrate of silver, gradually adding the ammonia, and stirring with a glass rod until the solution attains a beautiful, dark-blue color. Let it remain undisturbed for fifteen minutes. Then into another bottle insert a clean glass funnel, and in this place a piece of fine cotton cloth that is perfectly free from starch, and which has just been washed in distilled water. The contents of the wide-mouthed bottle are then to be poured into the funnel, to filtrate through the cloth. After draining for ten or fifteen minutes in this way, squeeze out what liquor remains in the residuum in the cloth. Neither the cloth nor the residuum are of any further use, and may be thrown away.

Then add the following solution, which must be prepared the day previous:

Sap-Green, pure and finely pulverized................................... ½ ounce.
Strong Liquor of Ammonia...3 ounces.
Diluted with Distilled Water..2 ounces.

When the solution is perfect, filter through paper.

Agitate thoroughly, by pouring the preparation from one wide-mouthed bottle to another, for five or ten minutes. Filter through paper, and let it stand in open bottles for twelve hours, to allow the ammonia to evaporate. Then add

Pure Loaf Sugar, finely pulverized......................................8½ ounces.

Agitate, and in fifteen minutes add

Pure White Gum Arabic, in fine powder..............................8 ounces.

Stir thoroughly with a glass rod for a few minutes.

After standing twelve hours, agitating occasionally, the process is completed. Bottle for use.

The above makes about forty fluid-ounces of a superior black marking fluid. It must be applied to a cloth (free from starch) with a gold or glass pen, or may be used with a stencil brush and a silver-plated stencil-plate. When first applied, it is of a light-green color, and after remaining five or ten minutes a hot flat-iron *must* be applied for a few moments, until the color becomes a beautiful black.

To prevent scorching, it is advisable to first cover the marking with a thin cloth; then apply the hot iron. This indelible ink will not injure the texture of the finest fabrics.

TO MAKE OLD WRITING LOOK LIKE NEW.

Ferro-cyanide of Potassium...............1 drachm.
Distilled Water...............2 ounces.

When dissolved, apply to the writing with a small camels'-hair brush.

After it has dried, make an application of the following preparation:

Muriatic Acid...............1 drachm.
Soft Water...............3 ounces.

Agitate well together.

When this diluted acid is applied, the writing changes to a deep blue color.

To prevent the spreading of the ink, apply the solution of potassium, with a glass or gold pen, to the writing, instead of with a brush.

TO GIVE NEW WRITING THE APPEARANCE OF AGE.

Saffron............... ¼ ounce.
Hot Water...............1 ounce.

Simmer for a few minutes, and add

Black Ink...............1 pint.

This ink, when spread upon paper, has the appearance of having been written for half a century.

TO REMOVE INDELIBLE INK OR STAINS OF NITRATE OF SILVER.

Moisten the parts with a solution prepared by dissolving one drachm of the iodide of potassium in half an ounce of water, which, when applied to the stains or ink, converts the black oxyd of silver into a colorless iodide of silver. Or a solution of the cyanid of potassium may be used, which also renders the oxyd of silver colorless; but the cyanid is a deadly poison, and great care must be exercised in its use; the cloth, also, must be immediately washed.

TO REMOVE INK-STAINS AND IRON-RUST FROM CLOTH.

Oxalic Acid...............2 ounces.
Bitartrate of Potassa...............1 ounce.

Pulverize and mix thoroughly together.

This mixture should be kept in bottles tightly corked, and marked "*Poison.*"

When used, apply a small portion of the powder to the stain or rust, and moisten it with water; or the foregoing quantity of the mixture may be dissolved in one quart of water. Have the cloth dry. Moisten the spots with the solution, and in a few minutes they will disappear. Then wash the cloth in clear water. It must be used only on *white* cloth.

ANOTHER PROCESS.

Apply the juice of ripe tomatoes, or of the pie-plant stalk, freely to ink-stains and iron-rust. Let it remain until dry, or repeat, if necessary, and then wash out.

ANILINE INKS OF VARIOUS COLORS.

Red Ink.

Aniline "Red Diamond," or " Fuchsine"..............................15 grains.
Gum Arabic Mucilage.. ½ drachm.
Pure Soft Water... 1 ounce.

Agitate a few moments, and it is ready for use.

Make other colored inks as follows: green, violet, purple, blue, crimson, orange, etc., by using the different colors of aniline, in the proportion of from ten to twenty grains to the ounce of water, according to the shade desired. Use only sufficient gum arabic to prevent the ink spreading. Use the aniline that is soluble in water, and not the aniline that is only soluble in alcohol.

The aniline is a dry powder, and may be conveniently used to make different colored inks at a moment's notice.

BLACK INK FROM ELDERBERRIES.

A German paper recommends that bruised elderberries be placed in an earthen vessel and kept in a warm place for three days, then pressed out and filtered. Add to twelve and a half quarts of this filtered juice one ounce of the sulphate of iron and the same quantity of crude pyroligneous acid. The result is an ink which, when first used, has a violet color, but when dry is an indigo blue-black. This ink does not become thick as soon as other inks, flows easily from the pen without gumming, and does not, in writing, run the letters together.—*Druggists' Circular and Chemical Gazette.*

AN EXCELLENT INDELIBLE INK.

Rub up one drachm of aniline black with a mixture of sixty drops of concentrated hydrochloric acid and one and a half ounces of alcohol. The resulting deep-blue liquid is then to be diluted with a hot solution of one and a half drachms of gum arabic in six ounces of water. This ink does not corrode a steel pen, and is affected neither by concentrated mineral acids nor by strong lye. If the aniline black solution be diluted with one and a half ounces of gum shellac dissolved in six ounces of alcohol, instead of with gum arabic water, an aniline black is obtained, which, after being applied to wood, brass, or leather, is remarkable for its extraordinary deep-black color.—*American Artisan.*

TO ASCERTAIN THE AGE OF OLD WRITINGS, AND HOW TO COPY THEM.

M. Carre, the author, states that as long as writing is not very old it admits of being copied, when moistened with water only, by means of the well-known copying press; further, that when writing has attained a certain age, an adulteration has taken place in the ink, which prevents the ordinary process of copying being successful; but, in that case, moistening with twenty parts of water acidulated with one part of hydrochloric acid effectually aids the copying process. M. Carre found that writing made in 1787 could not be reproduced by a copying press, even when previously moistened with acidulated water. Niepce St. Victor, however, gives a new process for copying very old writings. Ordinary copying paper is used, but is wetted with a thin solution of glucose or honey, instead of water. On coming out of the press the paper is exposed to strong ammonia, which brings out very clearly lines otherwise almost illegible.—*Druggists' Circular and Chemical Gazette.*

VARNISHES.

SHELLAC VARNISH—TRANSPARENT.

Bleached Gum Shellac, in powder...8 ounces.
Alcohol, 95 per cent..1 quart.

Agitate in a bottle occasionally during twenty-four hours, keeping it closely corked, and it will be ready for use.

Or it may be made in two or three hours' time by heating it in a water-bath, keeping the bottle tightly corked.

ORANGE SHELLAC VARNISH.

Prepared in the same manner as the above, with the exception that orange or common gum shellac is used (in the same proportion) instead of the bleached gum.

BLACK SHELLAC VARNISH.

To one quart of the common or orange shellac varnish add one ounce of pure lampblack, or sufficient to produce a deep black color.

Shellac varnishes are used principally by cabinet makers, model makers, etc., and should be applied with a varnish brush. They dry quickly, owing to the evaporation of the alcohol, leaving an air and water-proof coating. By repeating the application two or three times, drying each, and slightly sand-papering between applications, a smooth, glossy finish is obtained. When the varnish becomes too thick to be readily applied, more alcohol should be added.

SHELLAC VARNISHES OF OTHER COLORS.
(Red Shellac Varnish.)

Aniline Red (fuchsine)...1 drachm.
Alcohol, 95 per cent..1 ounce.

Agitate occasionally for a few hours until the aniline is dissolved. Then add

Transparent Shellac Varnish..1 quart.

By using the various colors of aniline, soluble in alcohol, other tints may be imparted to transparent shellac varnish.

TRANSPARENT VARNISH FOR IRON AND STEEL.

Gum Shellac, bleached and pulverized.........................2½ ounces.
Gum Sandarac, pulverized...1 ounce.
Alcohol, 95 per cent..1 pint.

Mix, agitate, and it will be ready for use in twenty-four hours.

This preparation forms a water-proof coating for iron and steel, which not only prevents them from corrosion or rust, but preserves their brilliancy.

COPAL VARNISH.

Camphor Gum..20 pounds.
Sulphuric Ether..30 gallons.

Dissolve the camphor in the ether, and add

Best Copal Resin, in powder.......................................80 pounds.

After standing twenty-four hours, with occasional agitation, add

Alcohol, 95 per cent..10 gallons.
Spirits of Turpentine...2½ gallons.

Keep the cask tightly bunged, rolling it about occasionally for one day, at the expiration of which time a thoroughly good copal varnish will be made.

INDIA RUBBER VARNISH.

India Rubber, in thin slices..1 ounce.
Naphtha..1 pint.

Agitate for a few days, until the rubber is dissolved.

Raw Linseed Oil...2 quarts.
Copal Varnish..2 quarts.

Heat altogether, gradually for about one hour, stirring occasionally.

TO BOIL LINSEED OIL.

Raw Linseed Oil	1 gallon.
Black Oxyd of Manganese	1 pound.

Boil for three or four hours, and strain through flannel while hot.

Instead of using the manganese, substitute

Litharge	4 ounces.

And proceed as before.

Litharge makes a darker oil than manganese.

BLACKING.

WATER-PROOF BLACKING FOR BOOTS AND SHOES, HARNESSES, CARRIAGE-TOPS, AND ALL LEATHER.

Boiled Linseed Oil	2 quarts.
Tallow	6 pounds.
Resin	3½ pounds.
Beeswax	2 pounds.
Neats-foot Oil	1 pint.
Castor Oil	½ pint.
Solution of India Rubber	8 fluid-ozs.
Lampblack	½ pound.

Melt together. To be applied in a melted condition, with a brush or sponge.

Directions for Use.—Have the leather clean, and moistened with a little water, so that it will be pliable; then apply the water-proof blacking freely, and rub thoroughly with the hands or brush until the leather is saturated; also, fill the crevice between the soles and upper. It is better to let the leather dry moderately for an hour or two before wearing. Renew the application whenever occasion requires, which will be very seldom unless the leather is greatly exposed to water or snow. This blacking preserves the leather in a pliable condition, and renders it snow-water-proof.

This preparation may also be applied to the soles of boots and shoes; for this purpose it must be used hot.

Have the soles of the boots or shoes dry, clean and warm, by holding them over the stove for a few moments while the composition is heating. Then, with a swab or brush, apply it freely to the soles. After each coat, hold the soles again over the stove, (but not where it is too hot), until the composition is absorbed. Renew the hot application four or five times, or until the sole-leather is fully saturated; then let the boots or shoes remain in a warm room an hour or two before wearing. No more applications are required, as the preparation cannot be displaced by water, it having formed an insoluble compound with the sole-leather, whereby it is toughened and rendered impervious to air, snow and water.

When prepared expressly for the soles of boots and shoes, the lamp-black may be omitted.

ANOTHER PREPARATION FOR THE SOLES,

Which we consider superior to the above.

Copal Varnish..1 pint.
Paraffin Wax... ½ pound.

Melt together, and apply while hot, as above directed.

CEMENT.

BEST CEMENT FOR GENERAL PURPOSES.

Cooper's Isinglass...2 drachms.
Water...2 ounces.

Soak the isinglass in the water for twenty-four hours. Then boil it down to one-half the quantity, and add

Alcohol...1 ounce.

While hot, strain through a linen cloth. Then add the following mixture, previously prepared:

Gum Mastic..1 drachm.
Gum Ammoniac.. ½ drachm.
Alcohol...1 ounce.

Melt together in a water-bath.

In cementing, warm the edges of the article to be united, and spread the cement thinly over the entire surface.

CEMENT FOR IRON AND STONE.

A very durable cement has been in use by parties in Saxony for several years, which is composed of oxyd of lead, litharge, and concentrated glycerin. It is said to harden rapidly, and to be unaffected by the ordinary acids, and by heat. The inventor claims that it is less easily broken than stone itself.—*Boston Journal of Chemistry.*

CEMENT FOR GLASS, CROCKERY, METALS, ETC.

Gum Mastic, white, in powder............2 ounces.
Gum Shellac, bleached, in powder............2 ounces.
Alcohol, 95 per cent............1 pint.

Mix in a tightly corked bottle, and agitate occasionally until dissolved. Into a tin vessel put

White Glue............½ ounce.
Warm Water............3 ounces.

Macerate for five hours. Then heat in a water-bath until the glue is dissolved.

Gradually heat the bottle containing the mastic, shellac and alcohol in a water-bath to 160° Fahr.

Both liquids are then to be poured together, at a temperature of 160°. Agitate occasionally until cooled.

Keep in vials tightly corked. When required for use, place the vial in a basin of hot water until the cement is dissolved. Warm the edges of the article to be joined, and apply a thin coating of the hot cement with a small brush. Set the cemented article aside for twenty-four hours before using.

GUM FOR LABELS, POSTAGE AND REVENUE STAMPS.

White Glue............½ pound.
Warm Water............1 quart.

Put into a tin vessel, and place it in a water-bath, about 100° Fahr., for eight hours.

Then add

White Sugar............14 ounces.
Gum Arabic, white, powdered............10 ounces.

Increase the heat in the water-bath to about the boiling point, stirring occasionally for one hour, or until all the substances are dissolved.

When partially cool, bottle for use. This solution is then spread upon paper, and dried in the open air.

CEMENT FOR ATTACHING LABELS TO TIN WARE.

Liquid Silicate of Soda, 25° Baume............1 quart.
Resin, in powder............1 ounce.

Simmer in a water-bath for one hour, stirring occasionally.

This cement may be applied either warm or cold. It will permanently fasten paper to tin, to which ordinary paste will not adhere. It may also be used to attach labels to bottles, wood, metals, etc.

MOUTH GLUE.

White Glue............1 ounce.
Cold Water............4 ounces.

Macerate for six hours. Simmer over a water-bath one hour, or until the glue is dissolved. Add

White Sugar...1 ounce.

Evaporate the whole in a water-bath until dry, and run into moulds, or cut into cakes, as preferred.

This is a convenient and substantial form of preparing glue to carry in the pocket for instantaneous use.

GRAFTING-WAX FOR FRUIT TREES.

White Resin...1 pound.
Beeswax...3 ounces.
Tallow...3 ounces.

Melt together.

This makes a good grafting-wax for various temperatures.

Grafting-wax should be of such a consistence that it will not crack in the cold winds of March or April, nor melt in the heat of summer.

RED SEALING-WAX.

Gum Shellac..1 pound.
Venice Turpentine... ¼ pound.
Vermilion, to color... ¼ pound.

Melt together, and run into sticks.

BLUE SEALING-WAX.

Use Prussian-blue, more or less, instead of vermilion, to color the wax.

BLACK SEALING-WAX.

Use lampblack, only sufficient to color the foregoing proportions of gum shellac and Venice turpentine.

GREEN SEALING-WAX.

Use verdigris in powder, combined with the above formula, to produce a green color.

OUR IMPROVED RED SEALING-WAX.

White Resin...4 pounds.
Beeswax...4 ounces.
Light English Vermilion..6 ounces.

Melt together.

Use for sealing bottles, packages, and other purposes. We find it equal to that made with gum shellac, at less than one fourth of the expense. American vermilion, which is cheaper, may be used instead of the English, but is not so fine a color. For different colors, use other pigments.

COMPARATIVE WEIGHT OF VARIOUS SUBSTANCES.

Platinum, heaviest known substance, a cubic foot weighs 1,218 pounds.
Platinum is fusible only by the oxy-hydrogen blow-pipe.

Gold melts 2,016°	cubic foot weighs 1,203 pounds.
Mercury (Quicksilver)	" " " 977 "
Lead melts 612°	" " " 709 "
Silver melts 1,875°	" " " 651 "
Copper melts 2,000°	" " " 555 "
Brass melts 1,900°	" " " 537 "
Cast Iron melts 2,800°	" " " 450 "
Lime-stone	" " " 198 "
Clay	" " " 135 "
Water	" " " 62 "
Ice	" " " 58 "
White Oak	" " " 45 "
Pine	" " " 31 "
Cork	" " " 15 "
Atmospheric Air	" " " 1¼ oz.
Coal Gas, lightest known substance	" " " ¾ "

TO RE-CUT AND RENEW OLD FILES OR RASPS.

Nitric Acid, commercial strength, by measure.......... 5 ounces.
Sulphuric Acid, commercial strength, by measure.......... 16 ounces.
Cold Water.......... 1 quart.

Mix together, in a *wide-mouthed*, two-quart bottle, or glass fruit jar, of sufficient width to admit of files and rasps being inserted. Gradually add, first the nitric, then the sulphuric acid to the water. If mixed quickly it might generate sufficient heat to break the bottle. Keep the jar corked when not in use, and have it labeled *Poison*.

To harden new files and rasps, dip them in the solution for fifteen seconds.

To recut old files and rasps, first wash them in strong, *hot* soap suds, to remove grease; then rinse in clear water, and immerse them in the acid solution from two to four minutes, according to the more or less worn condition of the metal. After the above treatment, wash them in clear, cold water; and, to prevent rusting, wash them in lime-water, made by putting two or three ounces of common lime into two or three quarts of water, and immediately dry the files by the fire.

QUICK PROCESS FOR PICKLING CUCUMBERS.

Good Vinegar.......... 1 gallon.
Mace.......... ½ ounce.
Cloves.......... 2 dozen.
Ginger Root, powdered.......... ½ ounce.
Salt.......... 1 teaspoon-ful.

Simmer altogether for ten minutes, in a porcelain kettle. Then put in the cucumbers, and simmer for fifteen minutes longer. Finally, pour all into a glass or wooden vessel, and closely cover them.

TO COLOR PICKLES.

Cucumbers, etc., are usually colored with verdigris, which is poisonous, and should not be used. The best plan to impart, or, rather, to retain the color in pickled fruits and vegetables, is to pour on them a scalding preparation made thus:

Common Salt .... 2 pounds.
Hot Water .... 1 gallon.

When the salt is dissolved, pour the hot solution on the vegetables, allowing it to remain three or four hours. Then pour off the salt water and pour on good vinegar, scalding hot.

Allow it to remain four days; remove and scald, and pour on again. Let them remain in the vinegar until required for use.

This process causes cucumbers, string-beans, peas, etc., to attain a dark-green color, without the use of poisonous substances.

COLORS FOR ARTIFICIAL FLOWERS.

For blue, sulphate of indigo in solution; for yellow, tincture of turmeric; for red, carmine dissolved in a solution of the carbonate of potash; for lilac, a solution of litmus; for violet, a solution of litmus mixed with blue. When the flowers are made of paper or muslin, they may be dipped in these colors; but when made of velvet they should be colored by the finger dipped in the dye.—*Boston Journal of Chemistry.*

STARCH POLISH.

Equal parts of spermaceti and white wax melted together. A piece as large as a chestnut is sufficient for one quart of starch.

A tablespoon-ful of gum arabic solution, mixed in the starch, imparts to the clothing, when ironed, a beautiful gloss.

PUTTY REMOVED FROM BROKEN WINDOWS.

With a small brush or swab apply muriatic or nitric acid over the dry putty that adheres to the broken glass and frames of windows. Make two or three applications within fifteen minutes, and in about one hour the putty will be softened, and can be readily removed.

WOOD GAS.

The following figures exhibit the remarkable products, and their values, yielded by *one cord of oak wood,* when subjected to distillation in close retorts:

5,000 feet Illuminating Gas, at $2 per thousand feet $10 00
50 bushels Charcoal, at 10 cents per bushel 5 00
2 barrels Tar, at $2 per barrel 4 00
5 gallons Naphtha, at 20 cents per gallon 1 00
100 gallons Vinegar, at 25 cents per gallon 25 00

Total value of products $45 00

WHITEWASH FOR WALLS.

White Glue...4 ounces.
Cold Water..1 quart.

Put into a tin pail and let it stand for twelve hours.

Place the pail in a water-bath over a fire, stirring occasionally until the glue is dissolved.

In another vessel mix

Paris White (*Sulphate of Baryta*)...........................9 pounds.
Hot Water, sufficient to make a mixture the consistence of cream..1 gallon.

Stir until well mixed. Then add the solution of glue (or sizing) prepared as above directed. Continue to stir until the materials are thoroughly combined, and apply while hot with a clean whitewash or other suitable brush. This makes an adhesive whitewash resembling paint. By the addition of a little yellow ochre, or other pigments, various colors may be produced. Applying this whitewash *hot* will prevent its rubbing off when dry. Freshly slaked lime may be substituted for the Paris white, if preferred, but does not give so white a finish.

FRESH MEAT PRESERVED IN HOT WEATHER.

Put fresh meat into earthenware or stone jars, covering it with skim-milk. The meat will remain sweet for eight or ten days after the milk has soured. The same result may be obtained by the use of fresh buttermilk.

HONEY (IMITATION).

White Sugar..12 pounds.
Honey, in the comb...3 pounds.
Gum Arabic, pulverized.......................................3 ounces.
Rose Leaves, dry...1 drachm.
Warm Water...2 quarts.

Mix, and simmer in a water-bath for one hour, stirring occasionally. Then beat up the whites of three eggs in a pint of warm water, add to the above, and continue to simmer for fifteen minutes. Remove the scum, and strain while hot through flannel cloth. When partially cool, add

Essence of Peppermint..20 drops.
Essence of Wintergreen.......................................15 drops.
Essence of Vanilla...10 drops.
Juice of Lemon...1 teaspoon-ful.

Stir well together, and put into bottles or jars for use. This is a good imitation of honey, and is perfectly wholesome.

MORTAR—TO PREPARE.

The mortar used by the ancient Romans gave their marvelous masonry far more stability and durability than that with which we are now familiar. The mortar of the present day hardens very slowly, *tears* after hardening, does not become very firm, crumbles easily after a time, and fails to unite with the building material; so that after a wall has thoroughly hardened little difficulty is experienced in removing a single stone or brick from the upper courses of the masonry.

Investigations of the ancient Roman mortar show that the greater portion of it was converted into *silicates*, closely combined with the particles of quartz with which they came in contact. It is well known that with modern mortar the formation of silicate is not effected until after considerable time has elapsed, and then only in a very slight measure. But the firmness of mortar relies upon these silicates, which at the same time give it power to resist the action of water. In accordance with this fact, the following formula for preparing a substantial mortar is here presented:

Lime, thoroughly and freshly slaked..................................1 part.
Sand, finely sifted...3 parts.
    Just before using, add
Lime, fresh and unslaked...$\frac{3}{4}$ part.
    While being mixed the mortar heats. It should be used immediately.

FIRE-PROOF PAINT.

To either slaked or unslaked lime add cold or hot water. Mix together as for whitewash, and allow the mixture to stand twenty-four hours before using, stirring occasionally.

Then, with a clean whitewash or paint brush, apply the mixture to either boards, stones, or bricks, giving them a thorough coating, and rubbing well with the brush, so that all the cracks shall be filled, the mixture being sufficiently thin to flow readily from the brush.

When the first application is about half dry, make a second one with the same mixture.

Within an hour afterwards, or when the second application is about half dry, with a clean brush apply freely over the first mixture (in the same manner as varnish), liquid silicate of soda, 25° Baume. This will dry in one or two hours, during which time it combines with the lime and forms an insoluble silicate of lime and soda.

A second application of the silicate of soda may be made at any time after one day. A third application, within a few days after the second, will be sufficient.

No salt, glue, grease, oil, or other substance, should ever be mixed with the lime or silicate of soda, as such materials prevent the chemical union of the silicate with the lime.

Never apply the silicate of soda before the lime, as the lime will not afterwards properly adhere.

Neither mix the silicate with the lime mixture, but use them separately, as above directed. It is much better to apply the silicate while the limed surface is somewhat damp, or half dry, than to defer its application longer.

The silicate of soda changes the color of the lime to that of cream. A nearly pure white may be produced by using oxyd of zinc mixed with cold water, and applying it in the same manner as recommended for the whitewash. Paris white, or whiting, mixed with water, may also be used.

[NOTE.—After the silicate of soda is applied, make no farther application of lime, zinc, Paris white, or any other pigment, as a subsequent coating will be sure to scale off in a short time.]

When other shades of color are desired, yellow or red ochre, or any pigment of a neutral or alkaline character, may be combined with the white, or mixed with cold water and used separately.

If this paint is applied to green lumber, it may crack somewhat when the wood dries and shrinks; but this can be obviated, in a measure, by making an application of shellac varnish, as a finishing coat, within a few days after the last application of the silicate of soda.

The bleached shellac varnish should be used on the white, and the common orange or liver-colored shellac varnish may be spread over the colors.

ARTIFICIAL STONE AND MARBLE.

All rocks which are not calcareous (containing lime) are silicious (containing sand).

Carbonate of lime is found of various colors and aspects, as *chalk*, *marble*, and *limestone*. It consists simply of carbonic acid and lime.

Silicon, in combination with oxygen, forms sand-stone, which constitutes 45 per cent. of the solid crust of the globe; occurring in a pure state, as *quartz*, (rock-crystal—also known as silicic acid, silex, or silica,) and almost pure in *chalcedony, flint agate* and *cornelian*. Sand-stone usually consists of the materials of older rocks, as granite broken up and comminuted, and afterwards deposited again.

When sand-stone crumbles, or is reduced to fine grains, it is called silicious sand, the most common and abundant form of silicic acid.

The grains of sand are sometimes cemented together firmly, or solidified, when they form *silicious rock*, or *sand-stone*.

Silicic acid, or quartz, in its ordinary form, is insoluble, and, therefore, inert, but when melted it becomes a powerful acid, combining with alkalies and metalic bases, producing a large family of salts—the silicates. Thus *glass* results from the melting and union of silica with potash, soda and lime. It is a mixture of true salts—silicates of potash, soda and lime. When combined with metals, silica exists in the same relationship. It forms compounds by uniting with bases which are salifiable.

It is on this principle that *artificial* stone is formed.

The materials used are common brown or white sand, (silica), sal-soda, and chloride of calcium.

The silica, which is the cementing agent, is mixed with carbonate of soda and exposed, in a furnace or glass-melting pot, to a strong heat, until the entire mass fuses uniformly. When completely melted, it constitutes the *silicate of soda* of commerce. (See process for manufacturing silicate of soda.)

TO PREPARE ARTIFICIAL STONE.

Take liquid silicate of soda, 30° Baume. Add sufficient sand to form, when thoroughly mixed, a mass having the consistence of dough, which is called "pug." It is very plastic, and may be worked by the hands as readily as wet clay or putty. When of the proper consistence, it may be pressed in a mould of the required pattern.

The mould may be in the form of a flower, rosette, or a leaf-ornament, a key-stone, vase, pedestal, or section of a mantel-piece. Any form, indeed, may be produced in a few minutes, more beautiful than a stone-cutter could produce after days of patient labor.

After the design is moulded into shape, it is immersed in a solution of chloride of calcium. It then hardens, by the result of their mutual decomposition and re-formation as *silicate of lime* and *chloride of sodium*; the former remaining as an indestructible bond throughout the *stone*—the latter soluble and easily removed by washing with water.

This valuable product, which is now taking the place of marble mantel-pieces, is prepared by using sand of various shades, and polishing the surface after it becomes thoroughly dry. It is a perfect imitation of marble, resembling the white or Italian variety, and, although it is more durable, the expense is about one-fourth that of true marble.

PRESERVATION OF BUILDING STONE.

Much of the building stone contains a small per-centage of protoxyd of iron, imparting to the stone the characteristic blue-greenish tint, and exposure to the atmosphere converts the protoxyd into hydrated sesquioxyd of iron, known as iron rust, which causes the stone to assume a dingy-brown appearance.

To remedy this defect, apply two or three coats of liquid silicate of soda, 25° Baume, allowing one or more days for drying between each application.

The unprotected stone fronts in buildings, after a few months' exposure, usually change to a brownish hue.

To give these fronts a new appearance, remove the oxyd by rubbing with sand-paper, which can be readily accomplished. Then immediately apply the liquid silicate of soda, 25° Baume, as above directed for new stone. This forms an insoluble coating, giving it a glass-like finish, and protects the stone from oxydation.

PRESERVATION OF TIMBER.

Immerse the timber in a hot solution prepared by dissolving two pounds of borax to the gallon of water. The timber should remain in this hot solution, in large water-tight vats, until the wood is thoroughly saturated. Then remove, and when dry apply the liquid silicate of soda, 25° Baume, in the manner of varnish. After drying for a day or two, apply a another coating of the solution of the silicate; this may be repeated two or three times, at intervals of at least one day. Instead of the silicate, fire-proof paint, mentioned on page 205, may be used. Timber impregnated by the solution of borax will not decay, and will not be attacked by insects, grubs, etc.

DECAY OF TIMBER.

The microscope shows that the decay of timber is largely due to parasites feeding on the albuminous substances of the wood. The following conditions are favorable to decay: The presence of parasites, or germs, albuminous matter, moisture, free oxygen, together with a warm temperature.

Boiling water destroys all parasitic germs, coagulates the albuminoids, and the pores being filled with the borax, the wood is rendered incombustible and almost imperishable.

The albuminoids are highly hygroscopic, and, in consequence, expand or contract with every atmospheric change; but wood treated with borax, which is a good antiseptic, and silicate of soda, as above directed, is no longer subject to such changes, and must remain in a perfect state of preservation for an indefinite period.

Various substances have been used for the preservation of timber, as sulphate of copper, sulphate of iron, chloride of zinc, corrosive sublimate, arsenic and common salt. These articles are good antiseptics, but require that the wood be thoroughly saturated with them, as with borax; but when they are employed for this purpose the silicate of soda cannot be used in combination with them.

To effectually preserve timber, it must be saturated with the antiseptic agent. When it is merely coated with the agent, or is penetrated but a short distance, cremacausis, or slow decay, is not prevented.

PLATING SOLUTIONS.

TO PREPARE ARTICLES FOR PLATING.

Wash the article in a weak lye—which may be made by dissolving a teaspoon-ful of saleratus in two-thirds of a tumbler-ful of soft water—to remove any grease. Rinse in clear soft water. Then dip the article into a solution of nitric acid diluted with an equal quantity of distilled water, to remove oxyds. Scour for a few moments with a hard brush and the *polishing cream*; after which rub clean and dry with a hard brush. Then dip the article for a moment in strong nitric acid, and immediately immerse it in the *electro-plating solution*, which is thus prepared for

PLATING WITH GOLD.

Cyanide of Potassium..1 ounce.
Pure Water..1 pint.

Put these into a wide-mouthed, flint-glass bottle that holds a little over a pint, and agitate. When dissolved, add

Chloride of Gold..1 drachm.

It is now ready for use.

Immediately after the article to be plated has been cleaned, as before directed, suspend it in the gold solution by a small strip of zinc not exceeding one-eighth of an inch in width, and this strip must hang on a copper wire that extends across the mouth of the bottle.

Once in about every fifteen minutes the article and the zinc should be taken out of the solution and rubbed for a few moments with a brush and the polishing cream. Then replace them as before in the solution. Repeat this operation every fifteen minutes, until the plating is sufficiently thick. Four or five immersions in the solution are generally enough. The point of attachment of the zinc to the article which is being plated should be changed once or twice during the process; otherwise the points of contact will remain unplated.

When it is not in use, the plating solution should be well corked, and so kept ready for use at any time. To preserve it still better, wrap a heavy blue paper around the bottle, tying down the cork with a cord, in order to protect the chemicals from light and air. The bottle should be labeled "Poison," and placed beyond the reach of children.

Electro-gilding, or plating, as above described, has the reputation of being an expensive process, and most of those engaged in the business deceive the public as to its cost. The actual expense may safely be estimated as follows: A silver thimble may be handsomely plated with gold for ten cents, a pencil-case for twenty cents, and a watch-case for considerably less than three dollars.

The relative difference in the price of plating with gold or silver is as sixteen to one, in the cost of materials. The value of pure silver required for plating a large-sized tea or coffee-pot ranges from $1.50 to $2.00. One and a half ounces of pure silver will plate a surface of 144 square inches as thick as ordinary writing paper. Estimate the value of silver coin, and you can readily arrive at the expense of plating as many square inches as you desire.

SILVER-PLATING SOLUTION—TO PLATE BRASS, COPPER, AND GERMAN SILVER, AND TO RE-PLATE ANY ARTICLE WITH SILVER, WITHOUT A BATTERY.

Nitrate of Silver..1 ounce.
Distilled Water..2 ounces.

Agitate in a bottle until the silver is dissolved.

Into another bottle put

Cyanide of Potassium, powdered......................................1¼ ounces.
Distilled Water..2 ounces.

Agitate until the potassium salt is dissolved.

Then add the contents of one bottle to those of the other, and agitate strongly for a few minutes.

Then add, and thoroughly incorporate,

Best Paris White...3 ounces.

Or sufficient to make a mixture of the consistence of cream, and it will be ready for use.

Polish the articles designed to receive the plating with finely powdered emery or Paris white, just before applying the silver-plating mixture, which should be applied with a cotton or linen cloth, and rub it thoroughly for a few moments, when the article will be plated with *pure silver.*

Immediately after plating, the articles must be washed in soap-suds, rinsed in clear water, and wiped dry.

Heavier plating may be produced by repeating the application; but it is impossible to produce a very thick, firm coating by this process, which is particularly applicable to articles not afterwards subjected to much wear or scouring.

ANOTHER PROCESS FOR SILVER-PLATING.

Thoroughly cleanse the brass or copper surface to be plated, by immersing it for a moment in nitric acid. Then apply the following mixture with a stiff brush, rubbing briskly:

Cream of Tartar..100 parts.
Chloride of Silver.. 10 parts.
Corrosive Sublimate.. 1 part.
Paris White... 40 parts.

Distilled water, sufficient to form the foregoing into a paste of the consistence of cream.

The plating is then to be polished in the usual manner, with a brush, or it may be "burnished" by rubbing it carefully with any very hard and smooth instrument.

POLISHING CREAM—TO CLEAN SILVER PLATE.

Water .... 1 quart.
Carbonate of Potassa .... 1 ounce.
Paris White .... 1 pound.

Mix in a porcelain or tin vessel, and boil in it the articles to be cleaned for twenty minutes. Then remove the dish from the fire, and when cool each article is to be polished well with soft chamois skin. A suitable brush may be used to polish all embossed or engraved parts.

Or the above may be applied cold, and the articles thoroughly polished with it.

TO PLATE COPPER AND BRASS WITH TIN.

Bitartrate of Potassa .... 1½ pounds.
Soft Water .... 1 gallon.

Boil until dissolved. Then add

Grain Tin, in shavings .... 2 pounds.

Boil again, for about one hour.

The article designed to be tinned is then put into the solution and boiled for one hour, or until a coating of tin is deposited on the surface of the article.

TO PLATE OR GALVANIZE IRON.

Thoroughly wash the oil or grease from the sheets of iron with strong soap-suds, or other alkaline solution. Then immerse them in diluted nitric acid, to remove the oxyd that remains on the surface, and immediately plunge them into a bath of melted zinc. As soon as the surface is thoroughly coated with the zinc, take them from the bath.

A more costly and troublesome process is to galvanize the sheets of iron with the aid of a battery, whereby they receive a deposit of zinc on the surface; but the above formula is preferable, owing to its simplicity and cheapness, and is substantially the process employed in large manufactories.

KEROSENE OIL AND ITS ADULTERATIONS.

The mixture of salt, soda, nitre, alum, or any other substance with kerosene oil or benzine, naphtha, etc., does not improve their illuminating qualities, or render them less inflammable or explosive.

Kerosene oil is frequently adulterated with gasoline, benzine, or naphtha, and sold under various names as new oils, and frequently at less prices than kerosene. These adulterants cost but about half as much as kerosene, which is the motive for their use.

Soda, borax, and other substances, it is said, are sometimes added to "neutralize" the explosive properties of these compounds, but they are perfectly useless, as the addition of any substance will not subdue the explosive nature of benzine without destroying its illuminating power.

Gasoline, benzine, or naphtha, should never be combined with kerosene for illuminating purposes, as it is the presence of these inflammable and explosive fluids that causes so many of the disasters recorded as kerosene-lamp explosions. Kerosene oil, below the *legal standard* temperature of 110° Fahr., is explosive.

The breaking of lamps which have not been properly annealed, by unequal expansion of the glass, is the cause of many disasters reported as "explosions."

To test kerosene oil, as to its liability to explode, take a tin cup of water heated to 100° by the thermometer, pouring into it a tablespoon-ful of the oil. Then hold a lighted match immediately over the cup, and if the vapor arising from the oil flashes or takes fire, it shows an excess of benzine in the oil, caused by the addition of benzine or naptha to the kerosene. If the oil or vapor does not take fire at 100°, gradually increase the heat of the water, and frequently repeat the test, occasionally adding fresh oil to the water, until it does flash or take fire, carefully noting the degree of heat at which this result is attained. If the oil does not generate sufficient vapor to burn or flash at 110° Fahr., it is to be considered a safe illuminating oil. In refining kerosene oil by "fractional distillation," some manufacturers purposely allow part of the volatile oils to remain, so as to increase the product and profit of their operations.

TO REFINE KEROSENE OIL.

To refine kerosene oil which contains an excess of benzine or naphtha, or other impurities, add one pound of coarsely powdered animal charcoal to each gallon of the oil. Shake well together. Then pour it into an open vessel, which is to be placed in a water-bath heated to 125° Fahr. Allow the oil to remain in the water-bath two hours, stirring it occasionally. At the expiration of that time more volatile oils will have sufficiently escaped to render the oil safe. Set the vessel aside for a few hours, to settle; after which the oil should be strained through cloth. It is then ready for use.

PETROLEUM.

It is a singular fact that in boring for oil the heaviest kind is first found, generally at a depth ranging from eighty to one hundred feet, while the lighter petroleum is seldom reached at less than eight or ten hundred feet. The oils nearest the surface were undoubtedly *once light*, but by absorbing oxygen their natures have been changed.

During the distillation of petroleum, the following products are expelled at the following (Fahrenheit) temperatures:

Chimogene	70°
Rhigolene	120°
Gasoline	170°
Naphtha	250°
Benzine	300°
Kerosene, light	400°
Kerosene	500°
Kerosene, heavy	600°
Paraffin	700°

PETROLEUM AS A WOOD-PRESERVATIVE.

Wood may be saturated by immersing it in vats of heavy petroleum oil, or by applying to it fresh coatings of the oil every day, with a brush, until the wood has entirely absorbed the oil. The volatile portions of the oil will soon evaporate, leaving the pores of the wood filled with a bituminous substance, which effectually excludes the air and renders it water-proof. Ordinary paint, made with linseed oil, preserves the wood by forming a coat which protects it from the effects of air and water, leaving the interior part liable to dry-rot; but petroleum, as before stated, penetrates every part of the wood, and, being a good antiseptic, prevents decay, and also the ravages of worms, insects and vermin. For large timbers, like the sills of buildings, etc., bore holes, half or two-thirds through the timber, three or four feet apart, fill them with petroleum oil, within three-fourths of an inch of the top, and tightly plug them up. The petroleum will soon penetrate every pore; but every few days the holes should be refilled with the oil, until the wood is thoroughly saturated. We have made numerous experiments, combining the petroleum oil with other oils, varnishes and pigments, in hopes of discovering an improved paint, but as a wood-preservative we have found the pure, heavy petroleum oil, used without the addition of any other substance, far preferable. As its price is only about thirty cents per gallon, it is probably the cheapest and most effectual wood-preservative known.

[NOTE.—During the process of saturating the wood with the petroleum oil, or applying it, and for a few hours afterwards, no fires, candles, or lamps should be brought near it, as the volatile portions of the oil (gasoline, benzine and naphtha) are highly inflammable; but they soon evaporate, leaving a preservative substance that will not readily ignite, composed of bitumen, paraffin wax, etc., and which are not soluble in water, or susceptible of decay. Wood thus prepared must remain in a state of preservation for ages.]

TO PLATE IRON OR STEEL WITH COPPER.

Sulphate of Copper	8 ounces.
Soft Water, hot	1 quart.

Stir, until the copper is dissolved.

Have the articles to be plated perfectly clean and free from grease, and polished bright. Then immerse them for a moment in diluted muriatic acid, (consisting of equal parts of muriatic acid and water.) Rinse the articles in clean water, and instantly dip them into the hot solution of copper. They will be immediately coated with copper.

TO PLATE IRON WITH TIN.

Prepare the sheets of iron as for galvanizing with zinc, (see page 211), using melted tin for the plating. But to make a perfect coating of tin, the sheets should be dipped in melted tallow just before their immersion in the bath of melted tin.

COLOR RESTORATIVE,

For instantly renewing the color to faded and worn coats, vests, pants and wearing apparel of black, brown, blue, and other dark-colored goods, but *not for white fabrics*, as the dye only chemically combines with the color already in the cloth, and reproduces the original color.

Extract of Logwood, pulverized............6 ounces.
Sulphate of Copper............½ ounce.
White Sugar............3 ounces.
Alcohol............1 quart.
Soft Water............1 pint.

Mix, and heat in a water-bath for two hours. Let it stand one day, agitating occasionally.

Directions for Use.—Add two ounces to a quart of *hot water*, and apply the hot solution to the garments with a clean brush, until the cloth is wet. Lastly, rub with the nap, to produce lustre. Dry the garments, and they will have the appearance of new goods.

A superior and more durable color may be produced by first cleaning the cloth with the cloth renovator; then dry for at least 24 hours before applying the color restorative.

INDIA RUBBER—PURE.

To preserve the gum in a liquid form, as it comes from the tree, the liquor is filtered; then mixed with about one-eighteenth of its weight of strong ammonia. On being poured out and exposed to a temperature of from 70° to 100° Fahr., the ammonia, which preserves it from the action of atmospheric oxygen, evaporates, leaving the gum in the shape of the vessel which contains it.

INDIA RUBBER SOLUTION.

India Rubber (pure gum), cut into thin slices............1¼ ounces.
Naphtha............1 pint.

Keep in a tightly corked bottle, and in a warm room, for two or three days, shaking occasionally, until the rubber dissolves.

The color of this solution is dark, but by leaving it undisturbed for a few weeks it will become nearly transparent, when the clear portion may be carefully poured off, the sediment remaining behind.

Rubber shoes, etc., will not dissolve in naphtha, as they contain sulphur, which forms an insoluble compound with the gum. Use only the pure india rubber, which is kept for sale at the principal rubber-stores, and is sold for about $2.00 per pound.

HARD INDIA RUBBER.

India Rubber (pure gum)	7 pounds.
Sulphur, in powder	1 pound.

Heat to a temperature of about 300° Fahr. Stir well together, and press into moulds of the required pattern. It will then be "vulcanized," and retain its form.

LIQUID POLISH BLACKING.

Ivory-Black, fine	1 pound.
Olive Oil	4 ounces.

Mix, and grind well together in a porcelain or wedgewood mortar. Then add

Strong Vinegar	2½ quarts.
White Sugar	10 ounces.

Grind well together. Lastly, add

Sulphuric Acid, by weight	4 ounces.
Muriatic Acid, by weight	4 ounces.

Stir thoroughly together, and it is ready for use.

This blacking should be applied to leather with a soft brush or sponge, and requires no rubbing to produce a polish.

PASTE (POLISH) BLACKING.

Ivory-Black	1 pound.
Molasses	12 ounces.
Sulphuric Acid	1 ounce.
Olive Oil	2 ounces.

First mix the ivory-black and molasses thoroughly. Then add the oil; then gradually the acid, and, afterwards, as much water as may be necessary to bring the mass to a proper consistence. Put into boxes for use. Moisten the blacking with water, and apply to the leather with a brush, rubbing thoroughly for a few moments, to produce a polish.

TOOTH POWDER.

Prepared Chalk, pulverized	2 ounces.
Orris Root, pulverized	¼ ounce.

Mix well together.

This makes an excellent tooth powder.

Charcoal and other hard substances should never be used for cleansing the teeth.

TOILET POWDER.

Wheat Starch, pure	1 pound.
Orris Root, pulverized	3 ounces.
Oil of Bergamot	30 drops.
Oil of Neroli	10 drops.

Mix thoroughly.

If a flesh-colored powder is required, a few grains of carmine, pulverized, may be added to give the required tint.

Bismuth and other poisonous substances should not be used for cosmetics.

FRANGIPANNI SACHET—PERFUME FOR CLOTHING.

Orris Root, powdered	8 ounces.
Rose Leaves, powdered	6 ounces.
Sandal-wood, powdered	2 ounces.
Musk	30 grains.
Tonqua Beans, powdered	2½ ounces.
Essence of Roses	½ drachm.

Mix well together.

When used for perfuming clothing, in trunks, closets, wardrobes, etc., half an ounce or more may be sewed up in sachets made of two thicknesses of silk, and placed among the garments.

TO CLEAN CLOTHES.

Take equal parts of alcohol and aqua ammonia. Mix them in a bottle, and keep tightly corked. Moisten a sponge with this mixture, and vigorously rub the garment to be cleansed. It will remove grease, etc., and is instantaneous in its action. When clothing is stained with acids it restores them to their original color.

PERFUMED GLYCERIN SOAP.

Transparent Soap, sliced	12 ounces.
Soft Water	8 ounces.
Alcohol	8 ounces.

Heat in a closely covered vessel, or tightly corked bottle, in a water-bath until the soap is dissolved; then remove the cover or cork, and continue to heat for half an hour longer, in order to evaporate a portion of the alcohol.

Into another bottle put

Glycerin	6 ounces.
Essence of Sassafras	1 ounce.

Shake well together, add to the solution of soap, and stir until thoroughly combined. Then press into moulds of any pattern preferred.

This is an excellent soap for chapped hands, rough skin, etc.

PRESERVATION OF POTATOES.

Liquor Ammonia, concentrated	3 ounces.
Cold Water	1 gallon.

Immerse the potatoes in the ammoniated water for one week; then remove and allow them to dry. The effect of the ammonia suspends or destroys the germinating principle in the vegetables, without proving detrimental to the nutritious properties of the potato. Potatoes cannot sprout after undergoing this process, and if kept in a dry place will remain in a good state of preservation for months.

If the common aqua ammonia is used, the quantity, as an equivalent for the concentrated, should be twelve ounces to the gallon of water.

The vessel containing the ammoniated water in which potatoes are immersed must be kept tightly closed, to prevent the escape of the ammonia.

POISONOUS POTATOES.

Sprouts of the potato contain an alkaloid (*solanine*), which is very poisonous if taken into the system. This also exists in the potato when it is accidentally exposed to light and air by the removal of the earth during the period of cultivation, which may be known by the potato having a bluish-green tint on one side. Such a potato should never be eaten, nor fed to stock.

DYEING WITH ANILINE COLORS.

Fabrics must first be washed in warm soap-suds, or solutions of sal-soda or silicate of soda, and then thoroughly rinsed.

For the dye-bath use a clean, enameled kettle, or an earthenware pot, which must be free from fat, and must not be used for any other purpose.

Old fabrics, which have once been dyed, may be freed from color by previously boiling them in strong soap-suds from a half to one hour.

Aniline colors are prepared from coal-tar by elaborate chemical processes.

VIOLET ANILINE PURPLE FOR WOOL.

(For 25 lbs. of Goods.)

Aniline Purple..4 ounces.
Alcohol, 95 per cent..1 gallon.

Mix in a stone jar, or tin pail, having a tight-fitting cover, through which a stick passes for the purpose of stirring. Place the jar or pail in a kettle of boiling water, constantly stirring, and allow the solution to boil for ten minutes.

After cooling, filter through paper, muslin, or flannel, but if it stands over night it will have to be filtered again, to prevent the color from crocking, or rubbing off.

Directions for Use.—Have ready sufficient boiling water to cover the goods, adding to it half a pound of oxalic acid and one-third of the aniline solution. After boiling for one minute, and stirring well, put in the goods, and continue to boil gently for ten or fifteen minutes, stirring them often. Then take them out, and add to the dye half a pound of sulphuric acid and the rest of the aniline solution. Replace the goods in the dye, keeping it at the boiling point, and stirring for half an hour. Wash the goods in cold water, and wring them. The more sulphuric acid used, the more blue will be the shade. Should the dye become too blue, pour in cold water until the temperature reaches 95° Fahr., when a little fuchsine may be added, making the shade of a more reddish cast.

VIOLET ANILINE PURPLE FOR COTTON.
(For 25 lbs. of Goods.)

Perchloride of Tin, in crystals	5 ounces.
Hot Water	1½ gallons.

Dissolve the tin in the water. Then immerse the goods for fifteen minutes in this solution, frequently turning and airing them. Remove the goods, and add to the solution

Aniline Violet	3 ounces.

Stir well until dissolved.

Immerse the goods again in the dye, stirring and airing them occasionally, for fifteen minutes. To render the color more permanent, mix

Alum	4 ounces.
Water, hot	1 gallon.

And in this solution wash the clothes, wringing and drying them.

ANILINE RED (FUCHSINE) ON WOOL.
(For 25 lbs. of Goods.)

Aniline Red (fuchsine crystals)	1½ ounces.
Alcohol, 95 per cent	8 ounces.

Dissolve in a tin pail, over a water-bath, as directed for the violet dye.

Directions for Use.—Heat water to about 170° Fahr., sufficient to cover the goods, and if twenty-five pounds of goods are to be dyed at one time, add all of the aniline solution to the water, and stir for a few moments. Into this dye immerse the goods, stirring them well to prevent streaks. Allow them to remain for thirty minutes. Then remove, and they will be completely dyed. Pass them through an ordinary clothes-wringer. On a large scale this may be done in a centrifugal machine. The same water may be used for ten or twelve hours, heating whenever required, and adding more of the aniline solution; but it must not be used after twelve or fifteen hours.

By adding a little ammonia to the dye, a brighter red is produced. Silk is treated in the same manner, but in *cold* water, to which half an ounce of tartaric acid has been added, and in which the silk has been steeped for half an hour before adding any color.

ANILINE RED (FUCHSINE) ON COTTON.
(For 25 lbs. of Goods.)

Sumach Bark..2 pounds.
Hot Water..4 gallons.

Simmer together for five or six hours. Strain the decoction, and while it is heated to about 170° Fahr., immerse the goods, allowing them to remain in the dye for two and a half hours, stirring and airing them frequently. Pass them through a clothes-wringer, and then immerse for 15 or 20 minutes in the red aniline (fuchsine) bath, prepared as for dyeing wool.

HOFFMAN'S DAHLIA, VIOLET, RED, AND BLUISH PARME SHADES.

Aniline..4 ounces.
Alcohol, 95 per cent..1 quart.

Use in the same manner as the aniline red.

ANILINE BLUE ON WOOL.
(For 25 lbs. of Goods.)

Soft Water, hot..4 gallons.
Sulphuric Acid..½ pound.

Boil for ten minutes. Have ready

Aniline Blue..4 ounces.

Dissolved in

Alcohol...1 quart.

Gradually add the aniline solution, stirring constantly.

Submerse the goods, and continue to boil until they have absorbed the color from the water.

A lighter shade will be imparted to the goods by using only one-half or two-thirds of the quantity of the aniline; or a darker shade may be obtained by adding more aniline to the water as often as its color is absorbed by the goods.

Silk is steeped first for an hour in luke-warm water, made acid in the same manner, and the color must be added in from four to five small portions, raising the temperature gradually to boiling heat, and continuing it at that point for from five to ten minutes, to produce a good color. The old bath is then replaced by fresh water, which is acidulated with sulphuric acid, and in which the silk is boiled for ten minutes; after which it is thoroughly washed in water, and then in soap-suds; afterwards, again, in water; then once more drawn through acidulated water; and, lastly, through water alone.

Violets and purples are produced on wool in the same manner as the blue; on *silk* the same method is used likewise, but the water must only be heated short of boiling.

ANILINE BLUE VIOLET ON COTTON.
(For 25 lbs. of Goods.)

Hot Water..4 gallons.
Nitrate of Iron..1 pound.
Chloride of Tin, in crystals..4 ounces.

Mix, and immerse the goods, allowing them to remain in the solution a few minutes.

Have ready a solution made as follows:

Prussiate of Potash..10 ounces.
Sulphuric Acid (by weight)...8 ounces.

Mix. Into this remove the goods from the solution of iron and tin, turning them over a few times.

They are then to be taken out and placed in a tub of tepid water. Turn them several times in this water, and then take them out. To the water add the following mixture:

Olive Oil..1 pound.
Sulphuric Acid (by weight)...2 ounces.
Alcohol...2½ ounces.
Hot Water..1 pint.

Agitate well together, and add to the tepid bath. Immerse the goods in this, turning them several times. Then take them out, and put them into a tepid solution of *reddish violet* and half a pound of alum added to sufficient water to cover the goods.

ANILINE BLUE ON COTTON.

For pure blue, prepare the goods as for fuchsine, and dye like violets. For a greenish and dark-blue, dye in a bath of prussiate of potassa and sulphuric acid, as mentioned in the formula for blue violet on cotton.

For very light shades, place the goods subsequently into a new tepid bath containing five ounces of perchloride of tin for every twenty-five pounds of goods.

SCARLET ANILINE ON WOOL.
(For 25 lbs. of Goods.)

Soft Water, hot..3 gallons.
Sulphate of Zinc...3 pounds.

When dissolved, submerse the goods in this bath, and boil for ten minutes. Remove them, and add

Scarlet Aniline...10 ounces.

Stir until dissolved. Strain and submerse the goods for fifteen or twenty minutes, by which time they will be of a brown color. Then add

Muriate of Ammonia..3 ounces.

Continue to boil for thirty or forty minutes.

By the addition of more ammonia a brighter shade may be produced.

ANILINE GREEN ON WOOL.

(For 25 lbs. of Goods.)

Iodine Aniline Green	4 ounces.
Alcohol, 95 per cent	½ gallon.

Dissolve, in a water-bath, as before directed.
Prepare a bath of

Water	3 gallons.

In which must be dissolved

Acetic Acid	3 ounces.
Acetate of Soda	3 ounces.

Add the solution of aniline green, and stir well together. Heat the bath to 100° Fahrenheit. Submerse and air the goods, in the usual manner, until an even shade is obtained. Then add

Castile Soap	1 ounce.

Dissolved in

Hot Water	1 quart.

And the brilliancy of the color will be increased.

ANILINE GREEN—SOLUBLE IN WATER.

(For 25 lbs. of Goods.)

Aniline Green	4 ounces.

Made into a paste with a little cold water. Then add

Boiling Water	3 gallons.
Sulphuric Acid	½ pound.

This dye will serve for both silk and wool. To produce a darker shade of green, the goods should be first dyed with light-blue.

IODINE ANILINE GREEN FOR COTTON.

The cotton has to be taken through a bath of boiling water; next, through one of castile soap, and, next, dyed in a luke-warm bath containing tannin, the color being shaded off with picric acid or fustic.

ANILINE YELLOW.

Dissolve aniline yellow in boiling water. For dyeing silk, add to the bath acetic or sulphuric acid in small quantity, and dye at 170° Fahr.

For wool, dye the same way, but add oxalic or sulphuric acid. If aniline yellow is shaded off with fuchsine, every shade from orange to scarlet may be obtained.

PICRIC ACID.

This acid yields a canary color, different from the golden yellow of the aniline yellow, which, by the way, is not made from aniline, but from naphthaline. For green and drab colors on wool and silk, picric acid is of the greatest value, as it dyes an even shade, not obtainable with other dyes, affords facilities for nice shading off, and makes a brilliant color.

For green, take the goods through a bath soured with sulphuric acid and alum, to which, subsequently, picric acid and indigo extract are added.

For drab colors on wool, the bath is to be soured with glauber salts and tartaric acid, the alum omitted, the picric acid being added, together with the indigo, orchil, or cudbear.

For family dyes, those mordants should always be added in the right proportion to the solution of the aniline, to render its solution simple. Perfection in this manner can at best be only approached, never realized.

[For many valuable suggestions in regard to dyeing with aniline colors, we are indebted to "THE ARTS," published by J. M. Hirsh & Co., Chicago, and the "DRUGGISTS' CIRCULAR AND CHEMICAL GAZETTE," published in New York by L. V. Newton, M. D.]

GENERAL SUGGESTIONS.

Instead of adding the whole amount of aniline dye to the bath at once, divide the prescribed quantity of aniline color into three parts. Begin the dyeing with one part, and do not heat the bath above 100° Fahr.

All the color having been taken up by the goods, add another part, allowing the heat to rise to the boiling point of water (212° Fahr.); and thus continue to add the color from time to time.

Heat and acids produce blue shades with all aniline colors. To obtain the redder shades of violet and blue, use less acid, and lessen the time of boiling.

OTHER PROCESSES FOR DYEING.

TO DYE COMPOUND COLORS.

Compound colors are produced by mixing together two simple ones; or, which is the same thing, by dyeing cloth first with a simple color, and then with another. These colors vary to infinity, according to the proportions of the ingredients employed.

From blue, red and yellow, *red olives* and *greenish grays* are made.

From blue, red and brown, *olives* are made, from the lightest to the darkest shades; and by giving a greater shade of red, the *slated* and *lavender grays* are made.

From blue, red and black, *grays* of all shades are made, such as *sage, pigeon, slate and lead grays*.

From yellow, blue and brown, are made *green olives* of all shades.

From brown, blue and black, are produced *brown olives* and their shades.

BLACK DYE FOR WOOLEN GOODS.

Blue Vitriol..1 pound.
Hot Soft Water, in a large iron kettle..3 gallons.

When the vitriol is dissolved, fifteen pounds of cloth may be dipped in the solution, taken out, and aired for a few minutes. Repeat this process for thirty minutes.

In another kettle place

Extract of Logwood	½ pound.
Hot Soft Water	3 gallons.

Boil until dissolved. Keep it hot, and immerse the cloth for one hour, airing it four or five times. Then wash in strong soap-suds, and dry.

BLACK DYE FOR COTTON GOODS.

Sumach Bark	2 pounds.
Hot Soft Water	3 gallons.

Simmer two or three hours.

This is sufficient for fifteen pounds of cloth.

Let the goods remain in the dye for ten hours, keeping it hot, and airing the cloth occasionally.

Then dip the cloth in lime-water for twenty minutes, afterwards allowing it to air and drain for half an hour.

Add to the sumach decoction

Sulphate of Iron	1 pound.

When dissolved, immerse the cloth again for one hour. Then remove, and allow it to drain for thirty minutes.

In another kettle have ready prepared the following:

Extract of Logwood	½ pound.
Hot Soft Water	3 gallons.

As soon as dissolved, immerse the cloth in this hot liquor for two hours, airing occasionally.

Then add to this liquor

Bichromate of Potassa	5 ounces.

Again immerse the cloth for one and a half hours, airing at intervals. Wash in cold water, and dry in the shade.

This process imparts a permanent black.

TO DYE STRAW AND CHIP HATS AND BONNETS BLACK.

Extract of Logwood	¼ ounce.
Hot Water	1 gallon.
Sulphate of Iron	¼ ounce.

Simmer until all are dissolved.

Boil the articles to be dyed in this liquid for a few minutes, every half-hour, until the desired color is obtained. Then rub them, inside and out, with a sponge moistened in olive oil, and proceed to block them.

TO VARNISH STRAW AND CHIP HATS BLACK.

Alcohol, 95 per cent	½ pint.
Best Black Sealing Wax	2 ounces.

Put them in a bottle together and cork it tightly, keeping it in a warm place. Shake occasionally, until the wax is all dissolved. Apply while warm, with a soft brush, in the sun or in a warm room.

This preparation stiffens old straw hats, bonnets, baskets, etc., imparts a beautiful gloss, and renders them water-proof.

ANNATTO AND ITS USES.

Annatto is a coloring substance derived from the red pulp or covering surrounding the fruit or seed of the *Bixa Orellana*, a tree indigenous to the West Indies and other hot climates. The fruit, (which resembles an orange), is used by the residents as a substitute for the tomato. The seeds not only impart a brilliant color, but a spicy flavor to a great variety of native dishes.

Annatto is sometimes called Arnotta and Rocou. It is frequently adulterated with red ochre, chalk, sulphate of lime, turmeric, etc.

It is used for coloring butter, cheese, soaps, pomades, soups, sauces, etc., and also for dyeing cloth.

Pure annatto is not in the least unwholesome. For its employment in coloring butter and cheese, reference is made to the processes set forth in the foregoing pages.

Soda and potash are usually recommended as the best solvents for extracting its coloring qualities, but they do not produce a bright or satisfactory color.

When annatto is used for dyeing, its coloring properties are best extracted by the following method:

Hot Water..1 gallon.
Liquid Silicate of Soda, 30° Baume................................2 ounces.
Pure Extract of Annatto..2 ounces.

Simmer in a water-bath for two hours, frequently stirring until the annatto is dissolved.

When used for coloring butter, cheese, etc., its color is best extracted by alcohol. (See pages 83 to 88.)

PARAFFIN WAX.

(Tar-Oil—Stearin.)

Paraffin Wax is a tasteless, inodorous, white solid, insoluble in water, but dissolves readily in ether and oils. It is obtained from both coal-tar and petroleum, and melts at 120° Fahr. The most energetic chemical re-agents, as strong acids, alkalies, chlorine, etc., fail to exert any action on this substance. In consequence of this want of affinity, it derives its name from two Latin words, *parum* and *affinis.* It is used in the manufacture of candles and chewing-gum, and we are using it extensively in deoxygenating and insulating eggs, and for preparing kerosene oil and other barrels, vats, butter-firkins, etc., as set forth in previous pages. In these processes it is unequaled.

GLYCERIN.

(The Sweet Principle of Oil.)

Glycerin is obtained from either oil, tallow or lard. It was discovered by Scheele, who called it "the sweet principle of oils and fats."

When perfectly pure, glycerin is colorless and odorless, having a sweet taste and sirupy consistence. It combines readily with water, alcohol or oil, dissolves many gums and resinous substances, does not crystallize nor ferment, like sugar, will not evaporate, and is destroyed by boiling.

Properties and Uses.—Glycerin is antiseptic and demulcent. Applied in many diseases of the skin as a lotion or poultice, it acts as an emollient and soothing application, absorbing moisture from the air, and preventing the parts to which it is applied from becoming too dry. It is used extensively, in combination with rosewater, for chapped hands, lips, etc.

Pills and extracts, incorporated with a small portion of glycerin, are preserved soft and free from mouldiness. It has also been highly recommended as a cure for deafness, by putting a few drops into the ear.

Pure glycerin does not produce any smarting or irritating effects when applied to tender and broken skin. When these effects are produced it is evident that the glycerin is impure and should not be used.

For consumptive and dyspeptic patients glycerin has a beneficial effect, in doses of a teaspoonful stirred into a wineglass-ful of water, two or three times a day. In this respect it is far preferable to cod-liver oil.

For its use for coloring butter, and giving it a lustrous appearance, see page 90.

Pure glycerin is perfectly wholesome.

CARBONIC ACID GAS.

Carbonic acid gas is obtained by the action of diluted sulphuric acid upon powdered marble, and by means of a forcing pump is thrown into a suitable receiver nearly filled with water, the bulk of the water being equal to only one-fifth of the quantity of carbonic acid gas in the receiver. Under common atmospheric pressure, water takes up a volume of carbonic acid gas equal to its own, and if the pressure be doubled the quantity of gas absorbed will also be doubled, and in like proportion with every increase of pressure.

Consequently, to saturate the water with five times its volume of carbonic acid gas, it must be subjected to a pressure of five atmospheres.

Carbonic acid water is a sparkling liquid, having a pleasant, pungent and slightly acidulous taste. It is familiarly known as "soda-water," a term derived from custom, as, originally, it contained a small portion of the carbonate of soda, which, however, is now wholly omitted in its manufacture. As a summer beverage, in connection with flavored sirups, it is drawn from fountains at many drug-stores, ice-cream saloons, etc. Most of the "mineral waters" are also charged with this gas.

The vessels which contain it should be kept in a cold place, and air-tight, or the gas will evaporate and the water lose its briskness; hence the necessity of drinking soda-water, when drawn, before the gas escapes.

Its specific gravity is 1.527—that of atmospheric air being 1.000—and it is so much (or one-third) heavier than common air that it may be poured from one vessel into another.

The sparkling and effervescing properties of many kinds of wine, beer, cider, etc., are owing to the presence of carbonic acid gas.

The acid gas with which soda-water is impregnated is obtained, as before stated, from the combination of marble dust and diluted sulphuric acid, because these are the cheapest materials for the purpose. Chalk may also be used, but is objectionable on account of its imparting an unpleasant odor to the carbonic acid.

The following is the ordinary formula for preparing it:

Cold Water..13 ounces.
Sulphuric Acid, commercial... 1 ounce.

Gradually add the acid to the water, in a porcelain or glass vessel, constantly stirring.

This constitutes what is known as diluted sulphuric acid. Add to this
Marble Dust...8 ounces.

Which must be stirred occasionally, during which time the gas is generated by the action of the acid upon the marble, and passes into the receiver.

LIQUID SILICATE OF SODA.
(*Liquid Silex.*)

It is also known as "water-glass," "soluble glass," etc.

Quartz, (*silicic acid*), pure and finely pulverized..................900 pounds.
Carbonate of Soda, dry and finely pulverized.....................460 pounds.

These are first well mixed, and afterwards exposed to a strong heat, in a "glass-melting pot," for six or seven hours, or until the whole mass is uniformly fused, the heat being about the same as that required to melt glass. After it has melted, it is removed from the fire and allowed to cool. It is then broken into small pieces, and is known in commerce as "dry silicate of soda," or "silicate of soda crystals."

To convert the crystals into liquid silicate of soda, to each one hundred pounds of crystals add twenty-five gallons of boiling water, the boiling point being maintained for four or five hours, with frequent stirring, until the crystals are dissolved. Hot water is occasionally added, as evaporation proceeds, to keep up the original quantity. When the crystals have dissolved, the solution should be strained, while hot, and put into vessels to settle. After standing two or three days, it is drawn off, its density being that of thick sirup, or 36° Baume.

It should be kept in bottles or casks, tightly stopped, as, if allowed to evaporate, it becomes thick and resembles jelly.

When used, this preparation is generally reduced with either cold, warm or hot water, and is extensively employed in various manufactures and the arts.

For its uses, see the processes for making artificial stone, fire-proof paint, the No. 2 process for coating barrels and vats, making soap, washing compound, the preservation of eggs, cement for labeling tin boxes, etc.

SILICATE OF POTASH.

This is used for the same purposes as the silicate of soda, and is prepared in a similar manner, substituting potash for the soda.

Silicate of soda and silicate of potash, when combined, are known as the "double silicate of potash and soda," and are used for the same purposes; but after a series of experiments with them, the silicate of soda has our preference.

[NOTE.—Some manufacturers of silicate of soda use the dry sulphate of soda, instead of the carbonate, in order to produce a cheaper article, but we cannot commend its use, although it is sold in the market for the genuine article. When used for the preservation of eggs, it will not answer the purpose. Hence it is essential that only the true silicate of soda should be used in the various processes set forth in this work. For the price of the true silicate of soda, see the last page.]

CARBOLIC ACID.

ITS PROPERTIES AND USES.

Carbolic Acid is one of the products of the distillation of coal-tar oil. It congeals in the form of long, colorless, prismatic crystals, which melt, at 95° Fahr., to an oily liquid, boiling at 356° Fahr., and in many particulars resembling creosote. It is deliquescent, attracts moisture from the atmosphere, quickly becomes liquid, and continues so at moderate temperatures. It is known by the names of "carbolic acid," "phenic acid," "phenol," "phenic alcohol," and "hydrate of phenyle." It was discovered by Runge, in 1834, who gave it the name by which we designate it. It possesses remarkable powers as an antiseptic, and most of the disinfecting powders now in use are composed of crude carbolic acid and plaster of paris. It prevents putrefaction, has the power to arrest fermentation in organic matter, and also prevents its development. In sloughing wounds, a solution composed of fifteen grains of the acid, dissolved in one ounce of water, produces a most remarkable healing effect. It destroys all fetor, facilitating the separation of the slough, and causes the parts beneath to assume a healthier appearance. It has also the effect of promoting the growth of healthy granulation, and of hastening the healing process of wounds. It has been used successfully in the various forms of skin diseases, etc.

Its *modus operandi* is supposed by some to be involved in mystery; but it is now believed, by many eminent physicians, that animal parasites are the chief cause of diseases. Some of these parasites live on the surface of the human body, (*epizoa*), and others in the interior (*entozoa*).

Experiments have proved that carbolic acid, even in a diluted form, will destroy all the lower forms of life, whether animal or vegetable. The air we breathe contains extremely active powers of destruction, as it holds, floating in it, myriads of the minutest germs of plants and animals, and these mysterious atoms, alighting upon the bodies of living beings, enter the blood, lungs and tissues, there develop and multiply exceedingly, and become the sources of disease, infection and death.

It was held by the British Pharmacy Conference, of 1869, that "these putrifying (septic) germs are great causes of putrefactive *fermentation;* that fermentation is intimately connected with *inflammation;* that most *diseases* result from inflammation; that carbolic acid (antiseptic) will kill all septic germs, and thus remove many causes of disease; that glycerin is a very powerful healing agent; that carbolic acid is freely soluble in glycerin, and that their united application has resulted in the speedy cure of some of the most dangerous diseases. It follows, therefore, that these new therapeutic agents demand very special attention."

We suggest, as a rule for general external application, the following:

Carbolic Acid, crystallized................................1 drachm.
Glycerin, pure..1 ounce.
Oil of Wintergreen...10 drops.

The oil of wintergreen is added to disguise the odor of the carbolic acid.

Mix, and shake well together.

This may be termed *carbolate of glycerin*, but of this strength it is to be used only upon sores and wounds which indicate a fungus growth.

When used for many other purposes it must be diluted with water.

We suggest the following formulas for the general use of carbolic acid, which we have prescribed and found efficacious the past two years:

As a gargle for diphtheria, sore throat, etc., add two grains of carbolic acid to one ounce of water.

As a lotion, sixteen grains to an ounce of water.

As an ointment, twenty grains combined with half an ounce each of lard and glycerin.

As a general application for healing wounds, burns, sores, cuts, boils, felons, bruises, frost-bites, etc., add four ounces of water to one ounce of the carbolate of glycerin.

Shake well together; bathe the affected parts several times a day, or apply to them a cloth saturated with the mixture.

For rheumatism and neuralgia, take

Carbolic Acid, crystals......................................30 grains.
Alcohol, 95 per cent..1 ounce.

Shake well together, and apply several times a day.

For ring-worm, salt-rheum, itch, etc.:

Carbolate of Glycerin..1 ounce.
Alcohol, 95 per cent..1 ounce.

Shake well together, and apply several times per day.

For cancer and scrofulous sores—first application, to remove the fungus flesh:

Carbolic Acid, crystals......................................1 drachm.
Alcohol, 95 per cent..2 drachms.

Shake well together, and apply once a day with a camels'-hair pencil. The parts will immediately turn white.

Within thirty minutes after, and two or three times a day, make an application of "Glycerin and Egg-Yolk Dressing." (See formula for preparing it on page 233.) After the fungus flesh is removed, apply carbolate of glycerin two or three times per day.

For asthma, bronchitis and catarrh, take six drops of the carbolate of glycerin in a wineglass-ful of water three or four times a day, and oftener in urgent cases.

CARBOLIC INHALATION.

For inhalation in pulmonary consumption, bronchitis, catarrh, and asthma:

Carbolic Acid, crystals..2 drachms.
Alcohol, 95 per cent., deodorized...6 drachms.

Shake well together, and keep the bottle tightly corked when not in use. Let the patient inhale, through the nose, the vapor that arises from the bottle when uncorked, for about one minute. This inhalation may be repeated several times a day.

For ague and fever:

Carbolate of Glycerin..10 drops.

Take three times a day, before meals, in a wineglass-ful of cold water. The patient should also inhale the carbolic vapor (described above) several times a day.

For tooth-ache: With equal parts of carbolic acid, glycerin and alcohol saturate lint, and insert it into the cavity of the tooth. The nerve of the tooth will very soon be destroyed, and the pain cease.

For diarrhœa, dysentery, etc.: Take four drops of the carbolate of glycerin in half a wineglass-ful of water every hour or two, until relief is obtained.

For poisonous bites of insects, snakes, etc.: With equal parts of carbolic acid (in crystals) and alcohol, cauterize the wound freely, and when the general system is affected by the bite, let the patient take ten drops of the carbolate of glycerin in half a wineglass-ful of water every fifteen minutes until relief is obtained. We also suggest this treatment for *hydrophobia*.

CARBOLIC ACID FOR DYSPEPSIA.

In dyspeptic cases, of the fermentive class, accompanied by the copious evolution of gas from the stomach, and the discharge of fetid evacuations from the bowels, it is usually attended with satisfactory results. *Dose*—from ten to fifteen drops of the carbolate of glycerin in half a wineglass-ful of water, three or four times a day. It arrests fermentation, and stops the evolution of gas.

TRICHINÆ SPIRALIS.

This malady arises from eating diseased pork, and often proves fatal. As a remedy, give the patient fifteen drops of carbolate of glycerin in a wineglass-ful of water, repeating the dose every two hours. Alternate it every two hours with twenty drops of *liquor sodæ bisulphis*, also administered in a wineglass-ful of water. In urgent cases repeat these agents every hour, and continue until relief is obtained.

Carbolic acid and sulphurous acid will effectually destroy the animalculæ and parasitic family. These anti-parasitic agents may be safely administered in a diluted form, as above described, and no injurious results can possibly occur to the most delicate constitution.

The *trichinæ* may be found throughout the system, and in order to reach them with carbolic acid we advise its admixture with glycerin, which is the most efficacious vehicle for its dissemination through every part of the body, as glycerin will rapidly penetrate both flesh and bone, and carry with it such chemical agents as it holds in combination.

The *sodæ bisulphis*, in addition to destroying parasitic life, reduces the inflammation, and allays the pain caused by the ravages of the *trichinæ*.

CARBOLIC ACID AS A REMEDY FOR MOSQUITOES AND FLIES.

Saturate pieces of cloth with crude carbolic acid and hang them about the room, and the mosquitoes and flies will leave. The process of wetting the cloths may be repeated three or four times a day.

NOT AN ACID.

Carbolic acid should not be called an acid, as when pure it does not redden litmus paper.

HOW TO DISSOLVE CARBOLIC ACID CRYSTALS.

One ounce of carbolic acid crystals is soluble in one pint of distilled water, by adding a few grains at a time, and agitating the water at every addition of the acid.

SPORES THE CAUSE OF DISEASE.

Recent investigations in science have proved that the cause of disease is due to microscopic spores floating in the atmosphere, which, by their subsequent development and propagation, are held to be the true source of contagion.

It has also been proved that the microscopic spores can be destroyed by the presence, and even the vapor, of carbolic acid, which at once arrests the progress of disease, thereby preventing further contagion.

Hence the use of carbolic acid as a disinfecting and deodorizing agent is commended during the prevalence of cholera, typhoid fever, and other contagious diseases.

PREVENTIVE OF CHOLERA.

The *Moniteur Scientifique*, of Paris, says that during a severe epidemic of Asiatic cholera, which caused the death of a large number of people, carbolic acid, mixed with water, was daily sprinkled in the rooms and passages of the houses, and the further spread of the disease was immediately arrested.

CARBOLIC ACID AND GLYCERIN AS PRESERVATIVE AGENTS.

Carbolic Acid, in crystals..1 ounce.
Alcohol, 95 per cent...8 ounces.
    Shake well together, and add
Pure Glycerin, concentrated...5 pints.
Distilled Water.. ¼ gallon.

This makes an excellent preparation for the preservation of animal bodies, where it is desired to preserve the color as well as the tissues. For naturalists, physicians and surgeons, this requisite is invaluable; and by using double the amount of carbolic acid, an excellent preparation for washing and preserving corpses is obtained.

ANTIDOTE FOR CARBOLIC ACID.

When an overdose of carbolic acid has been taken internally, take a tablespoon-ful of olive oil. Repeat the dose as often as may be required. When strong carbolic acid has been used on the skin, and it is desired to correct its corrosive effects, apply olive oil freely to the affected parts.

CARBOLIC CRYSTALS CHANGE TO A DARK COLOR.

Crystallized carbolic acid, when first prepared, is somewhat transparent, but by exposure to the light assumes a dark appearance. In relation to this subject, we copy the following from the "BOSTON JOURNAL OF CHEMISTRY," edited by James R. Nichols, M. D., the well-known manufacturing chemist: "Crystallized carbolic acid becomes *liquid* in warm weather, and solidifies again as winter approaches. The best acid assumes a pinkish hue (which is due to the action of light) by long keeping, but this in no respect renders its use inadmissible for the nicest purpose. We have had thousands of pounds, which, as it flowed from the retorts and crystallized, was as white and beautiful as the freshest snow, changing, in the course of twenty-four hours, so as to have some color. No specimen from the best European makers, that we have seen, is free from this liability. Redistillation, a dozen times repeated, does not always suffice to maintain it in a colorless condition for many months."

CRUDE CARBOLIC ACID.

This article is made from the alkaline portion of the liquors with which coal-tar is treated, which is reduced to dryness in iron stills, and decomposed by an acid. The portion which distills over, between 285° and 376° Fahr., is collected separately as crude carbolic acid. It has the appearance and consistence of thin, dark-colored molasses, and is not used in medicine, but as a disinfecting, deodorizing and antiseptic agent. Only the crystallized acid is used for medicinal purposes.

CARBOLIC SOAP.

Add one-fourth ounce of carbolic acid, crystalized, to the six ounces of glycerin, in the formula for making "perfumed glycerin soap," on page 216, and proceed in all other respects as there set forth. This makes a good disinfecting soap, for all purposes.

TO DEODORIZE CESS-POOLS, GUTTERS, PRIVIES, ETC.

Sulphate of Iron (copperas)..1 pound.
Hot Water...1 gallon.

When the iron is dissolved, pour or sprinkle the solution into the place to be purified, and in a few moments the offensive stench will be removed.

In hot weather, when cholera or fevers prevail, after using the above solution of copperas, also disinfect with

Carbolic Acid, crude..4 ounces.
Cold Water..1 gallon.

Agitate well together, and sprinkle over the infected places.

Or the carbolic acid may be used in the form of powder, prepared as follows:

Carbolic Acid, crude..1 pint.
Sulphate of Lime (known as gypsum, or plaster of Paris)......10 pounds.

Mix well together, and distribute wherever required.

For sick-rooms, hospitals, ships, cellars, alleys, out-houses, etc., this is an efficient and convenient disinfectant.

Either of the above-described preparations is far superior to chloride of lime, etc., used for the same purposes.

Carbolic acid, as a disinfecting agent, used during the ravages of the Asiatic cholera, has proved itself the best specific for arresting that terrible disease.

FAMILY MEDICINES.

GLYCERIN AND EGG-YELK DRESSING.

Glycerin..3 ounces.
Yelks of Eggs...4 in number.
Otto of Roses..1 drop.

Mix well together.

This preparation has the consistence of cream, and is highly beneficial as a healing agent for chapped hands, lips, chafes, wounds, etc. It renders the skin soft and white. It is also a valuable dressing for all kinds of skin diseases, sores, etc., as it allays inflammation and excludes the air from the parts affected.

STIMULATING DROPS.

For colic, cramps, spasms, cholera, diarrhœa, dysentery, and the first stages of a cough. Also, to promote reaction in cases of shock or injury, lock-jaw, etc.

Tincture of Myrrh..1 ounce.
Tincture of Capsicum..½ ounce.
Tincture of Peppermint..1 ounce.
Tincture of Camphor...½ ounce.
Tincture of Valerian..1 ounce.
Oil of Fireweed..½ ounce.
Oil of Sassafras...¼ ounce.
Bicarbonate of Potassa..½ ounce.
Simple Sirup..5 ounces.

Mix well together; shake well just before taking.

Dose: From 10 to 40 drops, according to age and requirements, in a wineglass-ful of water. The dose may be repeated every 30 minutes, and in extreme cases every 15 minutes, until relief is obtained.

In severe cases of pain, soak the feet in hot water for 15 or 20 minutes, and apply externally some of the mixture and a woolen cloth saturated in *hot* water over the region of the pain, which, together with the mixture taken internally, will remove pain and coldness, and produce a healthy perspiration.

COUGH SIRUP.

For coughs, colds, asthma, croup, bronchitis, consumption, and whooping-cough:

Black Cohosh Root, powdered		1 ounce.
Beth Root,	"	½ ounce.
Lobelia Herb,	"	1½ ounces.
Spikenard Root,	"	2 ounces.
Licorice Root,	"	1 ounce.

Mix, and soak for twelve hours in
Cold Water ....3 pints.

Then simmer for three or four hours. When cool, pour sediment and all into a bottle, and add

Alcohol ....½ pint.
White Sugar ....¼ pound.

Shake well together. Dose: From one to three teaspoons-ful several times a day.

Instead of using roots and herbs, as prescribed above, substitute for them the fluid extract of each in the same proportions, adding four times their weight of sugar-house or simple sirup, and omitting the alcohol, cold water and white sugar.

ALTERATIVE SIRUP.

Yellow-dock Root, powdered		2 ounces.
Bittersweet	"	2 ounces.
Blue Flag	"	1 ounce.
Yellow Parilla	"	1 ounce.
Burdock Root	"	2 ounces.
Tag-Alder Bark	"	2 ounces.

Place altogether in a clean iron or porcelain kettle, and add
Cold Water ....2 quarts.

Soak over night, or not more than twelve hours.

Then gently simmer over a slow fire for two or three hours. When cool, put all into a jug, and add

Good Gin ....1 quart.
Essence of Wintergreen ....1 ounce.
White Sugar ....2 teacups-ful.

Agitate thoroughly. Dose: One tablespoon-ful two or three times a day, shaking the jug each time after using.

Useful for all impurities of the blood, and excellent for scrofula, cancers, ulcers, etc.

[NOTE.—Instead of the roots and barks designated in this formula, the fluid extracts of all may be combined, in the same proportions, (which, as above, would make ten ounces), adding to them two and a half pints, or four times their weight, of either simple or sugar-house sirup. Omit the cold water, gin and white sugar, but the essence of wintergreen should be retained to flavor the sirup.]

LIVER SIRUP.

Fluid Extract of Blue Flag	1 ounce.
Fluid Extract of Yellow Parilla	2 ounces.
Fluid Extract of Mandrake	1 ounce.
Fluid Extract of Prickly Ash	½ ounce.
Fluid Extract of Black Root	2 ounces.
Sugar-house Sirup	1 quart.
Essence of Wintergreen	1 ounce.

Shake well together.

Dose: One teaspoon-ful at morning, noon and evening, half an hour before meal-times.

Lessen this dose, should it produce a cathartic effect; and if the bowels are constipated, or not sufficiently relaxed, gradually increase the dose.

For chronic inflammation, or inaction of the liver, constipation, etc., this preparation is unequaled; and for purifying the blood, a dose should be taken three or four times a week, in connection with the alterative sirup.

CATARRH.

Catarrh, or chronic irritability of the mucous surfaces of the air-passages, generally results from "taking cold," and from a want of attention to those hygienic measures which tend to fortify the system against sudden changes of temperature.

Catarrh, if long neglected, becomes difficult to cure, and tends to induce bronchitis and consumption.

General symptoms: A dull pain in the head; swelling and redness of the eyes; the effusion of a thin, acrid mucous from the nose; hoarseness, cough, fever, etc.

We submit the following as a reliable method of treating this disease:

CATARRH REMEDIES.

Chlorate of Potassa	1 ounce.
Hot Water	1 pint.

Stir until the potassa is dissolved. Into a bottle put

Pure Glycerin	2 ounces.
Carbolic Acid, crystals	1 drachm.

Shake well together.

When cool, add the solution of potassa. Shake well just before using.

Directions for Use.—Twice a day pour about a tablespoon-ful of the mixture into the palm of the hand, and inhale or draw it up the nostrils until it passes to the throat. This will allay all pain and inflammation, and heal the diseased membrane.

The patient should also use the following smoking compound:

Mullein Leaves, dried and pulverized	1 ounce.
Sage Leaves, " " " "	1 ounce.
Lobelia Leaves " " " "	1 ounce.

Mix well together.

Using a new clay pipe, smoke two-thirds of a pipe-ful, forcing the smoke through the nose. This should be repeated twice a day.

ANOTHER VALUABLE SMOKING COMPOUND FOR CATARRH.

Plantain Leaves	1 ounce.
Red Clover, blossoms and leaves	1 ounce.

Pulverize and thoroughly mix. Smoke as above.

We would suggest that the patient use one smoking compound one week, and then alternating with the other until cured.

An infusion of plantain leaves and red clover blossoms and leaves, (one drachm of each, simmered in a pint of water for an hour or two), is also excellent for catarrh, to be used the same as the solution of chlorate of potassa.

It is better to alternate these catarrh remedies, using one for two or three days, and then the other.

EYE WATER.

White Sugar	1 ounce.
Common Salt	$\frac{1}{2}$ ounce.
Soft Water	1 pint.

Agitate until the salt and sugar are dissolved. Strain through fine linen. Apply three or four times a day.

Useful to relieve weakness and inflammation of the eyes.

In cases of chronic inflammation and granulation of the eye, should the above preparation not have the desired effect, add to one pint of it one-fourth ounce of the sulphate of zinc, and shake well together. Use as previously directed.

For acute inflammation of the eyes, poultices made of raw potatoes or slippery elm bark are excellent.

COMPOUND LINIMENT FOR NEURALGIA, RHEUMATISM, ETC.

Oil of Hemlock	$\frac{1}{2}$ ounce.
Oil of Sassafras	$\frac{1}{2}$ ounce.
Oil of Origanum	$\frac{1}{4}$ ounce.
Tincture of Lobelia	4 ounces.
Alcohol, 95 per cent	1 pint.

Shake well together for a few minutes; then add

Aqua Ammonia	2 ounces.

Agitate, and keep in a closely corked bottle.

Shake immediately before using, and apply several times a day to the affected parts.

We have prescribed this liniment for several years with decided success, as a remedy for neuralgia, rheumatism, toothache, and for all purposes where a stimulating liniment was required.

RELAXING LINIMENT.

Tincture of Lobelia	2 ounces.
Tincture of Marygold	2 ounces.
Glycerin	2 ounces.
Oil of Sassafras	1 drachm.
Alcohol	2 ounces.

Mix, and apply to the affected parts several times a day.

Useful for relaxing stiff joints, calloused and contracted tendons and muscles, and reducing chronic inflammations.

FAMILY LINIMENT.

For healing wounds, burns, sores, cuts, and curing boils, bruises, felons, frost-bites, rheumatism, neuralgia, ringworm, salt rheum, etc.

Tincture of Guaiacum	8 ounces.
Tincture of Lobelia	4 ounces.
Tincture of Myrrh	4 ounces.
Oil of Hemlock	1 ounce.
Oil of Cedar	½ ounce.
Oil of Anise	½ ounce.
Carbolic Acid, (crystallized)	¼ ounce.
Glycerin	4 ounces.
Alcohol, 95 per cent	12 ounces.

Mix all together in a quart bottle, and shake well just before using. Saturate a soft cotton or linen cloth, or some lint, with this preparation, and apply to the parts affected several times a day. It will allay acute pain and reduce inflammation and swellings in almost every instance; prevent or arrest erysipelatous inflammation and mortification, and may be regarded as a general "cure-all," for the various diseases of the skin, for man or beast.

COOLING LOTION FOR INFLAMMATIONS AND VARIOUS DISEASES OF THE SKIN.

Borax, pulverized	1 ounce.
Chlorate of Potassa	½ ounce.
Glycerin	1½ ounces.
Essence of Peppermint	½ ounce.
Rosewater	4 ounces.
Soft Water	1 quart.

Agitate well together.

This also makes a cooling wash for the head, is a good hair dressing, and excellent for chapped hands, blistered feet, or chafing in any part of the body, as its effects are cooling and healing.

PRICE-LIST OF CHEMICALS, ETC.

If the chemicals used in the various processes described in this volume cannot be readily purchased in a pure state, or at reasonable prices, elsewhere, they may be obtained at the following rates, and warranted pure and reliable, by addressing the author:

NO. 1 LIQUID SILICATE OF SODA—($36°$ Baume), warranted pure for the purposes enumerated in this book, and weighing *twelve* pounds to the gallon—1 gallon (25 cents extra for package)..$1.50
    5 gals., ($1.00 extra for keg), per gal............................ 1.30
    10 gallons, ($1.25 extra for keg), per gal....................... 1.20
    1 barrel, containing 40 gals. ($1,50 extra for barrel), per gal. 1.00

NO. 2 LIQUID SILICATE OF SODA, the kind usually sold in commerce, which answers all purposes for making soap and washing compounds:
    For 10 galls. or less (extra for packages), per gal............... .90
    For 40 galls. (extra for the barrel), per gal...................... .75
    [This No. 2 Silicate of Soda will *not* serve for preserving eggs, making fire-proof paint, or the preservation of stone.]

NO. 1 TRANSPARENT RESIN, per bbl, (280 lbs)......................$7.00
    [The dark-colored resin must not be used for insulating barrels, or other purposes set forth in this book, as it contains too much tar, and will communicate an unpleasant flavor.]

PARAFFIN WAX, pure (less than 10 lbs), per lb........................ .45
PARAFFIN WAX, pure (10 lbs and upwards), per lb................... .40
ANNATTO, warranted fresh and pure for the purposes recommended in this book, per lb..$2.00
    [Adulterated Annatto may be purchased for a less price, but will not impart the desired color to butter, etc.]

CARBOLIC ACID, (crystalized), per lb..................................$2.00
CARBOLIC ACID, (crude), per gal., by the barrel..................... 3.25

Parties who have not the conveniences for refining Linseed and Paraffin Oils, may obtain them prepared of the author, at the following prices:

REFINED RESINOUS LINSEED OIL (See process of refining, page 72), pure, for insulating eggs for dry packing, as recommended on page 38:
    1 gal. (including package)...$2.00
    5 gals. (including package), per gal........................... 1.80
    10 galls. (including package), per gal......................... 1.60

REFINED PARAFFIN OIL.—(See process of refining, page 74); pure, for insulating eggs (see page 37); for deoxygenating and insulating eggs (see page 33); for insulating egg-preserving liquids, to prevent evaporation and the absorption of impurities (see pages 12, 15, 37, 59 and 60), 1 gallon, (including packages), per gal..$2.00

    Five gallons (including packages), per gal...................... 1.80

    Ten gallons (including packages), per gal........................ 1.60

GLYCERIN, pure and concentrated, for butter, etc., per lb............ .80

INDIA RUBBER, pure gum, for making solutions, per pound......... 2.00

NAPHTHA, pure and deodorized, for dissolving India Rubber—

    One gallon, (package 25 cents extra)................................. .50

    Five gallons, (package $1.00 extra)................................. .40

    Ten gallons, (package $1.25 extra)................................. .30

Persons who do not wish to prepare the butter Coloring, Butter Preservative, and Milk Preservative, can purchase them of the author, at the subjoined prices:

BUTTER COLORING (warranted pure), made according to the formulas of this book, sufficient

    To color 100 lbs of butter...$1.50

    To color 500 lbs of butter... 6.00

    To color 1,000 lbs of butter.. 10.00

About *two-thirds* of the cost is regained by the increased weight of the butter.

BUTTER PRESERVATIVE—

    10 lb package, sufficient to preserve 120 lbs................... $1.25

    50 lb package, sufficient to preserve 600 lbs................... 5.00

    100 lb package, sufficient to preserve 1,200 lbs............... 9.00

    200 lb package, sufficient to preserve 2,400 lbs............... 16.00

The preservative increases the weight of butter, so that its cost is more than recovered.

MILK PRESERVATIVE—

    Five pound package, sufficient to preserve 240 gallons of milk..$4.00

WIRE BASKETS—For deoxygenating and insulating eggs, according to size, from..$1.00 to $3.00

Persons wishing to procure chemicals of any kind can be supplied on short notice and reasonable prices, and also obtain information relating to chemical processes, by addressing

                         W. C. BRUSON, Practical Chemist

Office, 145 La Salle St.   P. O. Box 855, Chicago, Ill.

CHEMICAL, SCIENTIFIC AND AGRICULTURAL JOURNALS.

DRUGGISTS' PRICE CURRENT.

"The Chicago Druggists' Price-Current and Chemical Repository" is a practical journal of pharmacy, chemistry, and *materia medica*. Its editorial supervision is in able hands, H. D. Garrison, M. D., Professor of Chemistry in Bennett Medical (Eclectic) College, being at the head of its scientific and literary departments. Dr. Garrison is a gentleman of high attainments and celebrity in his profession, and the ability manifested in the "Price Current and Chemical Repository," is due to his editorial acumen. In its pages may be found various interesting topics, embracing Chemistry, the Arts and Sciences, etc.; together with a complete price-list of drugs and chemicals. All these advantages serve to make this paper a desirable one for druggists, chemists, and others engaged in scientific pursuits. Issued monthly—terms $1.00 per year.

BARNET & HANNA, Publishers,
186 Lake Street, Chicago.

THE PRAIRIE FARMER.

"The Prairie Farmer" has been established nearly thirty years, dating its origin in 1841. As the pioneer of agricultural journals in the west, it has always aimed at progress and improvement, and ably maintains a high position in its class, claiming justly to be a leader of opinion upon whatever pertains to agriculture, horticulture, stock-breeding and raising, mechanical, educational and home interests. For the western farmer it is a valuable repository of such information as he daily needs. Its circulation we are glad to know, is large, and a general air of prosperity seems to enliven its pages. Published weekly in a quarto form, of eight pages, handsomely illustrated, at $2.00 per annum, by the

PRAIRIE FARMER COMPANY,
112 Monroe Street, Chicago, Ill.

THE BOSTON JOURNAL OF CHEMISTRY.

"The Boston Journal of Chemistry as Applied to Medicine, Agriculture and the Arts," is published monthly, under the editorial supervision of the well-known chemist, James R. Nichols, M. D., and is considered excellent authority in all matters pertaining to chemistry, science, art, agriculture and medicine, aiming to furnish the freshest and best information on topics connected, directly or indirectly, with these departments. No one can read it without finding his intelligence increased upon subjects in which every thinking man should feel an interest. Terms, $1.00 per annum.

JAS. R. NICHOLS & CO.,
150 Congress Street, Boston, Mass.

THE SCIENTIFIC AMERICAN.

"THE SCIENTIFIC AMERICAN," besides being the largest and most widely circulated, is, we believe, the oldest journal of its class in this country, and the impetus which it has given to inventive genius is almost incalculable. Indeed, could the truth be known, it is probable that many of the most important and successful inventions of the age are indebted to its columns for their germination and perfection. Every week its sixteen handsomely printed pages are replete with valuable information for artisans, scientists, farmers, and inventors, including a full account of the principal inventions and discoveries of the day, with explanatory engravings. Its articles embrace nearly every department of popular science, which everybody can read and understand; also, reports of scientific societies, at home and abroad, patent-law decisions and discussions, practical recipes, etc.; together with an official list of all the patent claims, a special feature that commends it to inventors and owners of patents. Published weekly, at $3.00 per annum, by

MUNN & CO.,
37 Park Row, New York City.

THE DRUGGISTS' CIRCULAR.

"THE DRUGGISTS' CIRCULAR, AND CHEMICAL GAZETTE," is now in its *fourteenth* annual volume, and its continued and prosperous existence bears evidence to the fidelity with which it maintains its dignified and important character as a representative journal of American Pharmacy. Ably edited, it has become a valuable authority in practical chemistry as applied to the arts, sciences, and pharmaceutical preparations, carefully recording the most notable discoveries, and lending its aid, as a general business organ, to advance the interests of druggists, chemists and apothecaries. Its list of contents every month, is extensive, embracing a great variety of scientific and useful topics practically treated, including many "Notes and Queries," and a Miscellaneous Department of interesting items. Published monthly, in numbers of sixteen quarto pages each, at $1.50 per annum, by

L. V. NEWTON, M. D.,
36 Beekman Street, New York.

THE AMERICAN ARTISAN.

A very popular journal is "THE AMERICAN ARTISAN" among a large class of our intelligent builders, moulders and manufacturers, to whom, every week, it comes freighted with the information which they need for instruction and preservation. Its scope embraces everything relating to the advantages and use of new inventions and discoveries in art, science and manufactures, illustrated and embellished with good engravings; all of which make up a mechanical record of great value. Agricultural implements, labor-saving devices, and whatever of worth pertains to the growth of mechanical ingenuity or social science, finds place in its columns. The utility of a journal, competently conducted, like "THE ARTISAN," will commend it to capitalists, inventors and working-men throughout the country. Published at $2.00 per annum, by

BROWN, COOMBS & CO.,
189 Broadway, New York.

THE ARTS.

"THE ARTS: DEVOTED TO SCIENCE AND ARTS," edited by Joseph M. Hirsh, the able chemist and scientist, does honor to Chicago, as an evidence of the culture and refinement to which she is advancing. Forty years ago "a howling wilderness," it is something to know that to-day she can sustain a scientific journal like this, which displays great editorial ability, and has won hearty encomiums from the press, as well as the scientific men of the West. Its object is to introduce useful knowledge, of a theoretical and practical character, into every home, at a price within the means of all. Eminent men are numbered among its contributors, and their aid tends to bestow upon it an intrinsic and permanent value. Not only is it ably conducted, but neatly embellished, each number containing a lithographic portrait of some prominent scientist, with his biography, besides several illustrations in important papers. "THE ARTS" is still in its first half-year, and good as it is, we hope with age to see it gather increased ability and influence. Its external appearance is very attractive, and its mechanical execution creditable to the printer. Terms, $1.00 per year. Published monthly by

J. M. HIRSH & CO.,
10 & 12 South Wells Street.
Chicago, Illinois.

THE WESTERN RURAL.

"THE WESTERN RURAL: A WEEKLY FOR THE FARM AND FIRESIDE," published simultaneously in Chicago and Detroit, is devoted to the various departments of rural affairs, and particularly adapted to the needs of the West. Besides the important issues of agriculture and horticulture, which it liberally discusses, it gives also choice original and selected stories and miscellaneous reading for all classes, presenting a very complete and entertaining rural and family newspaper. It has attained a large circulation, and, under the supervision, editorially and financially, of H. N. F. Lewis, with able assistants, is one of the most successful publications in this country. Terms $2.00 per year.

H. N. F. LEWIS, Publisher,
113 Madison street, Chicago.

JOURNAL OF APPLIED CHEMISTRY.

"THE JOURNAL OF APPLIED CHEMISTRY," published simultaneously every month in New York, Philadelphia, and Boston, is devoted to chemistry as constantly developed and applied to the arts, manufactures, metallurgy and agriculture. Each number, of sixteen quarto pages, contains original articles on general chemistry in connection with the above-named departments; essays on indigenous and exotic products derived from the mineral, vegetable and animal kingdoms; expositions of the adulterations of commercial substances and the way to detect falsifications, with papers on particular fabrications, as petroleum, soaps, tanning, dyeing, etc. A suitable space is also devoted to practical recipes and interesting scientific intelligence. Full and carefully prepared market reviews and prices-current of drugs and chemicals of every description are given in each number, for New York, Boston and Philadelphia, with tables of imports, etc. Terms, $1.50 per annum. Published by

DEXTER & CO.
17 Spruce Street, New York.

FIRE! FIRE! FIRE! FIRE!
EXCELSIOR
Fire Extinguisher!

LATEST PATENT.

Portable and Self-Acting.

Price, $45.00. Six sets Chemical Charges Five Dollars. Ready for action in 3 seconds, by one turn of the Crank.

Puts out burning kerosene, varnish, turpentine, benzole, &c.

EASILY CARRIED: weighs 75 pounds filled; throws a stream charged with powerful chemicals 40 feet: Saves its cost in reduced rates of insurance. The public are hereby cautioned against purchasing Fire Extinguishers, having our device for instantaneous action, from any and all parties not duly authorized by us to act as Agents, on pain of immediate infringement. Manufactured by the

EXCELSIOR FIRE EXTINGUISHER CO.,

GEO. S. BOWEN, President.   EDSON KEITH, Vice-President.

Address all communications to J. C. DAVISON, Secretary, 92 Washington Street, Chicago, Ill.

Agents Wanted. Send for circular, containing indorsement of Chicago Fire Marshal and many others of the highest character.

GARRISON & MURRAY,
— MANUFACTURING —
CHEMISTS AND DRUGGISTS,
135 Madison St., Chicago,

Manufacture and offer to the Trade full lines of

FLUID EXTRACTS.   SOLID EXTRACTS.   RESINOIDS,
MEDICINAL SIRUPS, TINCTURES, ETC.,
PURE POWDERED DRUGS.

Fresh Herbs, Leaves, Barks, Roots, Etc., pressed neatly into 1 oz., ¼ ℔, ½ ℔, and 1 ℔ packages, in great variety.

DRUG GRINDING OF EVERY KIND TO ORDER.
HOPS PRESSED TO ORDER, AND FOR SALE AT LOW PRICES.

Western Chemical Works,

Office, 209 South Water St., and 10 & 12 South Wells St.,

CHICAGO, - - - ILL.

JOSEPH M. HIRSH & CO., Proprietors,

MANUFACTURERS OF

ANILINE COLORS, suitable for dye works and family dyes—all shades.
CARBOLIC ACID, for disinfecting. 25 cents per gallon.
CARBOLIC ACID, for burns. 50 cents per pound.
CARBOLIC ACID, for destroying insects. $1.00 per pound.
CARBOLATE OF GLYCERINE, for affections of the throat.
GLYCERINE, for printers, perfumers and druggists, warranted equal to the very best.
PEPSIN-WINE, for dispeptics. Used by the profession universally.
FLAVORING EXTRACTS, for household use.
LIQUOR and WINE ESSENCES.
DEXTRIN, substitute for gum arabic.
Pharmaceutical preparations generally.

The quality of our goods we always guarantee prime, and prices low.

ANALYTICAL LABORATORY

—— OF ——

J. M. HIRSH & CO.,

10 & 12 South Wells St,

Chicago, - - - - Illinois.

ANALYSIS AND ESSAYS of technical products, minerals, drugs, merchandise generally.
Pathological Specimens, etc., made at our office.
Correctness guaranteed.
PLANS OF FACTORIES and Estimates furnished for all branches of manufacture and mining. Advice given regarding the practicability of new or old processes of manufacture.

CONTENTS.

	PAGE.
ANILINE DYES	217—244
ANILINE INKS	195

APPLES—
    Antiquity of the apple............113
    Improved by culture............113
    Longevity of apple trees............113
    Number of varieties in the United States............113
    The best climate for apple raising............113
    Flavor of apples, whence obtained............114
    Apples as an article of diet............114

ANNATTO—
    History, names and uses of............224
    Concentrated tincture of annatto—how to make............85

ALBUMEN............5
ALDEHYD............140
ALTERATIVE SIRUP............234

BUTTER—
    How made in the best manner............76
    Necessity of keeping the cream cool............76
    Effect of boiling water on cream............76
    How butter and cream should be kept............77
    Cleanliness indispensable in butter making............77
    Why butter becomes sour and rancid............78

How to RESTORE SOUR AND RANCID BUTTER............79
    The number one, cold process............80
    Rancid butter converted into good table butter............81
    Various materials for refining butter............82
    Preparing butter for hot climates............82

How to COLOR BUTTER............83
    White and "streaked" butter made to resemble "June butter"............83 to 89
    Chemical composition of butter............91
    Difference between winter and summer butter............91
    Insulating butter firkins............91
    Packing butter in insulated firkins, etc............92
    Powdered ice used to cool butter when packing............92
    To prevent firkins shrinking or swelling............93
    Number two process for preparing butter firkins for packing...93
    New oak firkins not to be used without preparation............93
    Average yield of butter from good milk............97

CONTENTS.

BUTTER PRESERVATIVE— PAGE.
    The art of keeping butter sweet..................................89
    How to prepare the preservative................................90
    Directions for using it..90
    Preserving butter with honey....................................90
    Effect of glycerin with butter....................................90

BAKING POWDER—
    Formula and directions for using.............................180
    Making yeast cakes...180

BEERS—VEGETABLE AND ROOT—
    Corn beer...133
    Ginger beer..132
    Lemon   " 132
    Root   " 133
    Sarsaparilla compound root beer.............................131
    Spruce beer...131

BLACKING—
    Water-proof blacking for boots, shoes, harness, etc....198
    Water-proof for soles of boots and shoes..................198
    Liquid polish blacking...215
    Paste (polish) blacking..215

BUTYRIN..78
BUTYRIC ACID...78

CIDER—
    Known to the ancients..114
    Made in nearly all temperate climates.....................114
    Sweet cider...114
    Best method of fermenting apple juice....................114
    Cider vinegar..115
    What apples make the best cider.............................115
    Cider kept for 25 years..115
    Poor apples—cider from..115
    Preserving and flavoring cider.................................116
    Composition and specific gravity of cider...............117
    When cider should be bottled..................................117
    Rules for making cider..117
    Average yield of cider...117
    Alcohol in cider..117
    Philosophy of preserving cider................................118
    Champagne cider..118
    Cider wine..119
    Artificial cider..119
    Cider without apples...120

CIDER—*Continued.*   PAGE.
    Sweet cider—imitation of..120
    Cider—imitation of...121
    How to bottle or can sweet cider for preservation................121
CHEMICAL, SCIENTIFIC AND AGRICULTURAL JOURNALS......240
CHEESE—
    Composition of...100
    Chemical analysis of cheese..100
    Its flesh and muscle-making properties...............................100
    Obesity and its effects..102
    Digestibility of cheese..102
    Process of cheese making...103
    Rennet—what it is, and how prepared.................................103
    The difference between good and inferior cheese...............104
    Taking care of cheese..105
    Proper season for manufacturing...105
    Acid substituted for rennet..106
    Cheese vats and presses...106
    Salting cheese properly..106
    Coloring cheese—usual method; improved process...............107
    How to preserve cheese from flies, maggots, and dust—new method...107
CATARRH—Cure for...235—236
CANDLES—
    Refined tallow candles..182
    Paraffin wax candles...182
CHEMICAL PRICE-LIST..238—239
COUGH SIRUP..234
COLOGNES..158
CLOTH RENOVATORS—
    Useful for removing grease, oil, paint, tar, wax, varnish, etc., from clothing, silk, satin, ribbons, cotton, woolen, table-covers, carpets, etc.,..178
COLOR RESTORATIVE—
    To restore color to garments...214—216
CREAM—
    Its origin, and how to obtain the greatest quantity.............93
    Its chemical composition...94
    How to preserve it for months..94
CASEIN..76—100
CARROTS—
    The juice as a butter coloring..88
    How to use it for coloring butter..88
CAOUTCHOUC—(see India Rubber)..214

CONTENTS.

CEMENT—   PAGE.
- Best cement for general purposes..................199
- Cement for iron and stone..................199
- Cement for glass, metals, etc..................200
- Cement for labeling tin-ware..................200
- Gum for labels, stamps, etc..................200
- Mouth glue..................200

CARBONIC ACID GAS—
- Properties and uses of..................226
- How manufactured..................226

CARBOLIC ACID—
- Properties and uses of..................228
- As a disinfectant..................231, 232, 233
- Method of preparing carbolate of glycerin..................229
- The parasitic theory of disease..................228
- Spores the cause of disease..................231
- As a remedy for diphtheria, or sore throat; for healing wounds, burns, sores, cuts, boils, felons, bruises, frost-bites; for rheumatism and neuralgia, ring-worm, salt-rheum, itch, cancer, scrofulous sores, asthma, bronchitis, catarrh, pulmonary consumption and dyspepsia..................229—230
- Carbolic inhalation..................230
- Carbolic acid for dyspepsia..................230
- Trichinæ spiralis cured by carbolic acid..................230
- Carbolic acid for hydrophobia..................230
- Carbolic acid *not* an acid..................231
- How to dissolve carbolic acid crystals..................231
- Carbolic acid as a cholera preventive..................231
- Carbolic acid and glycerin as a preservative..................231
- Antidote to carbolic acid..................232
- Carbolic crystals become dark-colored..................232
- Crude carbolic acid..................232
- Carbolic acid as a protection against mosquitoes, flies, etc.....231

DYEING—

DYEING WITH ANILINE COLORS—
- Preparing cloth for dyeing..................217
- Violet aniline purple for wool..................217—219
- Violet aniline purple for cotton..................218
- Aniline red (fuchsine) on wool and silk..................218
- Aniline red (fuchsine) on cotton..................219
- Hoffman's dahlia, violet, red and bluish parme shades..........219
- Aniline blue on wool and silk..................219
- Aniline blue violet on cotton..................220
- Aniline blue on cotton..................220

CONTENTS.

DYEING WITH ANILINE COLORS—*Continued.* PAGE.
    Scarlet aniline on wool..220
    Aniline green on wool..221
    Aniline green soluble in water...221
    Iodine aniline green for cotton..221
    Aniline yellow..221
    Picric acid..221
    Picric acid for yellow, green, drab and other colors............221
    General suggestions on aniline dyeing..................................222
    Compound colors...222
OTHER METHODS OF DYEING—
    Artificial flowers..203
    Black for woolen goods...222
    Black for cotton goods..223
    Straw and chip hats and bonnets black................................223
    Straw and chip hats and bonnets varnished........................223
DEODORIZING Cess-pools, out-houses, etc.............................232

EGGS—
    Preservation of eggs—general remarks....................................5
    Effects of chemical agents in common use...............................6
    Eggs undergo a change in lime-water.......................................9
    Chemical composition of the "white" of eggs..........................9
    Become "watery" in lime-water..9
    Decomposition of the white vitiates the yolk...........................9
    Lime-water will not arrest decomposition..............................10
    Limed eggs held in low estimation...10
    Egg-yelk hardened by salt combined with lime.....................10
    How to prevent this result..10
    Salt or lime dissolves the white...11
    Why the "lime process" spoils the egg..................................11
    Formula for a new lime compound..11
    Directions for its use...11—12
    Proper barrels or vats for preserving necessary....................13
    Cautious use of salt recommended..13
    Objectionable substances prohibited....................................13
    Improved compound process..14
    Instructions for its use..15
    New method of preserving egg-preserving solutions...........15
    Improved dry process for preserving and packing...............16
    Antiseptic properties of the dry process...............................17
    Effects of salt, dry ashes, oats, sand, bran, straw, chaff, saw-
        dust and shavings, as packing for eggs.....................18—19
    Liquid silicate of soda as a dry coating.................................19

Contents.

Eggs—*Continued.*   PAGE.

How used, and its effects..20
Why stale eggs cannot be preserved by the common methods...20
Effects of certain chemical agents upon eggs—cream of tartar,
    diluted sulphuric acid, and alum...21
    Bisulphides of calcium and sodium; sulphate of lime;
        vinegar; tartaric, muriatic, oxalic, and acetic acids;
        carbonates of potassa and soda; borax and saltpetre..22
    Sulphites of lime and soda; chlorides of calcium and lime;
        bicarbonates of soda and potash; sulphite, hypo-
        sulphite and phosphate of soda; tartrate of potassa;
        tartrate of potassa and soda; chlorate of potassa;
        carbonate of ammonia; carbolic acid, pyroligneous
        acid and glycerin...23
    Sugar..24
Air-proof and hot water processes for preserving...................24
Eggs hatched one year after being made air-proof..................25
Why clouded eggs usually appear clear after coming out of
    lime-water, etc..26
Why eggs sometimes crack when in egg-preserving solutions,
    or after removal from them..27
How to prevent preserved eggs from cracking when boiling.....27
Why the shells of preserved eggs crack when boiling..............28
Why fresh eggs sink and stale eggs float in water..................28
Keeping eggs in stone jars..28
The secret of preserving eggs fresh, and the causes of the fail-
    ure of most egg-preservatives...29
Temperature for keeping eggs...29
Oxygen in the new-laid egg—its effect...................................30
Conditions required to induce putrefaction............................30
Chemical change during incubation.......................................30
Temperature favorable for germination..................................30
A deoxygenated egg cannot spoil in any climate.....................31
Eggs for preserving..31
Chemical operation of the deoxygenating process..................31
Fresh and new appearance of deoxygenated eggs..................32
Disadvantages of the egg dealer overcome by the deoxygena-
    ting process for preserving eggs.....................................32
The number one process of deoxygenating and insulating
    eggs..33
The new colorless solution for preserving eggs......................33
The process of deoxygenating and insulating eggs fully ex-
    plained..33—34
The best substance known in chemistry for deoxygenating and
    insulating eggs...35
Preserving eggs by the cold insulating process......................37

Eggs—*Continued.*   PAGE.

Insulating eggs for dry packing..38
Number two process for deoxygenating eggs..................39—40
Keeping deoxygenated eggs...41
Why the new colorless solution is preferable to other means of
    keeping eggs...42
Eggs rendered less liable to break, increasing their durability
    and value..42
Why limed eggs soon spoil after being taken out of lime
    solutions...42
Eggs kept fresh by cold air...43
Anatomy of the egg..44
Why the yelk of a fresh egg settles against the shell, and
    the egg soon after spoils..44
Deoxygenation and insulation as a preventive........................46
The size and weight of eggs..46
Salt water a test for fresh eggs...47
What class of eggs to select, and the best months for preserv-
    ing them..47
Testing and preparing eggs for the preserving process..........49
Instructions for packing and shipping eggs............................49
General suggestions concerning eggs in preserving solutions....50
The sex of eggs..51
Length of time required to hatch the eggs of various fowls....51
Why the large end of a new-laid egg feels cold.....................51
Magnitude of the egg trade...52
Table of statistics for 1869, showing the population of the
    United States and Territories, number of families, number
    of farms, number of dozens of eggs produced, and their
    value at 20 cents per dozen..53
Perfect chemical analysis of the egg..............................54—55
Its mechanical and medical uses...56
Interesting facts concerning albumen.....................................56
Dessicating or drying eggs..57
Animal warmth or germinating heat as affecting the decompo-
    sition of eggs..57
An egg never decomposes as long as it has life....................58
Barren or non-fecundated eggs the best for preserving..........58
A lime preparation for preserving, that will not pack around
    the eggs...59
All egg-preserving solutions cooled before using....................60
Cooked eggs keep sweet much longer than raw....................61
Elements of a fresh egg, and the changes which they undergo
    in decomposition...65
Process for insulating kerosene oil and other barrels and
    vats for holding egg-preserving solutions...............66 to 69

EGGS—*Continued.*   PAGE.
    New oak barrels—their effects on egg-preserving solutions.....70
    Vats—how to construct, for keeping eggs...........................71
    Result of experiments in coating eggs with—
        Refined resinous linseed oil.................................72
        Raw linseed oil..74
        Refined paraffin oil...74
        Olive oil..75
        Cotton-seed oil..75
        Castor oil...75
        Poppy oil..75
        Sperm oil..75
        Lard oil...75
        Tallow...75
        Lard...75
        Butter...75
        Beeswax..75
        Paraffin wax...75
        Caoutchouc...75
        Resin, etc...75

EYE WATER..236
ESSENCES—
    See Tinctures from Essential Oils..............................153
EXTRACTS—FLUID FORM—
    General rules for preparing fluid extracts................155—156
    Hydro-Alcoholic Extract of Golden-Seal..........................155
    Over three hundred kinds made by one drug house..........156—248
EXTRACTS AND RESINOIDS..243

FIRE-PROOF PAINT..205
FIRE EXTINGUISHER...243
FRUIT—
    Fruit and vegetables preserved by coagulating their albumen...61—62
FUSIBILITY of Various Substances....................................202
FILES AND RASPS—To renew and recut.................................202
FIBRIN..108

GLUE—See Liquid Glue..181
GLYCERIN—
    General properties and uses....................................225
    Used to improve butter...90
    Glycerin dressing for chapped hands, etc.......................237

CONTENTS.

HAIR AND HAIR DRESSINGS— PAGE.
    Hair "Restoratives," in general..183

HAIR OILS—
    Number One Hair Oil...184
    Number Two Hair Oil...184
    Hair Invigorator and Restorative..185
    Instantaneous Hair Dye..185
    Shampooing Compound..186
    Hair Curling Liquidine..186
    Cooling Hair Dressing..287

HONEY—
    Imitation Honey...204
    Used in making champagne cider...118
    Used in making mead..121

INSULATING BARRELS, Vats, Firkins, Pails, etc.—
    How to prepare or insulate carbon or kerosene oil, lard and linseed oil or other barrels, whether new or old (as well as wooden vats), and render them suitable for holding egg-preserving solutions, pork, beef, brine, cider, vinegar, alkalies, acids, sirups, butter, water, etc.—Number one process and formula..66–67
    Number two process for preparing barrels......................................68–69
    New oak barrels not adapted to hold egg-preserving solutions unless prepared...70
    The most suitable barrels for preserving solutions..............................71
    Philosophy of the insulating processes..71
    Vats for keeping eggs—how to prepare...71
    How to insulate butter firkins, pails, etc.....................................91

INKS—
    Blue-black Writing Ink..188
    Blue Writing Ink..188
    Marking Inks..188
    Black Ink—Writing or Copying..189
    Black Ink Powder..189
    Green Writing Ink...189
    Red Writing Ink...189
    Red (Carmine) Ink...190
    Gold Writing Ink..190
    Silver Ink..190
    Bronze Ink..190
    Crimson Ink...190
    Violet Ink..190
    India Ink...191
    Black Ink from Elderberries...195

CONTENTS

SYMPATHETIC, OR INVISIBLE INKS— PAGE.
 Blue Sympathetic Ink 191
 Green Sympathetic Inks 191
 Yellow Sympathetic Ink 191
 Black Sympathetic Ink 192
 Rose Purple Sympathetic Ink 192

BLACK INDELIBLE INK—
 Number one formula ....192—193
 Number two formula 193
 To remove indelible ink 194
 To make old writing look like new 194
 To give new writing an aged appearance 194
 To ascertain the age of old writings and how to copy them...196

ANILINE INKS—
 Red Aniline Ink 195
 Green Aniline Ink 195
 Violet Aniline Ink 195
 Purple Aniline Ink 195
 Blue Aniline Ink 195
 Crimson Aniline Ink 195
 Orange Aniline Ink 195
 Black Aniline Ink 195

INDIA RUBBER—
 Preparation of the pure gum 214
 Solution of india rubber 214
 Hard india rubber 215

KEROSENE OIL—PETROLEUM—
 Kerosene oil and its adulterations 211
 To refine kerosene oil 212
 To test kerosene oil 212
 Petroleum—Its distilled products 212–213

LIQUID SILICATE OF SODA—
 Its properties, manufacture, uses and price 227–238

LIVER SIRUP 235

LIME—
 As an egg preservative 6
 Effects upon eggs 6
 Its caustic properties 7
 Dissolves best in cold water 7
 Quantity required to saturate a barrel of water 7
 Air excluded from lime-water 7
 Necessity of renewing lime-water 8

CONTENTS.

LIME—*Continued.*   PAGE.
  Chemical properties of lime-water..................8
  Why it renders eggs "watery"......................9
  Does not arrest decomposition....................10
  "Cream of Lime Compound," to make...............11
  Used in whitewash...............................204
  Mortar, to prepare with lime....................204
  Used in fire-proof paint........................205

LIQUID GLUE, Etc.—
  India Rubber Compound Liquid Glue...............181
  Mouth Glue......................................200
  Gum for stamps and labels.......................200

LEMONADE—
  How to make portable lemonade...................130

LINSEED OIL—
  Refined resinous linseed oil—mode of refining and bleaching..................................72—73
  Its use in coating eggs..........................74
  Raw linseed oil as a coating for eggs............74
  To boil linseed oil.............................198

LACTIC ACID...76

LINIMENTS—
  Compound, for neuralgia, rheumatism, etc........236
  Relaxing Liniment...............................237
  Family Liniment.................................237
  Cooling lotion for inflammations and various diseases of the skin................................237

MEAT, ETC.—
  Meat, vegetables and fruits preserved by coagulating the albumen......................................61
  Canning meats, etc..............................62
  The presence of air produces fermentation.......62
  Inanimate organic matter, animal or vegetable, subject to vinous, acetous and putrefactive fermentations...63
  Elementary constituents of animal and vegetable substances, and their changes under fermentation........63
  Antiseptics used to preserve meat...............108
  The theory of preserving meats..................108
  Salt impairs the nutrition of meat..............108
  Methods of dry salting and pickling.........109–110
  Pickle for Beef, Pork and Mutton................110
  Articles used in preserving meat, and their effects...111
  Preserving meat with smoke......................112
  Insulating meat protects it from air, moisture, flies, dust, mould, etc...................................112

MEAT, ETC.—*Continued.*   PAGE.
    Pyroligneous acid for preserving meat.............................112
    Fresh meat preserved in hot weather 204
MEDICINES—
    To prepare for family use...233
MILK—
    Its composition and preservation....................................95
    Its specific gravity and average weight.............................95
    How to preserve milk for years......................................96
    How to detect watered milk..96
    Effects of heat and agitation.......................................97
    Composition of skimmed milk...97
    Average yield of butter from good milk..............................97
    Butter can be seen in milk with a microscope........................97
    Effect of boiling milk..98
    Never put milk in lead or zinc vessels..............................98
    How to prevent milk from souring....................................98
    Why lightning causes milk to sour...................................99
    Why stale milk curdles when boiled..................................99
    Milk should always be boiled in a water-bath........................99
    Used for clarifying vinegar..140
MARGARINE..77
MEAD—To make...121
MANGANESE—Black Oxyd...198
MALIC ACID..114
MORTAR—To prepare..204

OLEIN..91
OIL OF EGG YELK...84
OIL OF BUTTER...88
OINTMENTS—
    Articles that enter into their general composition.................159
    Bittersweet Ointment...160
    Green Ointment...159
    Poke-root Ointment (compound)......................................161
    Stramonium Ointment..160
    Venice Turpentine Ointment...159
    Yellow-dock Ointment...160

PARAFFIN OIL—
    Mode of refining and bleaching......................................74
PARAFFIN WAX—Properties and uses....................................225
PERFUMERY—
    Spirit of Bergamot...157
    Spirituous Hungary Water...157

Contents

COLOGNES—SPIRITUOUS— PAGE.
    Number One Cologne 158
    Number Two Cologne 158
PEARL WASH for the Complexion, removing tan, etc. 187
    Toilet Powder 216
    Frangipanni Sachets, for clothing 216
PERRY—"Wine of Pears"—how made 121
PICKLING—
    Quick process for pickling cucumbers 202
    To color pickles 203
PLATING SOLUTIONS—
    Preparing articles for plating 209
    Plating with gold 209
    Silver-plating metals without a battery 210
    Cost of electro-plating 210
    Another process for silver-plating 210
    Polishing Cream, for cleaning silver-plate 211
    To plate copper and brass with tin 211
    To plate or "galvanize" iron 211
    To plate with copper 213
    To plate with tin 214
PLASTERS—
    Adhesive and Strengthening Plaster 162
    Irritating Plaster 163
POTATOES—
    Poisonous potatoes 217
    Preservation of potatoes 216
PRESERVING DEAD BODIES 232
PRINTS—
    To prevent prints from fading 176
PUTTY—To remove from broken windows 203
PYROLIGNEOUS ACID—For meat 112
    For eggs 23

SIRUPS—
    Simple Sirup the basis of other sirups 123
    Simple Sirup subject to vinous fermentation 124
    Alterative Sirup 234
    Cough Sirup 234
    Liver Sirup 235
SODA, OR FLAVORED SIRUPS 125
    Blackberry Sirup 127
    Cream Sirup 126
    Coffee Sirup 128
    Cinnamon Sirup 129
    Ginger Sirup 126
    Lemon Sirup (genuine) 125
    Lemon Sirup (imitation) 125
    Mace Sirup 129
    Nutmeg Sirup 129
    Orange Sirup 126

CONTENTS.

SODA, OF FLAVORED SIRUPS—*Continued.* PAGE.
    Orgeat Sirup..128
    Peach Sirup...128
    Pine Apple Sirup (genuine)..127
    Pine Apple Sirup (imitation)..127
    Raspberry Sirup (genuine)...127
    Raspberry Sirup (imitation)..127
    Rose Sirup...128
    Sarsaparilla Sirup...126
    Strawberry Sirup (genuine)...126
    Strawberry Sirup (imitation).......................................127
    Vanilla Sirup...128
    Coloring for sirups..129
    Cochineal coloring—to make.....................................129
    Carbonic acid gas in soda-water.................................130

SILICATE OF SODA—
    Liquid silicate of soda—its manufacture.....................227

STEARIN..91

SOAP—
    Antiquity of its origin and use.....................................170
    The general composition of soaps...............................170
    Two varieties of soap—hard and soft..........................170
    Transparent Hard Soap, perfumed...............................171
    White Bar Soap, perfumed..171
    Almond Soap..172
    Soft Soap from Hard Soap (quick process)................172
    Improved Soft Soap..172
    Soft Soap—common..172
    Perfumed Glycerin Soap...216
    Carbolic Acid Soap..232

STAINS—
    To remove from silk, cotton, linen and other fabrics, and to
        restore their color...176
    (See, also, Cloth Renovator.)......................................178
    To remove ink-stains and iron rust....................194–195

STONE—
    Artificial Stone and Marble..206
    To prepare artificial stone...207
    Preservation of building stone....................................207

STIMULATING DROPS...233

STARCH POLISH...203

TANNING—
    Skins of animals—of what composed........................164
    How tannin is produced...164
    Converting skins into leather—three methods............164
    The Indian process..164
    Qualities of leather properly tanned............................165
    Philosophy of tanning..165
    Preparing skins for tanning...165
    Compound dressing, for keeping leather soft and rendering it
        water-proof...166

CONTENTS. XV

TANNING—*Continued.* PAGE.
    Tanning the skins of animals with the hair or fur on.....167–168
    How to renovate furs..167
    How to color furs or hair pelts..168
    Tanning skins with the hair off..169

TINCTURES—
    Their character and manufacture......................................150

TINCTURES FROM GUMS, HERBS AND ROOTS—
    Tincture of Bloodroot..151
    Tincture of Black Cohosh..152
    Tincture of Camphor (spirits of camphor)..............................150
    Tincture of Catechu...150
    Tincture of Capsicum (cayenne pepper)................................151
    Tincture of Columbo..152
    Tincture of Ginger...151
    Tincture of Guaiacum...150
    Tincture of Golden-seal..152
    Tincture of Lobelia (Indian Tobacco).................................152
    Tincture of Myrrh..150
    Tincture of Opium (Laudanum)...150
    Tincture of Peruvian Bark..152
    Tincture of Prickly Ash..152
    Tincture of Rhubarb..151
    Tincture of Senna..151
    Tincture of Senna, Compound (*Elixir Salutis*).......................151
    Tincture of Spearmint (Spirits of Mint)..............................153

TINCTURES FROM ESSENTIAL OILS—
    Tincture of Anise..153
    Tincture of Cinnamon...153
    Tincture of Lavender...154
    Tincture of Peppermint...153
    Tincture of Sassafras..153
    Tincture of Spearmint..154
    Tincture of Wintergreen..153
    Coloring and preparing tinctures.....................................154

TOILET POWDER..216

TOOTH POWDER...215

VARNISHES—
    Black Shellac Varnish..196
    Copal Varnish..197
    India Rubber Varnish...197
    Orange Shellac Varnish...196
    Red Shellac Varnish..197
    Shellac Varnishes of other colors....................................197
    Transparent Varnish, for iron and steel..............................197

VINEGAR (Acetum)—
    Ancients manufactured it from wine...................................139
    Effects of its moderate and excessive use............................139
    How formed by chemical action, its changes and their
        products..139—140
    Cider vinegar—how made..115–140
    Clarifying vinegar with milk...140

CONTENTS.

THE MANUFACTURE OF VINEGAR—   PAGE.
    Its chemical philosophy...141
    Quick processes—Nos. 1 and 2...................................141
    Quick process No. 3...142
    Slow processes—Nos. 1 and 2....................................142
    Instantaneous process..142
    Vinegar generators—mode of constructing.........142, 143, 144
    To decolorize vinegar..145
    Vinegars derived from fruits.....................................146
    Vinegars refined by boiling.......................................146
    Vinegars refined by distillation..................................146
    Gooseberry Vinegar..147
    Rhubarb Vinegar..147
    Adulterations of vinegar..147
    How to detect sulphuric acid in vinegar.......................148
    Wine vinegar—its properties.....................................148
    Sirups not to be run through generators......................148
    Vinegar—standards of strength.................................149
    Powers of saturation, and how numbered....................149

WAX—
    Grafting wax for trees..201
    Red, blue, black and green sealing-wax......................201
    Improved red sealing-wax.......................................201

WASHING COMPOUNDS—
    Objections to borax and sal-soda...............................174
    Washing Compound..174
    Improved Washing Compound..................................174
    Objectionable articles used in washing........................175
    To clean clothes..216

WATER—
    Made soft for washing..175
    To settle and purify muddy water..............................176

WHITEWASH—For walls...204

WINES—
    Domestic Wines..135
    Apple Wine..137
    Blackberry Wine...136
    Currant Wine...135
    Elderberry Wine...137
    Ginger Wine..138
    Isabella (or Catawba) wine......................................137
    Port Wine (imitation)...136
    Port Wine ("genu-wine")..136
    Raspberry Wine..137
    Rhubarb Wine..135
    Strawberry Wine..137
    Tomato Wine...135

WEIGHT—
    (Comparative) of various substances..........................202

WOOD-GAS—Products of Oak Wood..........................203

YEAST-CAKES—(See Baking Powder)........................180

www.ingramcontent.com/pod-product-compliance
Lightning Source LLC
Chambersburg PA
CBHW031347230426
43670CB00006B/464